"This important book cogently applies psychoanalytic thinking to a host of serious dangers that threaten democracy and even our very survival in the United States and in the rest of the globe. Starting with Donald Trump's unscrupulous rise to power and deeply damaging presidency, Messina studies the regressive dynamics of his supporters. She then broadens her discussion to include 15 additional countries being weakened by authoritarian leaders. Messina is a role model for psychoanalysts who want to apply their understanding of individual and group dynamics beyond the consulting room."

Richard M. Waugaman, M.D., Clinical Professor of Psychiatry, Georgetown University School of Medicine, USA

"In the fascinating *Resurgence of Global Populism*, Messina helps us understand the workings of the Populist-Authoritarian powermongers and how they con us and end up destroying everything in their path. This book is important and should be required reading in schools as a safeguard of true democracy."

Robert M. Gordon, Ph.D. ABPP, Forensic Psychologist

"Karyne E. Messina takes us on a global tour to explore how the fragile state of democracy has enabled the rise of authoritarian populist leaders—from Trump to Modi to Bolsonaro—who see themselves as heroes amidst a world of villains. Messina describes how the vitriolic blame game that these leaders employ is leading to immense human suffering and environmental damage. This important book stands as a stark warning that the mental health of elected leaders is a vital issue that impacts us all."

Ian Hughes, author, Disordered Minds: How Dangerous Personalities Are Destroying Democracy

"Karyne Messina has her psychoanalytic hand on the pulse of growing authoritarianism throughout the world. This book takes us on a guided world tour of corrosive trends from the United States to South America, Europe, the Middle East and Oceania to analyze the causes and effects of populist and authoritarian governments. What sets this book apart is her sure-handed use of a psychoanalytic lens to examine the developmental causes of threats to democracy and good governance, the invasive effects of social media, and the erosion of good governance worldwide. Students of international relations and all who care about the health of our planet will benefit from sharing her examination."

David Scharff, MD; Winner of the 2021 Sigourney Award in Psychoanalysis; Co-Founder, The International Psychotherapy Institute

"Messina brilliantly and eloquently applies the psychoanalytic defenses of splitting and projection to explain the appeal of populism and its powerful threat to democracies throughout the world. Her mastery of history, politics, authoritarian governments and their leaders makes for an exciting as well as invaluable read."

Maurine Kelber Kelly, Ph.D., Supervising and Training Psychoanalyst, Contemporary Freudian Society; Fellow of the International Psychoanalytical Association, Private Practice in North Bethesda, Maryland, USA

"Dr Messina offers a psychological explanation for current world politics. Narcissistic, charismatic leaders use projection to color complex situations black and white and tap into our unconscious desires to do the same. The world-wide rise of populist regimes, the hold on us of social media, and the sapping of political will to combat climate change are covered here in detail. If there is a fix, it rests in our discovering an ability to hear how the other is right."

Christopher Keats, M.D., Psychoanalyst

"*Resurgence of Global Populism* is one of the most important books that has been written in recent years because it illustrates the devastating effect of the Trump presidency that has reverberated around the world. While modern populists existed around the globe, the 45th president of the United States legitimized autocratic ways of thinking. Through the mechanism of projective identification, Messina explains how this way of shifting blame is destroying freedom as we know it. This is a must read for anyone interested in understanding how social media is also contributing to the erosion of representative government; a phenomenon that could lead to irreparable damage to democracy in America."

Harry Gill, MD, PhD; Medical Director, Embark at Cabin John; Medical Director, J Snyder Therapeutic Services; Clinical Assistant Professor of Psychiatry, George Washington University, USA

"While it is uncommon for psychoanalysts to venture into the realm of the political, Karyne Messina has done so with an astute eye, a deep well of social, historical and theoretical knowledge, and a willingness to face head-on the question on everyone's mind: "How did we get here?" Dr. Messina provides a framework for understanding how profoundly the psychological defense mechanisms of individuals in positions of power can reverberate on a global scale. Drawing on her understanding of the mechanisms of splitting and projective identification, Dr. Messina offers a comprehensive investigation into the dynamics that can precipitate a populist's rise to power."

Anne Adelman, Ph.D., Teaching and Training Analyst, Washington Baltimore Center for Psychoanalysis; Teaching Analyst, Contemporary Freudian Society; Co-Chair, New Directions in Psychoanalysis, WBCP

Resurgence of Global Populism

Resurgence of Global Populism provides a psychoanalytic perspective of the global implications of the populist movement in the U.S. and its relationship to other parts of the world, particularly focusing on the presidency and legacy of Donald Trump.

The book explores Trump's use of a psychological form of manipulation known as projective identification and how his use of this defense mechanism has influenced global institutions, political discourse, and quality of life in the long term. Messina explores the correlation between Trump's rhetoric and an increase in reported racism and prejudiced violence worldwide, disintegration of global values, and a radicalized political climate. She analyzes the dynamics between Trump and his supporters, political opponents and successors, considers the COVID-19 pandemic as a study of Trump's views of the world, and examines the roles of social and television media. The book concludes with an explanation of antidotes to projective identification, including thoughtful debate and meaningful discussions and scripted dialogues for global healing.

This insightful book will be of interest to psychoanalysts and psychotherapists, academics and students of political psychology and political movements, and readers interested in a deeper analysis of populism and political dynamics.

Karyne E. Messina, EdD, is a licensed psychologist and psychoanalyst at the Washington Baltimore Center for Psychoanalysis and serves on the medical staff of Suburban Hospital in Bethesda, Maryland. She maintains a full-time private practice in Chevy Chase and Rockville, Maryland. This is her third book.

Resurgence of Global Populism

A Psychoanalytic Study of Projective Identification, Blame-Shifting and the Corruption of Democracy

Karyne E. Messina

Routledge
Taylor & Francis Group

LONDON AND NEW YORK

Cover image: Getty

First published 2023
by Routledge
4 Park Square, Milton Park, Abingdon, Oxon OX14 4RN

and by Routledge
605 Third Avenue, New York, NY 10158

Routledge is an imprint of the Taylor & Francis Group, an informa business

British Library Cataloguing-in-Publication Data
A catalogue record for this book is available from the British Library

Library of Congress Cataloging-in-Publication Data
A catalog record has been requested for this book

ISBN: 978-1-032-06089-7 (hbk)
ISBN: 978-1-032-06451-2 (pbk)
ISBN: 978-1-003-20238-7 (ebk)

DOI: 10.4324/9781003202387

Typeset in Times New Roman
by Taylor & Francis Books

Contents

Acknowledgments

David and Jill Scharff taught me about projective identification over 30 years ago; a foundation that provided a theoretical scaffolding that has allowed me to explore many facets of the effects of this pervasive and far-reaching defensive maneuver. I am very grateful that they shared their wisdom with me.

I would like to thank Susannah Frearson, Senior Editor at Routledge, who encouraged me to broaden the scope of my work. Her advice led me to expand my ideas about projective identification and the role it plays in the resurgence of populism around the globe.

Barbara Basbanes Richter served as an excellent editor and researcher who deserves a great deal of credit for her diligent search for connections between populism and destructive mechanisms of defense that are initially cloaked in a smoke screen of good will but eventually lead to autocratic rule.

Robert Gordon provided invaluable encouragement and support for my ideas about projective identification and populism while recognizing how these concepts are affecting democracies around the world.

I am grateful to Rick Waugaman for his scholarly review of my work. He astutely described what I am trying to convey in a few brilliantly stated and noteworthy sentences.

Maurine Kelly has been a friend and pillar of support for many years. Her enthusiastic encouragement of this book is something I treasure a great deal.

I also want to thank Harry and Paul Gill for their unending support of this book and my commitment to raising awareness of the insidious power of projective identification and blame shifting here and around the globe.

Hannah Hahn offered invaluable insights about the psychoanalytic topics I write about as they relate to the political problems that are dividing our nation as well as countries throughout the world. Her steadfast support has been vitally important to me.

I greatly appreciate Olivia So's invaluable insights about the power of social media that is so pervasively affecting our world today.

Isabel So's research on South Asia helped me understand how complicated political systems on the other side of the world employ projective identification and blame shifting in ways that are similar to other countries around the globe.

Last but by no means least, I would like to thank my husband, daughters and their families who provide constant support which makes my writing possible.

Author's Note

One of the challenges with this book is that much of what it covers is happening in real time. As fragile democracies continue to face forces that threaten freedom, an unimaginable war has broken out in Ukraine, owing to Vladimir Putin's unprovoked aggression. To date, hundreds if not thousands of people have been killed, while many cities are being destroyed by Russian soldiers. As I submit this to the publisher, the Ukrainian people, led by their indefatigable president Volodymyr Zelensky, are resisting heroically. The final outcome is unclear.

Ultimately, all books must end. While some of the events chronicled in the pages that follow will be eclipsed by the passage of time, my thesis remains the same: Charismatic, democratically elected leaders unconsciously employ splitting and projective identification to manipulate their citizens and governments with the goal of consolidating power for themselves. They also use the more conscious technique of blame-shifting to control the people they govern. Owing to these mental maneuvers, populism is a hair's breath away from some countries, while authoritarianism has entered another.

I hope that the examples in this book may serve as a kind of warning to those who are tempted to take their democratic freedoms for granted. The peaceful people of Ukraine unfortunately have learned what can happen when a leader's tactics are fraught with persecutory anxiety. Putin is either purposely shifting blame to Ukraine and the West to rationalize his diabolical actions, or he is in a delusional state consistent with Melanie Klein's paranoid-schizoid position, wherein he is attacking because he thinks Ukrainians, NATO, and the United States are out to get him and will destroy Russia. Whatever the case might be, countries throughout the world are in great peril owing, at least in part, to the primitive mechanisms mentioned above that drive people to seek ultimate power and control of others.

Introduction

The Driving Force That Leads to the Emergence of Populism

Everything is not well with America in 2022. While there have been good times and bad times, something is different. As Ezra Klein put it, "It's easy to cast a quick look backwards and assume our present is a rough patch of our past, that the complaints we have about politics today mirror the complaints past generations had of the politics of their day (Klein, 2020, p. 1)." However, Klein goes on to suggest, and I agree, something is different, "...the Democratic and Republican Parties are not like the Democratic and Republican Parties of yesteryear (2020, p. 1). There is something that is different this time, something is changing that is more sinister. This something emerged during the Trump presidency that has moved the needle towards a populist stance that we as Americans have not known.

As a political phenomenon, populism defies easy definition because the concept encompasses various political movements throughout the world that appear to have few similarities. Though populism in some form or another has existed since ancient Greece was a thriving country, the term as it is currently employed hails from the nineteenth century. Today, strongmen—who oftentimes are themselves the source of populist power—capitalize on a long-standing sentiment of exclusion—the "sovereign people" against duly elected government officials and the so-called elite. On the surface, some populists make this concept sound laudable, however they rarely deliver on the promises they made. The vow of returning control to "the people" is generally little more than a stump pitch (Grzymala-Busse, 2019).

Other populist leaders attempt—and sometimes succeed—in deconstructing democracies, forming a new power structure based on paranoid authoritarianism. In another model, a populist takes power and rules with an iron fist—no returning of power to the people here—but he or she may improve economic conditions for many. In this case, the leader's popularity remains high despite the broken promise, offering the people bread and circuses in exchange for unfettered control. This method works just as well as making good on populist pledges.

DOI: 10.4324/9781003202387-1

The differences in populist leadership strategies are so varied that some scholars argue that the word "populist" no longer accurately applies. Giovanna Campani and Gabrielle Lazaridis suggest that "the sheer variety of political parties and movements labelled 'populist' has led some scholars to call the phenomenon itself a chameleon" (Campani and Lazaridis, 2017). However, I believe some explanations, especially from a psychoanalytic standpoint, are worthy of further exploration. This book is an attempt to do just that.

Populism is potent because it tugs at primal fears of being left out. Author Daniel Stockemer proposes that through a populist vantage point, "the political system is viewed as inherently opposed to the will of the people; it is inherently tied to the whims of the elite and must be challenged to once again work in service to the common man" (Cabovan 1999, p.3) (Stokemer, 2019, p.2). Populists employ defensive maneuvers to divide and conquer by literally or figuratively splitting their followers—the good and deserving people—from the bad oppressors who populists claim are taking advantage of their unsuspecting neighbors. Thereafter, these cult-like, charismatic leaders dictate what their base should say and do by convincing their followers that they are special and have been treated unfairly by their shared oppressors; those elites who would do harm—unless, that is, the people give the populist the power he wants.

Followers of a cult-like leader eventually isolate themselves from others, and the leader will do his or her best to keep followers from hearing or reading outside sources that might be contradictory. This has become easier than ever to achieve thanks in large part to social media that permits people to only associate with those who share similar world views. Once "siloed" into a particular group, it is as if other viewpoints do not exist or are not worthy of consideration. As I will demonstrate throughout the book, successful contemporary populist leaders lean heavily on social media to perpetuate acts associated with projective identification and reinforce their messaging.

The Role of Psychoanalytic Defense Mechanisms

Whether populists achieve their stated or unstated goals, this type of political and social movement often emerges when two unconscious psychoanalytic defense mechanisms—splitting and projective identification—are employed by leaders who cannot successfully acknowledge and process the good and bad qualities in their own lives and in the world around them or accept responsibility for their actions.[1]

These defenses occur together and are what permit many populists to control people. The first mechanism, *splitting*, is a mental maneuver through which the projector compartmentalizes good and bad qualities in themselves and others. *Projective identification* is the second psychological maneuver that enables populists to dispose of unwanted aspects of themselves by projecting these intolerable qualities or characteristics onto another person or other people. After splitting people into clearly defined groups and projecting bad and unwanted qualities onto others, many populists believe these characteristics reside in their enemies. It is, in its most basic manifestation, a primitive way to look at the world: *I am good. You are bad. There is no room for anything else.* When employed by a populist leader, this behavior can have significant, wide-ranging, and harmful consequences. Blame-shifting is another mental maneuver often used by people who control and manipulate. It is similar to projective identification but rather than being an unconscious defense mechanism, it is a conscious act. I will mention blame shifting in the text when I believe a behavior has led to an intentional act.

In addition to the use of splitting and projective identification by populist leaders, these defense mechanisms occur frequently in one-on-one situations and in small groups.

Bullies, for example, are also often guilty of attributing their thoughts and feelings to others to ward off difficult internal states of mind. A bully might call someone a "loser." Why? More than likely someone in the bully's life called him or her a loser, and it made the bully feel bad. Rather than finding a positive or constructive way to deal with those bad feelings, the bully passes them on to someone else. The person being called a loser might feel confused at the outset. However, before long, the victim may believe the bully. Eventually, the victim often feels like a bona fide loser. When this occurs, the receiver is identifying with the thought or feeling that the projector sought to dispel.

Basically, bullies are not happy with themselves. They were taunted at one point, but who wants to feel like an unpopular loser? The answer is, 'not many people,' which leads them to find various ways to cope. Some internalize these feelings, others might find someone to talk to, a third group might find another person to blame; someone who appears to be even scrawnier, less outgoing, or less intelligent. When this occurs, the bully does not feel like he or she is the loser. Instead, it is that other kid over there. In this example, the bully blames the other person by getting people to look at him or her. He or she is the one who is dumb or stupid or cannot play ball.

Projective identification happens in a split second, and though the recipient might feel stunned initially, over the course of repeated attacks, the projected thoughts might begin to represent those that are part of the receiver's mindset. This is especially true when bullies pick on the same people over and over again, which can make the process unbearable and hard to tolerate. Unconsciously, bullying ensures that the victim has the projected thoughts or feelings the bully is trying to deny.

I will demonstrate throughout this book how splitting, blame shifting, and projective identification occur between political leaders and their followers in a number of situations throughout the world.

Melanie Klein's Positions Reflect the Way People Relate to Each Other

Melanie Klein describes levels of functioning as *positions*: the paranoid-schizoid and the depressive positions. Her description of the paranoid-schizoid position, which is the one associated with these defense mechanisms, explores the need to mentally dispose of unwanted or threatening aspects of the self or others that are too much to bear. This is due to persecutory anxiety that is present in infancy but continues to plague adults when they become suspicious or extremely mistrustful of others. In this state of mind, a person will view others as one-dimensional: either good *or* bad, not both. When in the paranoid-schizoid position, people retaliate against those who they believe have harmed them or will harm them in the future. It is a way of relating to others where raw aggression and aggressive tendencies are ever-present.

Examples of Splitting, Blame Shifting, and Projective Identification in an Individual

As detailed in the first chapter, Trump serves as the prime example of how splitting and projective identification manifest on a large scale. As president, he routinely divided people into two categories: those who he believed were *for* him—the good base—and those who he thought were *against* him, the bad people. He continues to do this as a private citizen, notably in his claims that the election was stolen from him. It might seem like this is an over-simplification, but this reduction of people to "good" and "bad" is how splitting and projective identification work.

In Trump's case, he chastised those he determined as the bad people and blamed them for what *he* thought or had done. He also demeaned people from other countries who have lived in less-than-optimal conditions. For example, he often cast aspersions on poor people even though his own mother was an impoverished immigrant from Scotland who came to the United States to become a domestic worker (Kruse, 2020). Because he cannot stand the fact that he is the son of a woman who lived in poverty—a fact that more than likely causes him to feel insecure or inferior—he projects those unwanted parts of his background onto Central American migrant children were keep in cages at the U.S.-Mexico border (Sherman, Mendoza, and Burke, 2019).

While populism is expanding in the United States as well as in other parts of the world, I suspect many Americans have previously been unfamiliar with this new emerging way of life because most of us thought we were living in a democracy until recently.

This book will focus on the global implications of the latest version of populism bred on American soil that will not simply disappear because of Trump's current defeat. While populism in politics is hardly new, proponents of this iteration rely heavily on the psychoanalytic mechanisms *of splitting and projective identification* which are unconscious mental maneuvers that Trump employed when he was president that inspired and legitimized despotic leaders around the world. These phenomena will be thoroughly described in Chapter 1 as will the reasons why I believe that Trump unconsciously uses these mechanisms of defense to cover up his deeply seated insecurities.

Historical Examples of Group Splitting, Blame Shifting, Projective Identification, and Reconciliation

Studying genocides reveals how splitting and projective identification affects groups (Lemkin, 1944).

One example of the use of these defensive maneuvers occurred with the Armenian genocide that has never been acknowledged by the Turkish government or a number or other countries. Although Joe Biden acknowledged this genocide in April 2021, he was the first U.S. president to do so. Overall, this is an example of a failed reconciliation (Biden, 2021).

Since the Turkish government denies that the genocide occurred, repair is not possible because of this massive refusal to take responsibility for their crimes against humanity. You cannot heal or attempt to correct something that you insist never happened, so hatred and bitterness prevail rather than healing and reconciliation.

In contrast, few deny the occurrence of the Rwandan genocide where some 800,000 people were killed in one hundred days. This genocide happened in part because the colonialists—German and then Belgian soldiers—who occupied Rwanda projected their aggression onto the people who theretofore lived together peacefully. These Rwandans later projected this hatred towards each other. The Europeans preferred the lighter-skinned Tutsis and considered them superior to the Hutus, even going so far as issuing identification cards distinguishing one group from another. Tutsis were already perceived as "elite" among East African tribes, and this favoritism exacerbated tensions. When the Belgians left, the Tutsis gained greater power, further shoving the Hutus to a second-class status. Eventually, the rift was overwhelming and turned deadly (Messina, 2019).

In this book I will examine countries where a new brand of populism fuses the time-tested dictum of the people against the elite with contributions from Trumpian populism. These countries include Brazil, the Philippines, Venezuela, Nicaragua, Australia, New Zealand, India, Hungary, Poland, Austria, Turkey, Germany, the United Kingdom, France, and the United States.

While it is unlikely that populism will ever disappear, a greater understanding of the psychological underpinnings of this phenomenon could alter this trend as practiced by the new crop of Republican extremists loyal to Donald Trump and other leaders around the globe.

Each chapter will explore how the populist in question came to power and the conditions that made it possible for a political shift to occur. I will also examine the presence of splitting and projective identification to determine how these mechanisms might have influenced the change in the structure of each government.

A brief assessment of the economic, political, and social conditions that followed the new leader's rise to power will be examined, as well as how American Trumpism resembles or differs from populism in other areas of the world. Each populist leader employs splitting, blame shifting, and projective identification differently, and as such their outcomes will vary, but these mechanisms in various forms are at the root of each populist's rise to and grip on power.

Othering and Tribalism Emerge Due to Splitting and Projective identification

Othering and tribalism will be woven into the discussion in various chapters since these phenomena presuppose an "us/they" dichotomy inherent in populism. Both concepts pit one group against another group (or groups). In the "us" camp resides an identification with sameness that highlights the special qualities of a group that feels disenfranchised, ignored, or left behind. The *if we stay together, we can survive* mentality protects members from a barrage of assaults from anyone who is not part of that special group.

While sameness for the sake of identification can be positive, such as in a family, school, neighborhood, sports team, non-profit, or charitable organization, the problem arises when the "us" group is excluded—either actively or in more passive ways—from the "they" group. Sometimes, all it takes is for the perception that one group is being excluded, which allows widespread grievances to fester.

What causes this to happen? Here is projective identification at work again, except on a larger scale. The need to rid the "us" group of something that cannot be tolerated within is projected onto another group. Thereafter, the first group accuses the "they" group of possessing that which has been cast off. Thereafter, a vigilant eye monitors the "they" group to make sure what was projected remains a part of "them."

This process protects the "us" group because there is fear of becoming irrelevant or being mistreated by the majority. The possibility of this dynamic occurring in any group exists and will be included in relevant chapters for the purpose of assessing the balance between "us" versus "they" in each country or area being discussed.

Who Is Qualified to Talk About Psychoanalytic Defense Mechanisms?

While there have been recent discussions about whether it is right or ethical for mental health professionals to publicly discuss the psychological state of a president or world leaders, my last book, *Aftermath: Healing from the Trump Presidency* (Messina, 2020), closes with a disclaimer that I am not Trump's psychoanalyst, nor have I treated any of the other public figures discussed in this book. Instead, I am offering my opinion based on publicly observable behavior, and on nearly three decades of experience working with traumatized patients, and the research I have done for my two previous books on projective identification, including *Misogyny, Projective Identification and Mentalization: Psychoanalytic, Social and Institutional Manifestations* (Messina, 2019) and *Aftermath: Healing from the Trump Presidency* (Messina, 2020). Most importantly, as a psychoanalyst I have an obligation to warn the public about dangers that are inherent in Trumpian politics.

I think it is important to state here that The American Psychoanalytic Association (APA) takes the position that psychoanalysts should offer relevant psychoanalytic insights to aid the public in understanding a wide range of phenomena in politics, the arts, popular culture, history, economics, and other aspects of human affairs. The added depth of understanding that psychoanalytic commentary can provide regarding public affairs benefits society and the profession. However, the APA expects psychoanalysts to exercise extreme caution when making statements to the media about public figures.

Note

1 These concepts are psychoanalytic defense mechanisms that were described by Melanie Klein when she initially talked about the early state of mind that emerges in infancy. Since that time, these ideas have been defined as unconscious defense mechanisms that cause a person to split-off and then project aspects of the self that cannot be tolerated onto another person or group of people. Thereafter, the original projector blames the other(s) for possessing the characteristic(s).

References

American Psychoanalytic Association (2012). Position statement regarding psychoanalysts' providing commentary on public figures. https://apsa.org/sites/default/files/2012%20Position%20Statement%20Regarding%20Psychoanalysts.pdf.

Biden, J. (2021, April 24). Statement on Armenian Remembrance Day. White House, Washington, DC. www.whitehouse.gov/briefing-room/statements-releases/2021/04/24/statement-by-president-joe-biden-on-armenian-remembrance-day.

Burke, G, Mendoza, M, and Sherman, C. (2019). US held record number of migrant children in custody in 2019. *Associated Press*, November 12.https://apnews.com/015702afdb4d4fbf85cf5070cd2c6824.

Campani, G. and Lazaridis, G. (2017). *Understanding the populist shift: Othering in a Europe in crisis*: London: Routledge.

Grzymala-Busse, A. (2019, March 1). "How is Democracy Threatened," Presentation at Global Populism Project, Stanford University. https://fsi.stanford.edu/global-populisms/global-populisms.

Klein, E. (2021). *Why We're Polarized*, New York: Avid Reader Press.

Kruse, M. (2017). The Mystery of Mary Trump. *Politico,* November. www.politico. com/magazine/story/2017/11/03/mary-macleod-trump-donald-trump-mother-bio graphy-mom-immigrant-scotland-215779 (accessed March 9, 2020).

Lemkin, R. (1944). Chapter nine: Genocide, *Axis rule in occupied Europe: Laws of occupation analysis of government – proposals for redress,* Washington, DC, pp. 79–95.

Messina, K. (2019). *Misogyny, Projective Identification and Mentalization, Psychoanalytic, Social and Institutional Manifestations,* London: Routledge.

Messina, K. (2020). *Aftermath: Healing from the Trump Presidency,* Washington, DC and Chevy Chase, MD: IPI Press.

Olsen, H. (2021). Europe is proof that right-wing populism is here to stay. *The Washington Post,* March 18. www.washingtonpost.com/opinions/2021/03/18/europ e-is-proof-that-right-wing-populism-is-here-stay.

Stockemer, D. (Ed.) (2019). *Populism around the world: A comparative perspective,* Chams: Springer International Publishing.

Chapter 1

Corrupt Systems: Understanding Trumpian Populism

Donald Trump is an expert when it comes to exonerating himself and blaming others for his actions. This aspect of his behavior was illustrated when he was discussing the COVID-19 testing situation at a White House press conference on March 13, 2020. During that event he said, "I don't take any responsibility at all." His bombast and inability to accept responsibility has hurt millions of people and legitimized the rise of populism worldwide. As discussed in the introduction, *splitting and projective identification* are phenomena employed by those who unconsciously dislike something about themselves. Instead of taking responsibility for their actions, they separate good and bad aspects of themselves and others and project those unwanted feelings, thoughts, and actions onto someone else or other people. Trump represents, to my mind, the premier populist example of someone exhibiting these defense mechanisms. This chapter draws from my book on Trump entitled *Aftermath: Healing from the Trump Presidency* in which I explore the Trumpian mindset from a psychoanalytic viewpoint. This chapter will serve as the barometer by which the populists described in subsequent chapters will be measured, since Trump, I believe, exemplifies the Kleinian definition of projective identification.

The defensive maneuvers of splitting and projective identification were conceptualized by British psychoanalyst Melanie Klein, originally used them to describe how babies psychologically split-off and separate good and bad parts of their mothers and themselves. They then project bad phantasies of themselves while retaining only the good ones. They do this to protect themselves while holding in mind a "good object" since babies need a mother to care for them.[1]

Klein and her followers later applied the term to adult behaviors. These are now considered defense mechanisms wherein people divide people into "good" and "bad" categories and then rid themselves of intolerable aspects of themselves by projecting them onto another person or other people. Thereafter, in the projector's mind, these traits exist in the recipient.

Having completed the act of casting off intolerable aspects of the self, the projector temporarily feels like the unwanted characteristics are gone. Relief!

DOI: 10.4324/9781003202387-2

But much like a dopamine hit, this sensation is short-lived and must be repeated to achieve similar results.

The receiver of the projection often initially feels stunned. It is as if he or she does not know what happened. Eventually, however, this person might start to *believe* that the projected characteristic(s) belongs to him or her. When the projector is a politician projecting onto a group, potentially millions of people begin to believe what they hear. These primitive emotional control mechanisms cause tremendous pain to recipients and when doled out by populist leaders, wreak havoc on governments and destabilize societies. This silent erosion of self-confidence is soul crushing and often leads to feelings of widespread despair, skepticism, and paranoia.

As mentioned earlier, I can think of no better example of a public figure who employs splitting and projective identification as a defense mechanism than Trump. Perhaps the most glaring example of the former president's deployment of these processes came in the weeks leading up to and including January 6, 2021, when his messages galvanized a mob to commit violence acts against elected officials.

Trumpian populism embodies the toxic elements of intense blame and condemnation that is projected onto anyone who dares to differ with Trump's own shifting set of beliefs. In 2021 Trump turned this behavior onto his Vice-President, Mike Pence, who was among his most loyal followers until he refused to illegally overturn the 2020 presidential election results.

This trend gained traction in America when Trump made his bid for the White House in 2015. His campaign underscored his lack of willingness to take responsibility for his behavior. Rather than accepting blame or attempting to resolve difficult and often negative situations, Trump shifted blame onto others. He positioned himself as being against the establishment in a bid to gather credibility with "the people," yet at that point few considered him to be a real contender for the presidency. Instead, many believed that his recently discovered zeal for politics was a publicity stunt.

Love him or hate him, it is hard to deny that Trump is charismatic—he understands how to talk to people while assuring them that he is listening. And he is speaking to more than the stereotypical base composed of white, poor, uneducated American men. His base expanded to include those who believe they have been left behind in the race to the hyper-connected, digital future. Throughout his campaign and even during his presidency, Trump has cast himself as an outsider, that he is leading the people against a vast, frightening government conspiracy trying to force Americans to comply with burdensome programs and progressive policies. As such, his claims and his lies become irrelevant when wrapped up in theories of hijacked freedom and the American way. Even before Trump was considered a serious presidential contender, change was afoot in the United States with a chasm growing ever wider between the urban coastal areas and the Midwest. A lack of facts and a mastery of social media allowed Trump to weaponize misinformation and hurl it at those who questioned him or showered him with data.

Learning from Trump: A Psychoanalyst's Perspective

Trump supporters are nothing if not fiercely loyal: the Trump base believes they will be saved from current and future calamity by the former president. He has and continues to reassure them that he understands them and their plight and promises that life will get better for them—that, to quote his campaign slogan, he will make America great again. Whether or not he has fulfilled his promise to the base is debatable, but today, America is clearly split between cultural extremities: the coastal liberals and the vast rural populace. It appears that the differences have become downright toxic.

Trump cultivated such a following among conservative, rural, working, and middle class, white Americans, owing in large part to his charisma, and charismatic leaders often fill their arguments with heated emotion rather than sticking to facts. Further, by casting himself as an outsider, he added heft to his positions by creating the narrative that his ideas were anti-establishment and cultivated with the best interests of the people.

This position helped his cause considering that the 2020s are an era when Americans are inclined to doubt science—consider parents who refuse to vaccinate their children for fear of catching autism, even though there is no link between the two (Centers for Disease Control and Prevention, 2021). A 2020 Gallup poll found that the number of Americans who believe vaccines are important fell from 94 percent in 2001 to 84 percent in 2019. And though most respondents said that vaccines are less dangerous than the diseases they prevent, 46 percent said they were unsure whether vaccines caused autism—down from 52 percent in Gallup's last poll in 2015, but still high enough to suggest that misinformation continues to influence the decision-making process. Now, many of those same families are reluctant to vaccinate their children against COVID-19 (Ivory, Leatherby, and Gebloff, 2021).

The Trump Show

We must consider why Trump lashes out the way he does, shadowboxing with opponents real and imaginary. There is a method to Trump's actions. In *Audience of One: Donald Trump, Television, and the Fracturing of America*, author James Poniewozik asserts that:

> Donald Trump belongs to the attention machine because Donald Trump *is* an attention machine…. That the best response to any controversy or crisis is to heighten the conflict. (The lesson of TV news.) That people perform best when set to fight against one another for survival.
>
> (Poniewozik, 2019, p. xxii)

Whether tweeting into the internet or locking horns with journalists, Trump sells a certain image of himself while shifting an aspect of his personality that he finds unappealing onto those around him. This characteristic that Trump feels he must expel from his psyche seems to stem from his childhood and social background—the Trump who was the son of a poor immigrant mother who came to America as a domestic worker.

It is his ability to harness this aspect of his personality that enables people to feel close to him, as if he is a neighbor or friend. Trump is hardly an average American living in a split-level ranch style home in suburbia; his ancestors were poor, let alone middle-class. Somehow, it is this hidden history that helps him connect with ordinary people, despite his preferred Mar-a-largo self, the media-crazed self that is rich, famous, and can boast of having dined with the Queen of England. Some Trump supporters take his word as near gospel, but the result can be deadly: consider the man who drank fish-tank cleaner after hearing the president tout one of the product's ingredients, chloroquine, as a potential cure for coronavirus. (Read, 2020). We will see this again in the lead-up to the January 6 insurrection.

Despite Trump's outward bravado and boasting of a wonderful childhood, many accounts suggest that his early years were difficult. Trump's father, Fred, was a notorious hardnose, while his infirm mother was emotionally unavailable when Donald was a young boy and deferred much of his emotional upbringing to nannies and her husband. By many accounts, Fred Trump ruled the roost, and his disciplinarian ways were harsh, given that young Donald proved to be a challenging child. Some might have called Donald a bully outside the home from a very early age, but behind closed doors he marched to Fred's perfectionist drumbeat.

Although voted out of office, Trump's political rhetoric continues to appeal to Americans who felt their needs were ignored by other Republican politicians and previous administrations.

The 2020 election vote counting fiasco has been no different and is a good example of what he does. Trump continued to say the election was fraudulent and was stolen from him, which is simply not true. Joe Biden received over seven million more votes than Trump. Numerous election officials have verified the legitimacy of the election results—even Trump's own (Republican) director of cybersecurity, Chris Krebs, called the elections the most secure in America's history. Yet Trump continues to inflame his base by telling lies about the process and the results.

Stochastic Terrorism and Donald J. Trump

Stochastic terrorism involves a violent action that is taken by a follower after he or she has been emotionally stirred up by a charismatic leader who subtly incites a person to commit unlawful acts (this can involve a few people as well, not just a single person). While some people believe this concept is the same as the lone-wolf theory, I do not think it is the same thing. A stochastic terrorist riles up a group that leads one person or a small group of people to commit "terrorist acts that are statistically predictable but individually unpredictable" (Braddock, 2020, p. 224). In other words, acts of violence committed seemingly at random but that are triggered by a fiery demagogue, usually via mass media. These acts are likely to occur, but it is impossible to pinpoint precisely when or where a riled-up follower or group of followers will strike.

Some experts think the acts are carried out by "lone actors" which is a term they believe is a better and more apt characterization. This is the underpinning of the lone wolf theory, except that if the relentless egging on by a demagogue or political leader had not occurred, the terrorist(s) would probably not have acted. Consider, for example, Jacob Chansley, aka the QAnon Shaman, who stormed the Senate floor dressed as a shirtless Viking. The former actor and Navy sailor became one of the most recognizable faces of the riots. After he was arrested, Chansley, through his lawyer, argued that he went to the Capitol at the behest of Trump (Feuer and Hong, 2021). It is unlikely that Chansley would have ever participated in the riots had he not been encouraged by Trump.

Though his professional career has been built on sowing fear and paranoia—in September 2020, *The New York Times* analyzed the ways Trump has manipulated American paranoia for personal gain—Trump's ability to reach millions of Americans from the presidential lectern was unparalleled (Haberman and Rogers, 2020). As such, he built up a domestic terrorism movement that continues to threaten American democracy, culminating to date in the attacks on the Capitol on January 6, 2021. Leading up to an election that pollsters and members of his own team did not believe he could win, Trump pegged January 6 as an important moment in the movement: the day the election would be certified by Congress.

Through the summer and fall leading up to the election, Trump and his allies flooded social media and ultra-conservative news outlets with stories about how the election would have been rigged if he lost because there was, in Trump's world, no statistical way he could lose. From saying that mail-in voting would be inherently rife with fraud—that "millions and millions" of ballots were sent to dogs, cats, and dead people—to suggesting that he might even somehow have the power to postpone the elections, owing to the pandemic.

Throughout December 2020, he tweeted:

"Big protest in D.C. on January 6th. Be there, will be wild!"
"Statistically impossible to have lost the 2020 Election."
"Never give up. See everyone in D.C. on January 6th."
"Rigged & Stolen."

"We will never concede. You don't concede when there's theft involved."

And, on January 6, 2021 from a lectern overlooking thousands of the Trump faithful gathered in Washington, D.C.:

"You'll never take back our country with weakness. You have to show strength. If you don't fight like hell, you're not going to have a country anymore."

On December 20, 2020 Trump shared a video produced by jewelry auctioneer Seth Holehouse entitled, "The Plot to Steal America," in which he said that Biden clearly stole the election with an assist from the Chinese government. That video was retweeted 200,000 times and viewed more than 2 million times. Unknown to most viewers, however, was that Holehouse is a former creative director for *The Epoch Times*, a right-wing newspaper tied to Falun Gong, a Chinese religious movement that believes Trump will summon the apocalypse (Sommer, 2020).

These sensationalized claims represent a sliver of examples of how Trump summoned a mob to desecrate the Capitol building where five people died. This is stochastic terrorism as practiced by the president of the United States. What is more, in a move that could have been pulled from a textbook on projective identification, he denies he had anything to do with it or that he incited the mob, but he told people where to go, what to do, and why they should feel the way they did. It is only natural that someone of the many millions of his supporters would take him at his word.

Trump exhibits projective identification, and we the people pay the price, trapped in this relationship unbroken by an election loss. When the former president cannot control his emotions and projects his innermost insecurities onto others, the behavior loses its shock value. We become desensitized to what is otherwise abhorrent behavior.

Micro-targeting is another tactic used to manipulate public sentiment. It is the practice of flooding the internet with false information and conspiracy theories meant to toy with people's emotions. It is a misuse of social media and can be harmful to those in fragile or precarious mental states who are likely to take someone's words as literal calls to action. Brad Parscale, for example, who headed up Trump's "Death Star" operation, a sophisticated high-tech facility in Rosslyn, Virginia, was in sync with the kind of campaign blessed by his boss, one replete with race-baiting, immigrant-bashing, and truth-bending, that disseminated an eye-popping amount of false information. This type of campaign can be detrimental to people who are unable to differentiate truth from fiction. It can also affect partisan voters because of the powerful nature of misinformation.

While Trump is most certainly an independent actor, as we can see from his litany of personal disavowals and declarations, he by no means acts alone. There is a vast public and private machinery that functions in his midst—simultaneously driven by Trump but also driving him. Much of how the Trump administration operated relied on one or more forms of psychological exploitation implemented narrowly or broadly, depending on the goal at hand. Micro-targeting, disinformation, and manipulation are a few of the preferred methods Trump and his team use to control the narrative. This is an important consideration for mental health professionals to focus on since people are being exposed to these and even greater incidences of psychological control including splitting and projective identification. It appears to be worse now than during the election campaigns of 2016 and 2020.

President Biden became charged with leading a country that has never in modern history been as politically divided as it is today. Upwards of 70 million citizens cast ballots for Trump—almost 48 percent of total voters—and many continue to support him. In fact, this Trump-enabled amplification of existing tensions among Americans is all too real, a potential clash we need to deal with imminently for the good of our nation and our collective mental wellbeing. Much of this is driven by unconscious psychological manipulation on the part of the 45th President.

Trump's actions have no doubt influenced the behavior of other world leaders. His way of operating serves as an important addendum to the playbook other populist leaders use to run their countries, rendering it vital to fully understand the man that exemplifies this style of leadership since splitting and projective identification are the defense mechanisms that serve as a common thread linking these leaders in their actions. These maneuvers of control have contributed to emerging trends in conservative-leaning populist countries worldwide.

Trumpism is here to stay. The Brookings Institution found a correlation between Trump rhetoric and an increase in racism and violence, which appears to have given legitimacy to right-wing groups around the world (Gelfand and Williamson, 2019).

Americans who felt their needs had been ignored by other Republican politicians and previous administrations gravitated to Trump. And now that rhetoric is spreading worldwide. It is a brand of thinking that has emerged throughout Europe, Asia, and South America. Trump's behavior has also contributed to a disintegration of global values. He is certainly far from the first divisive American president, but he might be the first president to exhibit traits associated with splitting and projective identification in such a destructive way. I will look at other world leaders who are taking a page or two out of the Trump rulebook, as well as those who have felt the Trump effect firsthand.

Basic facts were called into question under Trump's presidency. When truth is less important than a sense of moral superiority, there's little wiggle room for finding middle ground.

Trump was defeated in 2020, but he is floating the possibility of another run in 2024. And Trumpism in America is not dead: acolytes in the U.S. are jostling for his mantle, while other leaders around the world are continuing in a similar vein of politicking—if it can work in America, it can work anywhere. Sometimes, Trumpian populism works better in countries where democracy is tenuous.

What follows are a few examples of how Trump employs projective identification and its consequences for the American people. This is hardly a definitive list but provides examples of the more salient representatives of how projective identification as practiced by a populist leader can harm the government, people, and the environment.

The Economy: Growth or Decline Under the Trump Administration

Despite Trump's boastful statements about building the greatest economy in U.S. history, the facts do not back up the claims. His promises of boosting the economy 3.5 percent or higher never came to fruition. Part of this disappointing news came during the pandemic when over 10 million people lost their jobs. However, even before the country suffered from the devastating effects of COVID-19, what we saw was Trump's inheritance from the Obama administration. The final three years of Obama's second term were better than Trump's best year, which occurred in 2018 (Jones, 2020).

Another indicator of economic growth is gross domestic product (GDP). There was not a meteoric rise in the GDP during Trump's single term in office. While it did rise by 3 percent as 2018, it had risen by 3.1 percent in 2015 during Barack Obama's second term, another indication that Trump rode into office on the coattails of the 44th President. Even in his own party, the increase in the GDP under George W. Bush from 2004 to 2005 was 3.8 percent and 3.5 percent, respectively. These numbers were lower than the historic high numbers of the 1950s and 1960s, which were in the 5 percent range (Jones, 2020).

The Rise and Fall of the Stock Market During the Trump Presidency

There is no question that the stock market index rose during the 45th President's term in office, peaking on February 12, 2020 to an all-time high. That day the Dow Jones Industrial Index rose to 29,551.42 points. It closed on December 31, 2020, at 30,606.48 (Zacks, 2020).

What occurred on the streets in most cities and towns in the U.S. during the pandemic was not reflected in Wall Street's numbers. This is a sad commentary on where we're at in the United States and perhaps what gave rise to Trump's popularity. While he campaigned as being anti-establishment, someone who would fight for the people ignored by the elite, he was part of those he railed about—the American elite: *Forbes Magazine* estimated Trump's value at $2.5 billion, much of that generate from his $40 million inheritance. Facts notwithstanding, he convinced those Americans that he was one of them. This is a false image of the 45th president that Trump's followers still believe. Several hypotheses about why Trump's base continues to be faithful to him were published in a review in *The Journal of Social and Political Psychology*. UC Santa Cruz professor Thomas Pettigrew and a group of psychologists found five reasons that help to explain Trump's popularity: Authoritarian Personality Syndrome, Social Dominance Orientation, Prejudice, Intergroup Contact, and Relative Deprivation.

Authoritarianism is the advocacy of strict fealty at the expense of personal freedom. Those suffering from the syndrome might display "aggression toward outgroup members, submissiveness to authority, resistance to new experiences, and a rigid hierarchical view of society. The syndrome is often triggered by fear, making it easy for leaders who exaggerate threats or fear mongers to gain their allegiance." Is Trump fearful of landing in jail? Perhaps. He certainly views the world from an "us" versus "them" viewpoint, and anyone who tries to give nuance or context to a situation is shot down.

Though like authoritarian personality syndrome, social dominance orientation refers to people who prefer the hierarchy of groups—there are clearly defined leaders and losers. Self-interested and tough personalities rule with social dominance orientation. Trump revels in this while appealing to others holding a similar worldview. White supremacists would agree.

Not all of Trump's supporters are prejudiced, but he caters to bigots and racists by coding his language with "dog whistles" that are shockingly overt: Muslims are "dangerous" and Mexicans are "rapists" and "murderers." This is one example of where his unrelenting deployment of projective identification comes into full effect.

Decreased intergroup contact—that is, interaction with people from different backgrounds—increased the likelihood that people would hold prejudicial viewpoints. Throw social media algorithms into the mix that allow users to only see self-reflecting truths, and you have a perfect brew customized for the modern Trumpian populist.

Finally, relative deprivation is this widespread sense of marginalization—that people in these groups are being unfairly targeted, whether by economic decisions or social ones. What impact, if any, has Trump's presidency had on our ability to deal with the rapidly escalating climate change crisis? While some might argue that Trump is not personally responsible for climate change—and he did not set in motion the situation we're in— his administration's policies and proclamations reveal another story.

Sending mixed messages during the early days of his presidency, Trump at times publicly acknowledged that climate change is not a "hoax," even as he memorably refused to believe the 2017 National Climate Assessment produced by U.S. government scientists. The announced withdrawal from the Paris Agreement only months after it had gone into effect under the Obama Administration (Trump, 2017), along with unprecedented rollbacks of major climate and environmental policies (Popovich et al., 2020), has not instilled much hope in those Americans who recognize that climate change is real and must be addressed to avoid further global catastrophe.

Trump demonstrably flopped on clean air, according to an Associated Press analysis of EPA data (Borenstein and Forster, 2019) which shows a 15 percent increase in the number of high air pollution days in the first two years of the Trump administration as compared with the last four years of the Obama administration. That is a setback from a long-term decline in air pollution under the previous four presidents, whereby emissions of sulfur dioxide—a component of acid rain—fell by 88 percent, to below pre-1990 levels. Lead particulate in the air was down 80 percent over the same period. Ground-level ozone, which causes smog, decreased 22 percent (Guillen, Snider and Wolff, 2019).

A statement released in 2020 by a group of nine leading agencies decried the Trumpian attack on the environment:

> Donald Trump's administration has unleashed an unprecedented assault on our environment and the health of our communities. His policies threaten our climate, air, water, public lands, wildlife, and oceans; no amount of his greenwashing can change the simple fact: Donald Trumphas been the worst president for our environment in history. Unfortunately, our children will pay the costs of this president's recklessness. Our organizations have repeatedly fought back against these attacks, and we will continue to fight to ensure that our kids don't bear the brunt of the Trump administration's anti-environmental agenda.
>
> (LaRue, 2020)

While a growing chorus of neuroscientists, psychologists, psychiatrists, and researchers in many other fields of study echo the urgent need for us to interact with our outdoor environment to be mentally healthy, what we need to do— have clean, breathable air—is becoming less available. According to Martin Hayden, Vice-President of Policy and Legislation at Earthjustice, Trump assaulted the "basic safeguards" we have in place to protect or clean up our water and air. He calls out multiple parties, including "Coal and oil lobbyists installed at the highest levels of government tasked with eviscerating our bedrock environmental laws," and "Secretive schemes to ensure that the public never gets a chance to hear about or speak out against any of it." (LaRue, 2020) Hayden added, "The only power that's restrained these corporate cronies in office is the power of the law."

We have a reasonable idea who the bad actors are in this scenario (chapter twelve is dedicated to examining the link between populist leaders and the increase in global warming), but to make progress, we need a sustained paradigm shift that involves changing the way we pollute our planet. Who will the good actors be, and what will their good actions look like? Only by engaging in an open dialogue about global warming—and facing what Al Gore so many years ago called the "inconvenient truth" about what it will take to save our planet—will we be able to take action to halt or mitigate the destruction.

Global warming is at an all-time high and the 'point of no return' might occur as early as 2035 (Sorab, 2019). The climate changes that started years before Trump became president deteriorated during his presidency. The Brookings Institution tracked regulatory changes that the 45th President made or relaxed. By February 2020 there were 74 (Brookings Institution, 2020).

The Political and Social Climate in America Following the Trump Presidency

Will Donald Trump fade into the annals of history as one of the worst American presidents or will he remain the unofficial leader of the GOP until he can return to power in 2024? No matter how this question is eventually answered, Trump deepened an ever-widening divide in America that might not lend itself to repair. This has caused family members and friends to sever their long-standing relationships, refusing at times to attend holiday events together even before the pandemic put a stop to such gatherings.

Trump, the New-York businessman-reality TV star, reshaped the presidency to focus on him, not the good of the people, but exploited American paranoia by opening the Pandora's box of deep-seated hatred and fear (Gittleson, 2021).

When some pro-Trump Republicans and Democrats managed to gather either virtually or in-person, the rule was that there would be no talk about politics. That might have prevented heated discussions at Thanksgiving dinners across the country, but it did not improve feelings that developed during the four years when Trump purposefully created an atmosphere that pitted people of all persuasions against each other. This is projective identification without anyone trying to heal the damage. Americans living with these beliefs about themselves and one another have had disinformation foisted upon them by the Commander-in-Chief. There's no easy fix, though I will share some ideas about damage control in a later chapter.

As a psychoanalyst, I know it is important to discuss problems versus avoiding them. Nothing can be resolved without talking about conflicts between and among people. When issues and differences of any kind are merely swept under the rug, they fester and can make bad situations worse. Like energy, aggression cannot be created or destroyed, we are born with aggressive tendencies that do not simply go away but are modulated by good caregivers. They help us learn how to tolerate and work through angry, rageful feelings that would otherwise be difficult or impossible to manage. That is acceptable for infant-parent dyads but what about adults whose pent-up anger or aggressive feelings need addressing?

Americans simply do not trust each other anymore. As former Secretary of State George Schultz wrote in a letter published in *The Washington Post* in 2020, "Trust is the coin of the realm. When trust was in the room, whatever room that was — the family room, the schoolroom, the locker room, the office room, the government room or the military room—good things happened. When trust was not in the room, good things did not happen. Everything else is details."

In high-truth societies, such as Canada and Sweden, people feel good and do well. The inverse is true where people are paranoid and distrustful (Wilke, 2008).

We need what Peter Fonagy and Elizabeth Allison (2014) call "epistemic trust," which refers to people's capacity to take in and believe what someone else has said or communicated to them without questioning everything (Messina, 2019, p. 1). In order words, in a world filled with fake news, misinformation and deliberate falsehoods given to others by those who wish to create chaos, where people purposely deceive others, we must be able to believe in the sources that give us news; we must be able to believe in the people who tell us what is going on in the world.

In his nomination speech at the July 2016 GOP convention, Trump himself identified the magnitude of a president's responsibility, saying, in hindsight, what comes across as almost farcical, "The most basic duty of government is to defend the lives of its own citizens. Any government that fails to do so is a government unworthy to lead."

Note

1 A 'good object' simply means the person whom the infant begins to expect will satisfy it."

Bronstein, C. (Ed.). (2001). *Kleinian Theory: A Contemporary Perspective.* London and Philadelphia: Whurr Publishers.

References

Blow, C. (2019). What Trump is teaching our children. *The New York Times*, July 19. www.nytimes.com/2019/07/17/opinion/trump-american-children.html.

Borenstein, S. and Forster, N. (2019). US air quality is slipping after years of improvement. Associated Press, July 18. https://apnews.com/d3515b79a f1246d08f7978f026c9092b.

Braddock, K. (2020). *The Strategic Role of Persuasion in Violent Radicalization and Counter-Radicalization.* Cambridge: Cambridge University Press.

Brookings Institution (2020). Tracking deregulation in the Trump Era. February 1. www.brookings.edu/interactives/tracking-deregulation-in-the-trump-era.

Centers for Disease Control and Prevention (2021) National Center for Emerging and Zoonotic Infectious Diseases. Vaccine safety: Autism, August 26. www.cdc.gov/va ccinesafety/concerns/autism.html.

Cooley, W. (2013). User clip of President Trump with coronavirus task force briefing. CSPAN, March 13. www.c-span.org/video/?c4861158/user-clip-no-dont-responsibili ty-all.

Dueck, C. (2019). Understanding conservative populism. *The American Mind*, November 19. https://americanmind.org/features/understanding-conservative-populism.

Feuer, A. and Hong, N. (2019). 'I answered the call of my president': Rioters say Trump urged them on. *The New York Times*, January 22.www.nytimes.com/2021/ 01/17/nyregion/protesters-blaming-trump-pardon.html.

Fonagy, P.and Allison, E. (2014). The Role of mentalizing and epistemic trust in the therapeutic relationship. *Psychotherapy*, 51(3), 372–380. doi:10.1037/a0036505.

Gelfand, V. and Williamson, V., (2019). Trump and racism: What do the data say? Brookings Institution, August 14. www.brookings.edu/newsletters/china_bulletin_ 01_25_2017/page/734.

Gittleson, B., (2021). How Trump obliterated norms and changed the presidency. ABC News, January 19. https://abcnews.go.com/Politics/trumps-legacy-obliterated-norm s-chipped-institutions-end/story?id=75275806.

Guillen, A., Snider, A., and Wolff, E., (2019). Fact check: Trump's environmental rhetoric versus his record. Politico, July 8. www.politico.com/story/2019/07/08/fa ct-check-trumps-environmental-claims-1573352.

Haberman, M. and Rogers, K. (2020) Trump's tactic: Sowing distrust in whatever gets in his way. *The New York Times*, September 3.www.nytimes.com/2020/09/03/us/poli tics/trump-2020-election.html.

Israel, J. and Provencher, D. (2020). Fact check: No, Trump didn't build 'the greatest economy in the history of the US. *The American Independent*, September 29. https://americanindependent.com/donald-trump-economy-fact-check-2020-election-ba rack-obama-growth.

Ivory, D., Leatherby, L., and Gebloff, L. (2021). Least vaccinated U.S. counties have something in common: Trump voters. *The New York Times*, April 17. www.nytimes. com/interactive/2021/04/17/us/vaccine-hesitancy-politics.html.

Jones, C. (2020). Obama's last three years of job growth all beat Trump's best year. Forbes.com, February 7. www.forbes.com/sites/chuckjones/2020/02/07/obamas-la st-three-years-of-job-growth-all-beat-trumps-best-year/?sh=450d60e76ba6.

LaRue, P. (2020). Environmental and public health advocates agree: Trump is the worst president for our environment in history. *Earthjustice*, February 4. https://ea rthjustice.org/news/press/2020/trump-worst-president-for-environment-in-history.

Messina, K. (2019). *Misogyny, Projective Identification and Mentalization, Psychoanalytic, Social and Institutional Manifestations.* London: Routledge.

Poniewozik, J. (2019). *Audience of One: Donald Trump, Television, and the Fracturing of America.* Liveright, p. xxii.

Popovich, N., Albeck-Ripka, L., and Pierre-Louis, K. (2020). The Trump administration is reversing nearly 100 environmental rules. Here's the full list. *The New York Times*, October 15. www.nytimes.com/interactive/2020/climate/trump-environment-rollbacks.html.

Read, B. (2020). A man drank fish tank cleaner after hearing Trump's medical advice. *The Cut*, March 24. www.thecut.com/2020/03/man-drank-fish-tank-cleaner-dies-as trump-touts-chloroquine.html.

Shultz, G., (2020). The 10 most important things I've learned about trust over my 100 years. *The Washington Post*, December 11. www.washingtonpost.com/opinions/2020/12/ 11/10-most-important-things-ive-learned-about-trust-over-my-100-years/?arc404=true.

Sommer, W. (2020). Trump made him a viral star. He's got a hidden backer, too. Yahoo Money, December 29. https://news.yahoo.com/newest-trump-boosted-viral-maga-095054427.html.

Sorab, V. (2019). Too little, too late? Carbon emissions and the point of no return. *Yale Environment Review*, March 26. https://environment-review.yale.edu/too-little-too-late-carbon-emissions-and-point-no-return.

Trump, D. (2016). Donald J. Trump Republican Nomination Acceptance Speech. Transcript printed in *The New York Times*, July. www.nytimes.com/2016/07/22/us/politics/trump-transcript-rnc-address.html.

Trump, D. (2017). *Statement by President Trump on the Paris Climate Accord*, The White House, June 1. https://trumpwhitehouse.archives.gov/briefings-statements/statement-president-trump-paris-climate-accord.

Wilke, W. (2008). *Where trust is high*, crime and corruption are low, Pew Research Center, April 15. www.pewresearch.org/global/2008/04/15/where-trust-is-high-crime-and-corruption-are-low.

Zacks (2020). Stock Market News for Dec 31, 2020. NASDAQ. December 31. www.nasdaq.com/articles/stock-market-news-for-dec-31-2020-2020-12-31.

Chapter 2

O Mito

Jair Bolsonaro, Blame Shifting, and Anti-Democratic Tendencies

Throughout Brazil, Jair Bolsonaro is known by his nickname, "O Mito," or "The Myth" in part for his stance against the political establishment, a savior supposedly arrived from the hinterlands to save the country from the socialist left. A legend, a hero, seemingly sprung forth out of nowhere, to protect the people. This type of mythmaking is in step with populist leaders who exploit normal psychological inclinations such as uncertainty and fear for political gain. Employing splitting, blame shifting, and projective identification permits a populist leader to both shift the perceived and real woes of the populace onto the "elite" while also providing legitimacy to the complaints aired by the aggrieved. The similarities between former President Donald Trump and Brazilian President Bolsonaro are staggering; both clawed their way to the heights of power through lies, fomenting distrust, and employing splitting, blame shifting, and projective identification to sway their base. Bolsonaro appears to be pleased to be in the same category as Trump. In a joint news conference on March 19, 2019, he said, "[M]ay I say that Brazil and the United States stand side by side in their efforts to ensure liberties and respect to traditional family lifestyles, respect to God, our Creator, against the gender ideology or the politically correct attitudes, and against fake news."

After Trump lost the presidency in 2020, the bond between the two men continued. In the days after the January 6, 2021 riots at the U.S. Capitol, Bolsonaro grudgingly recognized that Biden won the American election. Even as the riots were just barely being contained, Bolsonaro announced that "there were a lot of reports of fraud," leading up to the November election. And his thoughts of the riots themselves? "I followed everything today. You know I'm connected to Trump, right? So, you already know my answer" (Reuters, 2021).

At times—and even after accepting publicly that Biden is America's 46th President—Bolsonaro reaffirmed his assertions that the U.S. election was stolen from Trump. Why continue to make such a fuss when the dust seemed to have settled? Because he is using these statements to prop up his own claims that his presidential loss in Brazil's late 2022 elections would also only be due to election fraud. "What happened in the American elections?" he began in an interview. "Basically, what was...the cause of the whole crisis?

DOI: 10.4324/9781003202387-3

The lack of confidence in the vote." Without evidence, Bolsonaro repeated the baseless claims that people had voted multiple times and that dead people cast ballots, too. These statements let Bolsonaro pivot to his own argument for dispensing with electronic voting in Brazil's forthcoming presidential election. "Here, in Brazil, if you have electronic voting, it will be the same. Fraud exists. If we don't have the paper ballot printed in 2022, a way to audit votes, we're going to have bigger problems than in the U.S."

This type of rhetoric should sound familiar to anyone who followed the 2016 and 2020 American presidential elections because this kind of blame shifting works, at least on some levels. No, blame shifting did not keep Trump in office, but he's maintained a vice-like grip on his position as kingmaker in the Republican party, and many members of his base continue to believe his claims that the election was stolen from him. If it worked in America, why could it not work in Brazil? Like Trump, Bolsonaro understands where he derives his power and exploits it to full effect, as we will explore here.

This chapter will consider Bolsonaro's unprecedented rise to power over the course of thirty years spent bouncing around the military and in local politics, as well as the situations that permitted him to not merely inflict pain on Brazil's fledgling democracy but to potentially crush it. His various social and economic policies are rooted in splitting, blame shifting, and projective identification, worsening preexisting social division and unrest while, like Trump, his COVID-19 blame-game has been nothing short of a deadly disaster for the Brazilian people.

Whether tweeting into the ether or locking horns with journalists, Bolsonaro is always on brand and selling a certain image of himself. At the same time, he is shifting an aspect of his personality that he finds unappealing onto those around him. We could interpret that a characteristic Bolsonaro feels he must expel from his psyche stems from his childhood— perhaps something scared Jair who, along with his siblings, had to take cover under their parents' bed as gunfire ricocheted through the town square when local people were settling disputes. One can imagine how frightening those early experiences must have been, which might have caused him to identify with the aggressive fighters and their guns to defend against anxiety.

Knowing about his difficult childhood does not absolve Bolsonaro of his actions, nor does it fully explain his vice-like grip on national sentiment. Successful populist leaders manage to identify and articulate both real and perceived injustices in the public and exploit these feelings. Employing projective identification solidifies the authoritarian dynamic.

A Slow Rise

On the heels of his inauguration in January 2019, Bolsonaro's brand of politics included a plan to root out government corruption, prioritize law and order, and jumpstart Latin America's largest but stalled economy. Bolsonaro's ascent seemed to materialize out of thin air—an "outsider's" origin story if ever there was one—and his upbringing hardly portended a life on the national stage. As one of six children, Jair Bolsonaro was born on March 12, 1955, in a small town called Glicerio, located in the southeastern corner of the state of Sao Paulo. His father performed illicit dentistry—apparently a common practice in the 1960s until certified dentistry forced him to switch to a career fitting prosthetics—and the family moved frequently until finally landing in Eldorado, a decidedly not-mythical banana farming town in the Atlantic rainforest. Bolsonaro's childhood was chaotic and at times, violent, living in remote villages on the outskirts of the Amazon with a father whose job was itinerant and, sometimes, illegal.

The young Bolsonaro developed an early adoration for the military after a particular shootout that occurred between a military guerrilla group and local police:

> After the shootout, dozens of soldiers took over the town, searched houses and interviewed locals. It caused some tensions, but Bolsonaro and his teenage friends sympathized with the wounded policemen, got to know the troops, and used their local knowledge of the area to try to help them find Lamarca (a rebel army captain).He told them (the army) where the guerrillas might have gone.… In the weeks that followed, Bolsonaro made friends with the soldiers. After this he always used to say that he wanted to join the army. He thought what they did was great… His interest in the military became obsessive. Bolsonaro's infatuation with the army was, in a way, surprising.… Gerardo was investigated by the security forces for his political activities and then arrested for practicing dentistry. But there was little money for Jair and his two brothers and three sisters. And maybe Brazil's armed forces represented-as they did for many less well-off families-a potentially important source of economic security and social mobility.
>
> (Lapper, 2021, location 350)

Bolsonaro's infatuation with the army could be linked to his splitting of good versus bad: the army is good, everyone else is bad. After attending the Preparatory School of the Brazilian Army and the Aguljas Negras Academy, Bolsonaro enlisted in 1977 as a parachute infantryman and by the time of his discharge in 1988 had attained the rank of captain, though not without controversy; in 1985, his commanding officers ordered his detention for fifteen days in response to an opinion piece he wrote for *Veja* magazine criticizing the military's salary structure. Unsurprisingly, the story was denounced by his commanding officers, but lower-ranking members of the military supported his stance. It would be the first, but hardly the only, time Bolsonaro would find support among the Brazilian populace by blaming the military elite for being out of touch with the average soldier. The next year, Bolsonaro was court-martialed for allegedly attempting to disrupt the public water supply but was acquitted (*Veja*, 2020).

Discharged from the army in 1988, Bolsonaro launched a career in politics and ran for a seat on the city council of Rio de Janeiro. He leapfrogged from that to winning a seat in the federal Chamber of Deputies, where he remained for seven consecutive four-year terms. During his tenure as a legislator, Bolsonaro earned a reputation for spewing truly hateful ideology, from calling for the murder of "some 30,000 corrupt people, starting with President Fernando Henrique Cardoso" in 1999, to telling a fellow female legislator live on television in 2003 that he was not "going to rape you because you don't deserve it," to advocating for the death of a hypothetical homosexual son rather than accept him as he was. For these statements, Bolsonaro was censured, reprimanded, and fined, but did not lose his position and continued squawking from the bench. According to Ignacio Cano in Rio de Janeiro, Bolsonaro was "marginal and pretty much considered harmless" (Winter, 2018), which also meant that no one felt his words rose to a level that required action.

Of course, Bolsonaro had no plans to go anywhere but up, and in the intervening years his sons Flavio, Carlos, and Eduardo won seats as state legislators, city councilmen, and federal representatives. They, too, promulgated right-wing ideology without restraint, cementing the family's status as ambitious and hungry for greater power.

It was not until Bolsonaro's improbable run for president in 2017 that fellow politicians began to view him as a threat. His unwavering, decades-long message of law-and-order and of vowing to hold corrupt government officials responsible had touched a nerve among Brazilians, especially those who felt ignored by the Workers' Party, a left-leaning political body born out of the 1964 coup d'état and the ensuing twenty-years of military dictatorship. Then, in 2017, Bolsonaro's message—as with other nationalist leaders around the world—touched a collective nerve.

As I have discussed previously, a significant component of a person's life experiences is a result of those prejudices and biases, culture, and values that are cultivated from birth. Unconscious motivation is a powerful mechanism that drives people to do what they do, and at work in Bolsonaro's case, I believe, is a deep-seated need to eradicate intolerable elements of his persona. Understanding this allows us to better reckon with his leadership style and policies since he has successfully employed splitting, blame shifting, and projective identification to subdue his opponents and maintain power among his followers.

Bolsonaro's inflammatory way with language unleashed a simmering distrust among much of the Brazilian electorate of establishment figures, disgust for members of the military, and outright hatred for minorities, Indigenous Brazilians, and homosexuals. These unaired grievances reached a boiling point after the first decade of the 21st century, which, paradoxically, brought Brazil tremendous leaps in prosperity in almost equal measure with an increase in government corruption and seemingly endless political scandals.

In fact, it was a scandal involving the Workers' Party that catapulted Bolsonaro to the forefront of national politics. A criminal investigation launched in 2014 dubbed Operation Car Wash uncovered a massive money laundering and corruption scheme at state-owned oil company Petrobras to the tune of approximately $5 billion in embezzled funds. Among those caught in the snare were multiple high-ranking officials and former presidents Fernando Collor de Mello, Luiz Inácio Lula da Silva, and Michel Temer.

During his presidential campaign in 2018, Bolsonaro minced no words about his feelings for those under investigation. Like Trump, Bolsonaro turned to social media to reach a wide audience clearly hungry for his brand of bombast. With 6.6 million Twitter followers (eclipsed by Trump's 80+ million before being booted from the site) and another 18.2 million on Instagram, Bolsonaro's off-the-cuff, straightforward style resonated with his audience. He blamed a corrupt, left-leaning government for lining their own pockets while leaving the average Brazilian cleaning up after them and wondering whether they would become one of the nearly 60,000 homicide victims the country mourns each year. "Let's make Brazil Great! Let's be proud of our homeland again!" was his successful Trumpian stump pledge (Phillips, 2018). Trump ushered in and legitimized a new era for authoritarian-esque, gun-toting conservatism. And in Brazil, coupled with Bolsonaro's 30 years spent priming his base for paranoia and skepticism, the time was finally right for the rise of Bolsonaro.

In the four years prior to Bolsonaro's election, the country had suffered a historic drought, a rise in extreme poverty, unchecked deforestation, and an accidental but ruinous fire at the National Museum resulting in the loss of irreplaceable treasures, including collections relating to Indigenous and extinct languages in Brazil. Bolsonaro arrived on the national scene in October 2018 when people were looking for a champion—someone who would loudly and unapologetically fight for them.

Once in office, Bolsonaro began to make good on his promises, arguing for: zero tolerance for violence and calling for police to be comfortable employing lethal force ("a policeman who doesn't kill isn't a policeman,") (Anderson, 2019); repealing environmental regulations; ending abortion; and ending affirmative action and immigration. He might have earned the title of the "most misogynistic, hateful elected official in the world," from journalist Glenn Greenwald, but the people liked his brand of tough-guy action, especially given the recent parade of calamities that had decimated various elements of the country (Greenwald, 2015).

When he was firmly ensconced in his position as president, Bolsonaro continued to split people into desirable and undesirable groups and began to hurl aggression outwardly which made people feel bad. This appeared to be of little concern to him. Instead, it was *c'est la vie*.

This behavior has continued. When he targets others and treats them as receptacles for his unwanted and intolerable feelings and thoughts, he is quite possibly again employing projective identification; the primitive defense that allows Bolsonaro to deal with his internal angst with minimum of discomfort.

Let's recall that projective identification is an unconscious mechanism whereby a person rids him or herself of an intolerable quality by projecting it onto another person or other people. Thereafter he or she temporarily feels free, claiming the characteristic(s) resides elsewhere.

In general, when populist leaders exhibit these traits, the underlying factors seem to be rooted in a desire to expunge intolerable aspects of themselves while also maintaining a laser-like grip on those who answer to their beck and call.

What follows are some of the policies Bolsonaro has enacted during his tenure as president and an examination of how he has manipulated his foes and his base through the use of projective identification as a defense.

Homicides and Firearms Legislation

Homicides in Brazil began to increase dramatically in the early 2000s, when gun violence exploded in equal measure with Brazil's seemingly meteoric economic rally. In 2003, over 30,000 Brazilian citizens were killed by gun violence. By 2018 that number had doubled to over 60,000 annual homicides, equaling roughly 170 deaths a day. People at all points on the political spectrum were fed up. Populists draw power by capitalizing on widespread grievances when people believe they are being ignored. This is especially troubling in democracies with systems in place (such as courts with laws meant to promote justice and allow for redressing offences) (Ditto, 2021). Populists who employ projective identification will blame a broken system for all that ails a country, and then, once in power, will likely not do much of anything to help those who helped him gain his position.

Rallying the Brazilian electorate meant making assurances that Bolsonaro would not take away their guns—on the contrary, one of his first acts upon taking office was to ease gun ownership rules. In January 2019 Bolsonaro signed new legislation that increased the valid period of gun ownership from five years to ten years, and each Brazilian over the age of twenty-five was able to possess up to four firearms. Requirements for owning a weapon included providing proof of "the existence of a safe or a secure location for storage," which, in some cases could be the trunk of a car (Mazui and Barbieri, 2019).

Bolsonaro has continued to make it easier to acquire weapons, and as a result, gun ownership soared by 65 percent during his presidency, with an assist from abolishing the import tax on firearms and dropping restrictions on high-caliber weapons once reserved for the military and the police.

Interestingly, by June 2019, Brazil's murder rate plummeted by about 20 percent over the previous year. In an interview with the Wall Street Journal, Brazilian Justice Minister Sergio Moro (a judge who led the Car Wash corruption probe) said, "Our expectation is that this trend continues and that's what we're working towards" (Magalhaes and Pearson, 2019). Though his administration considered this statistic a win, most policy experts cannot attribute this trend to Bolsonaro's pro-gun policies. "There is no evidence that [Bolsonaro's] administration has had anything to do with improvements," (Stargardter, 2019) said Robert Muggah at the Brazil-based think tank Igarape Institute. "To the contrary, there are signs that certain forms of violence, not least police-related killings, may have increased since the election" (Stargardter, 2019). Ceasefires between rival gangs might have also led to a decrease in murders. At the same time, police engaged in more frequent and deadly encounters with the public, which Bolsonaro praised. His reigning stump mantra continued to be, "A good criminal is a dead criminal," (Darlington, 2018). Most homicide victims in Brazil tend to be young, Black, male, and living in favelas—vast slums in which organized crime flourishes, giving his credo more than a patina of racial prejudice (Darlington, 2018).

Interestingly, most Brazilians reported feeling that greater restrictions on gun ownership would result in less crime, yet Bolsonaro's sustained blame game launched a new wave of fervent gun culture fueled by blame-shifting rhetoric. To chum the waters, he turned to his most effective propaganda tool, Twitter, where he extolled the rights of average Brazilians to protect their families like the wealthy elite:

> With disarmament laws, who gives up access to firearms, the decent citizen who only wants to protect himself, or the criminal, who by definition doesn't follow laws? The right to legitimate self-defense cannot continue to be violated! Not everyone is in a position to have armed security guards.
>
> (Bolsonaro, 2019)

At the same time, Bolsonaro and his sons lobbied foreign arms manufacturers to build weapons in-country and then export them to countries like Saudi Arabia and India. Congressman Eduardo Bolsonaro called Brazil's arms market "elitist" because domestic red tape keeps prices high and competition out (Folhapress, 2020).

Amazon Wildfires and Indigenous Blame

The world watched in despair as the largest rainforest burned at a record rate in 2019. The Amazon is more than merely a rainforest in South America; this diverse ecosystem spans eight countries in South America—over 40 percent of the total land mass—and is home to unique species of flora, fauna, and approximately 30 million people. The Amazon is so diverse and uncharted that a new species of animal or plant is discovered every two days, according to the World Wildlife Fund (Gibbens, 2017). Rampant habitat destruction also means that some species might go extinct before they are even discovered.

The fires devastated the international community, which watched the incineration of the world's lungs—20 percent of the planet's oxygen is produced in the Amazon. These fires have increased in intensity, owing to deforestation, which in turn contributes to global warming. To understand the devastation unchecked wildfires in the Amazon could continue to have, I will discuss how projective identification and blame shifting strategies appear to have influenced policy decisions.

Historically, fires in the Amazon were not unusual, but the forests were generally resistant to widespread destruction thanks to a vast canopy of dense forest that creates its own weather systems, (Rasmussen, 2017) although major fire events did occur once every hundred years or so (Nepstad, 2007). In the past 50 years a combination of events led to "major ecological transformations" in the region, most bearing a human touch: increased logging, ranching, and the introduction of flammable grasses created a tinderbox waiting for a match. Now, the landscape has transformed; with fewer old-growth trees and dense forest canopy, the Amazon and its surroundings are more vulnerable to intense fires. According to the WWF: "[W]ith every new burn, the forest becomes more susceptible to a subsequent fire. The ecological tipping point of Amazon forests is reached when they become so flammable that frequent periodic burning is virtually inevitable" (Nepstad, 2007). In fact, some ecologists fear that if current deforestation trends do not reverse, the Amazon could become a source of CO_2 rather than a carbon reservoir.

To combat deforestation, Bolsonaro's modus operandi was to fuel the flames rather than put them out. In fact, he and his government have been called "a threat to the climate equilibrium" by Greenpeace (Nelson, 2020). During a pre-recorded speech at the United Nations in September 2020 Bolsonaro denied that the fires were causing any significant damage and that the blazes being broadcast on international news were set by poor locals and Indigenous people. "The fires practically occur in the same places, on the east side of the forest, where peasants and Indians burn their fields in already deforested areas" (Boadle, 2020). The reality on the ground reveals a far more organized slash-and-burn policy tacitly authorized by the Brazilian government. Most fires in the Amazon are caused by humans and occur in land previously clear-cut as a measure to prevent new growth. But it is not poor farmers who are causing the bulk of these fires—it is cattle ranchers and loggers enlarging their footprints with the backing of the country's powerful agribusiness lobby known as *ruralistas*. Researchers can determine the difference between natural and human-caused fires by satellite imagery (Borunda, 2019): thick plumes of smoke rising into the atmosphere are fueled by massive amounts of tinder—trees that have been previously felled and left to dry, making them easier to burn.

At the height of the fires in 2019, when 76,000 distinct blazes were tallied across the Brazilian Amazon, Bolsonaro basically told the international community to mind their own business. "You have to understand that the

Amazon is Brazil's, not yours. If all this devastation you accuse us of doing was done in the past the Amazon would have stopped existing, it would be a big desert" (Phillips, 2019). And rather than accept \$22 million in international assistance (though he later relented), a senior Brazilian official told French president Emmanuel Macron to focus inward and "take care of his home and his colonies." Instead, Bolsonaro pointed fingers at foreign governments with tarnished environmental policies: "No country in the world has the moral right to talk about the Amazon. You destroyed your own ecosystems" (Phillips, 2019).

Even when faced with satellite data from Brazil's National Space Research Institute (INPE) showing a dramatic increase in deforestation, Bolsonaro alleged that the images were fake. Suggesting photographs are doctored is a classic populist strategy designed to sow doubt—how can you, the public, be sure that these pictures were not manipulated by some nefarious foreign actor? Repeating such dubious inquiries and allegations agitates, aggravates, and confuses people, which is precisely what populist leaders want. "I am convinced the data is a lie. We are going to call the president of INPE here to talk about this and that's the end of that issue," he said (Bragança, 2019). Fittingly, he fired the man in charge of monitoring deforestation in the Amazon after that outburst (McCoy, 2019).

Adding insult to injury and further, undermining the public's trust in the "elite" political machine, Bolsonaro tacitly encouraged violence against Indigenous peoples living in the Amazon—people who just so happened to be standing in the way of businesses trying to profit from the untapped wealth of the forest. According to the Pastoral Land Commission (CPT), seven of twenty-seven reported deaths caused by Amazon-related conflicts were Indigenous leaders who attempted to block illegal loggers from further destroying the jungle. The CPT claims that these deaths are a direct result of institutionalized violence (Figueiredo, 2019).

Bolsonaro's campaign against Indigenous people has not been limited to the fight over the Amazon; in a move that accelerated a trend led by fellow conservative politicians before he became president, Bolsonaro directed the government to dramatically decrease funding of the National Indian Foundation, known as Funai, an agency charged with protecting Brazil's tribes. In 2017 a Funai official, speaking anonymously, talked about the mounting effort to cut costs at his agency as part of a larger move to disenfranchise the nearly one million Indigenous people who live in Brazil. "Without doubt, this is one of the worst crises for the rights of Indigenous people," he said, comparing the atmosphere surrounding his agency to that of the dictatorship of 1964 to 1985 (Phillips, 2017). Funai's budget cuts led to a diminished presence on the ground, paving the way for illegal land grabs by mafia-led logging and ranching concerns. At the same time, the pro-agrobusiness *ruralistas* increased their power and presence within Bolsonaro's party and produced a 3,000-page report that, among other things, accused Funai staff of inappropriately awarding land to Indigenous people and falsifying anthropological studies—in essence, blaming Funai for the Indigenous woes.

Bolsonaro has taken these aggressions further by continuing the push to open the rainforest to commercial development. "Where there is Indigenous land, there is wealth underneath it," he said in 2018. He has dismantled protections for Indigenous people previously ensured by the Brazilian Constitution in 1988 and has refused to grant further protected status to Indigenous lands, suggesting that 21st-century progress is the only true path forward. "The Indigenous person cannot remain in his land as if he were some prehistoric creature," he said in February 2020 (Schuch, 2020). A bill brought before Congress would legalize the illegal mining operations already underway throughout the Amazon and is a major contributor to increased river pollution.

What fuels such intense animosity towards Indigenous people? Is it possible, after growing up in the Brazilian backwaters, that he resented the Indigenous people who lived there? As someone who has largely identified himself as a provincial political outsider knows, he might resent Indigenous people for preventing, by virtue of their very existence, other (white/European descent) Brazilians from flourishing economically. Also, unlike in other populist-run countries, immigration is not such a big issue there, so the role of a de facto scapegoat in Brazil will be filled, at least in Bolsonaro's mind, by indigenous peoples. The Raposa Serra do Sol is one example where Bolsonaro has clearly designated native people as bad and blocking progress. Even though the area was marked as indigenous territory, Bolsonaro wants to open the land to mining for diamonds and gold and has turned a blind eye to farmer encroachment and violence. He could resent the fact that such a large area is protected and cannot be cultivated for economic gain. In fact, he has called Indigenous people "animals in zoos" and that protecting these lands is akin to keeping them locked in prehistoric times (Reuters, 2020).

COVID-19

Bolsonaro's handling of the pandemic proved that the policies of blame-shifting populists can turn deadly. The illegal mining and logging brought outsiders into the rainforest, putting previously isolated people into contact with carriers of COVID-19. As of March 2021—the last time these figures were updated—Brazil's Special Indigenous Health Service reported that the number of Indigenous COVID-19 deaths was at about 900, with some 50,000 people infected. However, that number does not include the roughly 400,000 Indigenous people who no longer live on reservations, and so the actual tally is likely much higher. In the small Amazonian Indigenous community of the Yanomami, ten children died from COVID-19 in January 2021, and the disease has spread to every known Indigenous community in Brazil (Assembleia Nacional da Resistência Indígena, n.d.).

Indigenous people live in communities that already suffer from smallpox and measles outbreaks and the recent homegrown mutation of COVID-19 will continue to decimate Amazon tribespeople. In March 2021 90-year-old Aruka Juma, the last member of the Juma tribe, succumbed to the mutant variant, most likely brought to his isolated region by illegal loggers carrying the disease. A tribe that once numbered around 15,000 members had dwindled to Mr. Juma and his children by 2002 (Knox, 2021). Meanwhile, the government has not attempted to stop the illegal logging and other invasions onto indigenous lands.

Bolsonaro has doubled down on his policies, telling the Brazilian public to "stop whining" about the virus. Even after he contracted it in July 2020, Bolsonaro did not publicly take the pandemic seriously. The first case was confirmed by Brazil's Health Ministry on February 26, 2020, and in March the presidential communications secretary tested positive for COVID-19 upon his return from Florida where he and Bolsonaro had met with President Trump. Rather than quarantine as public health guidance advises after exposure to COVID-19, Bolsonaro posed for selfies at a rally in Brasilia. By the end of March, Bolsonaro was urging municipal leaders to roll back lockdown measures and fired Health Minister Luis Mandetta for warning the public that the virus could result in a nationwide collapse of the healthcare system.

How Bolsonaro has viewed and handled the COVID-19 pandemic is perhaps the most obvious example of how he perceives the world and his role within it. His political and personal responses are sometimes one and the same and highlight how projective identification can be a very powerful and primitive defense which fosters confusion, frustration, and mistrust. When, as in this case, it is the leader of a country who is using this defense, those on the receiving end of the behavior are at risk for sickness and death. As of September 2021, Brazil's total reported cases of COVID-19 stood at 21 million, with nearly 600,000 reported deaths. As of publication, the country only trails the United States with the world's second highest COVID-19 death toll.

As Mandetta warned earlier in the pandemic, Brazil's health system is collapsing with intensive care units throughout the country operating at over 80 percent capacity (Castro, 2021). A special bulletin published by the COVID-19 Fiocruz Observatory warned that:

> "for the first time since the beginning of the pandemic, there has been a simultaneous worsening of various factors throughout the country, such as the growth in cases and deaths, the maintenance of high levels of Severe Acute Respiratory Syndrome (SARS), the high positivity of tests and the overload of hospitals."
>
> (Castro, 2021)

Brazil did not end up in this situation by some horrible misfortune. This is the result of a coordinated and willful suspension of working within the realm of reality.

From the start, Bolsonaro sought to diminish the severity of the virus and minimized the role preventative measures would have on keeping his people safe. The way projective identification manifests in a person in authority dealing with complex, alarming, and unpredictable situations can take numerous forms, from blame-shifting and gaslighting to magical thinking and minimizing. Bolsonaro has engaged in these thought processes since it became clear that shutting down his country to save his people would result in economic havoc. There is no indication that he will change his tone, either: in November 2020, he announced that he would not be taking the vaccine and called the use of masks, "the last taboo to fall."

Bolsonaro resisted promoting sound advice in favor of rallying against the scientific community. "I tell you; I will not take [any vaccine]. It is my right and I am sure that Congress will not create difficulties for whoever doesn't want to take a vaccine," he said. "If it is effective, lasting, reliable, whoever doesn't take it will be doing harm only to himself, and who takes the vaccine will not be infected. There's nothing to worry about," Bolsonaro said on social media. By December 2020, he was warning Brazilians that the vaccine could turn people into crocodiles. "In the Pfizer contract it's very clear: 'we're not responsible for any side effects,'" he said.

> "If you turn into a crocodile, it's your problem. If you become superhuman, if a woman starts to grow a beard or if a man starts to speak with an effeminate voice, they will not have anything to do with it."
>
> (Ibrahim, 2020)

Projective identification does not only happen among individuals, governments and their leaders employ this defense mechanism as well. COVID-19 is the disease caused by the SARS-CoV-2 novel coronavirus that was first identified in Wuhan Province, China. Just as President Trump insisted on calling it the "Chinese virus," the "China virus," "Wu Flu," or "Kung Flu," President Bolsonaro similarly revealed his penchant for name-calling and bullying as it pertains to the virus. The COVID-19 pandemic did not originate in Brazil, but once community spread was identified, the responsibility for how the virus was handled lay squarely on the shoulders of Brazilian leadership. But rather than wage war on coronavirus, Bolsonaro laid the blame for the crisis on everyone from Brazilian mayors, governors, his former health ministers, the media, to Indigenous people living in the Amazon.

Bolsonaro has avoided taking responsibility for his actions and for undermining local leaders' efforts to implement stay-at-home orders. For example, when the Brazilian Supreme Court sided with local jurisdictions in their ability to impose isolation requirements, Bolsonaro walked to the court and demanded a reversal of the order. "Some states went too far in their restrictive measures, and the consequences are knocking on our door," he said in May 2020 (Biller, 2020). He went on to suggest that local authorities attempting to take control of the virus in their own communities was tanta-mount to a descent towards authoritarianism.

By blaming the "global left-wing media," his mayors and governors, China, and Indigenous Amazonians for the COVID-19 crisis, Bolsonaro and his sons have institutionalized a strategy to spread the virus throughout Brazil. When a person in a leadership position expresses a conviction or a mood, their appointees often blindly parrot and even amplify their senti-ments. Bolsonaro's sons have readily spread his message of blaming out-siders and Indigenous people. And when government officials have tried to stem the outbreak, such as health minister Luiz Mandetta, Bolsonaro fires them. His second health minister, Nelson Teich, resigned after barely a month on the job. Though he did not explicitly say why he was leaving—at a press conference he said he had, "accepted it [the position] because I thought I could help the country and its people." It is widely believed that he clashed with the president's continued insistence to tout hydroxy-chloroquine as a treatment for COVID-19 (Londono, 2020). As of May 2020, eight Cabinet ministers had either resigned or were fired by Bolso-naro, further plunging the government into chaos.

In June 2020 the COVID-19 data was hardly rosy but publicly available. Soon, that data disappeared from public view. Why? "The cumulative data… does not reflect the moment the country is in," Bolsonaro said via Twitter. It took a Supreme Court ruling to restore the data (Dockery, 2020).

With the arrival of a vaccine, Bolsonaro flip-flopped on his feelings about it. First, he said it might turn patients into crocodiles. Then it became a "triumph of science," when the fourth health minister, Marcelo Quieroga, provided the gloss of authority and a fresh start. As new cases and deaths surged, the economy tanked along with his approval ratings. At that point, Bolsonaro and his surrogates embraced the slogan, "the vaccine is our weapon" and "embark[ed] on a more aggressive phase to combat the virus," which he said at a press conference when announcing Mr. Quieroga's appointment (Magalhaes and Pearson, 2021).

Mismanagement and denial left Brazil in tatters, and only when ratings appeared to be the driving force for the change in tone did Bolsonaro heed science. And yet, he was not totally on board with the new messaging: in March 2021 he hailed an experimental nasal spray from Israel as "miraculous" and returned to his mantra that social distancing, curfews, and mask wearing was unnecessary. "You didn't stay at home," he said to supporters. "You weren't cowards. We need to face our problems" (Londono, Casado, and Rasgon, 2021).

The problems, sadly, are tremendous. Harvard University professor Marcia Caldas de Castro minced no words: "Brazil is going down in history as a case study of what failed leadership can do in a health emergency, and the way we measure the cost is in lost lives" (Londono, Casado, and Rasgon, 2021).

Promoting a Populist Agenda via Projective Identification

The use of social media by populist leaders will be a common refrain throughout this book. Bolsonaro is second only to Trump in his ability to influence and manipulate millions via Twitter, Facebook, YouTube, and Instagram. Now that Trump is off mainstream social media, Bolsonaro might have taken the lead. His presidential victory and sustained hold on the electorate was assured by his dominance of both digital and legacy media. contemporary populists have something of a love-hate relationship with the media, engaging with voters via social channels fosters an air of authenticity—a "man of the people." In Bolsonaro's case it bolstered him rather than his party. When traditional media seemed to flatter him, Bolsonaro shared it across his channels, offering these tidbits as legitimizing his views; when criticized by traditional journalists, Bolsonaro returned fire, saying traditional news sources were frauds and fakes.

Consider, for example, when Bolsonaro shared a screenshot to his Instagram on May 30, 2020. In the headlines from Forum, a photograph purports to show Bolsonaro supporters giving him a Nazi salute. "FakeNews" he writes. "Olha a manchete (look at the headline)." Forum suggests his constituents are saluting, whereas he says that it is a group of shepherds raising their hands in prayer for him (Bolsonaro, 2020). Certainly, to some, the image looks like a group giving the "Sieg heil", but the background does look like farmland, so perhaps it could be shepherds simultaneously raising their arms in prayer that, at that moment the picture was shot, looked like a salute. In short, there's enough doubt sowed by Bolsonaro's PR team that his followers do not have to work hard to believe him.

Always with an eye to the future, Bolsonaro has gone into damage control. After seeing Trump booted from Twitter and the Facebook-owned WhatsApp in January 2021, Bolsonaro began urging his followers to also dump these social media platforms in favor of Telegram Messenger, a competitor messaging service to WhatsApp. But moving 6.6 million Twitter followers is no easy feat. Slow and steady wins the race: as of March 2022 Bolsonaro had grown his Telegram following to some 1.2 million—the largest such channel in Brazil and third most-followed international political figure on the platform (*Rio Times*, 2022). The mythmaking continues.

References

Anderson, J.L. (2019). Jair Bolsonaro's southern strategy. *The New Yorker*, March 25. www.newyorker.com/magazine/2019/04/01/jair-bolsonaros-southern-strategy.

Assembleia Nacional da Resistência Indígena (n.d.). (2021). *Overview of COVID-19 within the indigenous population*. Retrieved September 13. https://emergenciaindigena.apiboficial.org/en/dados-covid-19-novo.

Biller, D. (2020). In Bolsonaro's Brazil, everyone else is to blame for virus. Associated Press, May 25. https://apnews.com/article/virus-outbreak-health-caribbean-ap-top-news-brazil-7a7e8a0d3c524986412245ec9a23fad0.

Boadle, A. (2020). *Reuters*. Brazil's Bolsonaro blames indigenous people for Amazon fires in U.N. speech. September 22. www.reuters.com/article/uk-un-assembly-bra zil-idUKKCN26D1ZF.

Bolsonaro, J. (2020). *Instagram*, May 30. www.instagram.com/p/CA1Au7XBbcT.

Bolsonaro, J. (2019). *Twitter*, June 18. https://twitter.com/jairbolsonaro/status/ 1141159828003459072?s=20.

Borunda, A. (2019). See how much of the Amazon is burning, how it compares to other years, August 29. *National Geographic*. www.nationalgeographic.com/envir onment/article/amazon-fires-cause-deforestation-graphic-map.

Bragança, D. (2019). *Bolsonaro says INPE director may be 'at the service of some NGO*. OECO, July 19. www.oeco.org.br/salada-verde/bolsonaro-diz-que-dir etor-do-inpe-pode-estar-a-servico-de-alguma-ong.

Castro, C. (2021). *Covid-19: technical note points to a worsening pandemic*. AFN News, March 2. https://agencia.fiocruz.br/covid-19-nota-tecnica-aponta-agravam ento-da-pandemia.

Darlington, S. (2018). A year of violence sees Brazil's murder rate hit record high. *The New York Times*, August 10. www.nytimes.com/2018/08/10/world/americas/brazil-m urder-rate-record.html.

Ditto, P. (2021). Chapter 2. *The Psychology of Populism*. New York: Routledge.

Dockery, W. (2020). Coronavirus in Brazil: Bolsonaro government stops publishing Official Death Toll Figures, Drawing Outrage. *IBTimes*, June 8. www.ibtimes.com/ coronavirus-brazil-bolsonaro-government-stops-publishing-official-dea th-toll-figures-2989981.

Figueiredo, P. (2019). Number of deaths of indigenous leaders in 2019 is the highest in at least 11 years, says Pastoral da Terra. GI, October 12. https://g1.globo.com/google/amp/ natureza/noticia/2019/12/10/mortes-de-liderancas-indigenas-batem-recorde-em-2019-diz-pastoral-da-terra.ghtml.

Folhapress. (2020). Eduardo Bolsonaro wants foreign factories to increase access to weapons. Dol, January 26. www.diarioonline.com.br/noticias/brasil/548659/edua rdo-bolsonaro-quer-fabricas-estrangeiras-para-aumentar-acesso-a-armas.

Gibbens, S. (2017). New Amazon species discovered every other day. *National Geographic*, September 1. www.nationalgeographic.com/science/article/ama zon-brazil-new-species-discovered-spd.

Greenwald, G. (2014). The most misogynistic, hateful elected official in the democratic world: Brazil's Jair Bolsonaro. *The Intercept*, December 11. Retrieved May 4, 2015. https://firstlook.org/theintercept/2014/12/11/misogynistic-hateful-elected-official-dem ocacratic-world-brazils-jair-bolsonaro.

Ibrahim, N. (2020). Did Brazil's president Bolsonaro imply COVID-19 vaccine turns people into crocodiles? Snopes, December 22. www.snopes.com/fact-check/bolsona ro-covid-vaccine-crocodiles.

Knox, P. (2021). Last surviving man of Amazon's Juma tribe dies of mutant Covid spread by invading loggers. *The Sun*, March 15. www.the-sun.com/news/2516602/la st-surviving-man-amazon-tribe-dies-mutant-covid.

Lapper, R. (2021). *Beef, bible, and bullets: Brazil in the age of Bolsonaro*. Manchester University Press.

Londono, E. (2020). Another health minister in Brazil exits amid chaotic coronavirus response. *The New York Times*, May 15. www.nytimes.com/2020/05/15/world/am ericas/brazil-health-minister-bolsonaro.html.

Londono, E., Casado, L., and Rasgon, A. (2021). As Covid deaths soar in Brazil, Bolsonaro hails an untested nasal spray. *The New York Times*, March 6. www.nytim es.com/2021/03/06/world/americas/brazil-covid-bolsonaro-nasal-spray.html.

Magalhaes, L. and Pearson, S. (2019). Brazil's sky-high murder rate begins to fall. *The Wall Street Journal*, September 10. www.wsj.com/articles/brazils-sky-high-m urder-rate-begins-to-fall-11568122084.

Magalhaes, L. and Pearson, S. (2021). Brazil is getting a new health minister. *The Wall Street Journal*, March 15. www.wsj.com/articles/brazil-gets-new-health-m inister-11615859274.

Mazui G. and Barbieri, L. (2019). Bolsonaro assina decreto que facilita posse de armas [Bolsonaro signs decree that facilitates possession of weapons]. G1, January 15. https://g1.globo.com/politica/noticia/2019/01/15/bolsonaro-assina-decreto-que-fa cilita-posse-de-armas-ghtml.

McCoy, T. (2019). Brazil's Amazon monitor, fired after dispute with Bolsonaro, speaks out on deforestation. *The Washington Post*, August 19. www.washingtonpost.com/ world/the_americas/the-amazon-monitor-who-was-fired-by-bolsonaro-speaks-out-on-deforestation/2019/08/06/f436af92-b844-11e9-bad6-609f75bfd97f_story.html.

Nelson, K. (2020, September 22). Bolsonaro deflects responsibility for deforestation while the Amazon burns. Greenpeace. https://www.greenpeace.org/usa/news/bolsonaro-de nies-brazil-is-burning-blames-indigenous-people-for-fires-in-disturbing-speech-at-unga.

Nepstad, D. (2007). The Amazon's Vicious Cycles: Drought and fire in the greenhouse. EEF International. Switzerland. https://amazonwatch.org/documents/amazonas_ eng_WWF.pdf.

Phillips, D. (2017). Brazil's indigenous people outraged as agency targeted in conservative-led cuts. *The Guardian*, July 10. www.theguardian.com/world/2017/jul/10/ brazil-funai-indigenous-people-land.

Phillips, T. (2018). Jair Bolsonaro makes Trumpian pledge as poll shows big lead. *The Guardian*, October 7. www.theguardian.com/world/2018/oct/07/brazil-election-ja ir-bolsonaro-makes-trumpian-pledge-as-poll-shows-big-lead.

Phillips, D. (2019). Bolsonaro declares 'the Amazon is ours,' and calls deforestation data 'lies.' *The Guardian*, July 19. www.theguardian.com/world/2019/jul/19/jair-bol sonaro-brazil-amazon-rainforest-deforestation.

Rasmussen, C. (2017). New study shows the Amazon makes its own rainy season. NASA, July 17. https://climate.nasa.gov/news/2608/new-study-shows-the-ama zon-makes-its-own-rainy-season.

Reuters (2020). Brazil's indigenous to sue Bolsonaro for saying they're 'evolving.' Reuters, January 24. www.reuters.com/article/us-brazil-indigenous/brazils-indigen ous-to-sue-bolsonaro-for-saying-theyre-evolving-idUSKBN1ZN1TD.

Reuters (2021). Brazil's Bolsonaro reaffirms Trump ties, cites baseless vote fraud claims. Reuters, January 6. www.reuters.com/article/us-usa-election-brazil/brazils-bolsonaro-reaffirms-trump-ties-cites-baseless-vote-fraud-claims-idUSKBN29C01X.

Rio Times(2022). President Bolsonaro has the biggest Telegram channel in Brazil which will now be monitored and censored. March 23. www.riotimesonline.com/brazil-news/ brazil/president-bolsonaro-has-the-biggest-telegram-channel-in-brazil-which-will-now-be-monitored-and-censored.

Schuch, M. (2020). Indio nao pode ficar na sua terra como um ser human pre-hisor ico, diz Bolsonaro. *Valor*, February 18. https://valor.globo.com/politica/noticia/2020/ 02/18/indio-nao-pode-ficar-na-sua-terra-como-ser-pre-historico-diz-bolsonaro.ghtml.

Stargardter, G. (2019). Brazil murders maintain downward path in first three months under Bolsonaro. *Reuters*, April 18. www.reuters.com/article/uk-brazil-violence/brazil-murders-maintain-downward-path-in-first-three-months-under-bolsonaro-data-idUKKCN1RU1TM.

Veja (2020, July 30). O artigo em VEJA e a prisão de Bolsonaro nos anos 1980. July 30https://veja.abril.com.br/blog/reveja/o-artigo-em-veja-e-a-prisao-de-bolsonaro-nos-anos-1980/.

Winter, B. (2018). System failure: behind the rise of Jair Bolsonaro. *Americas Quarterly*, January 24. www.americasquarterly.org/fulltextarticle/system-failure-behind-the-rise-of-jair-bolsonaro.

Chapter 3

Populism in Hungary and the United States

The Similarities between Donald Trump and Viktor Orbán

Viktor Orbán has new-found popularity among conservative, right-wing American politicians. He, like many populists profiled in this book, is a study in contrasts: He hates immigrants and is alleged to be dismantling democracy—yet people call him a hero. However, the EU sees it differently, "A recent European Court of Justice ruling underscores that Hungary is not only in breach of the rule of law but violates the very rights and values on which the EU is founded" (Dordevic, 2020).

In spite of the fact that some European leaders have shunned Orbán because of his authoritarian behavior, according to Donald Trump, "Viktor Orbán has done a tremendous job in so many different ways"... (Jackson and Shesgreen, 2019). Many Hungarians would agree. His speeches have routinely attracted large groups of followers.

Every political institution in Hungary has been affected in what increasingly seemed to be Orbán's country. As Orbán gathered more control, all manner of events and atrocities occurred daily with little political fanfare, while the press faced daily scathing criticism for undermining his authority. In Hungary, policies are often changed without public support. In this case, many legal but questionable changes occurred after a democratically held election brought Orbán to power. In a space of a few short years, he refashioned the government in his image.

Similarities Between Viktor Orbán and Donald Trump

Orbán, the Prime Minister of Hungary and Donald Trump, the former President of the United States have a lot in common when it comes to leadership style. In short, both leaders do what they please without fear of repercussions. They are brash, bold, and undeniably charismatic. But neither seem to have defined political beliefs, save for one: whatever the people will follow.

They do this, in part, by psychologically splitting people into two categories: a "good" category and a "bad" one. Thereafter they blame people in the "bad" group for the projected, intolerable thoughts and deeds. This defense mechanism is followed by continual checking on the recipient's or

DOI: 10.4324/9781003202387-4

group's behavior to make sure the "badness" remains where they have placed it. This is how projective identification works.

Trump and Orbán are strikingly similar in the way they lead and interact with others. They are strongmen who appear to say and do what is on their minds irrespective of the truth. For example, Trump said a myriad of absurd and inappropriate things during his presidency—see Chapter 1 for a more fulsome examination—but for our purposes here, consider a claim he made on February 27, 2020, at a White House meeting about COVID-19: "It's going to disappear. One day it's like a miracle, it will disappear" (Holmes, 2020). By September 13, 2021, over 670,000 people had died in the United States (Centers for Disease Control and Prevention, 2021), yet Trump has faced no appreciable consequences for his egregious mishandling of the pandemic.

He also advised people to take a chemical that is not intended for human consumption, saying to reporters at the White House, "I think people should take hydroxychloroquine." The suggestion was followed by some Americans and proved to be fatal to at least one person and perhaps others as well (Yu, 2020).

Later, during a phone call with Brad Raffensburger in which he tried to coerce the Georgia secretary of state to "find 12,000 votes," Trump said:

> I think I probably did win it by half a million. You know, one of the things that happened, Brad, is we have other people coming in now from Alabama and from South Carolina and from other states, and they're saying it's impossible for you to have lost Georgia.

The facts were quite different, though, with Trump ultimately receiving some 74 million votes, and Joe Biden garnering more than 81 million (Wasserman et al., 2020).

Another lie Trump repeated at least 493 times: "We also built the greatest economy in the history of the world...Powered by these policies, we built the greatest economy in the history of the world" (*The Washington Post*, 2021). This was hardly the case. Numerous modern leaders of the United States have grown the economy faster and more than Trump ever claimed to, including Dwight D. Eisenhower, Lyndon B. Johnson, and Bill Clinton. For example, during Clinton's presidency, in 1997, 1998, and 1999, gross domestic product grew 4.5 percent, 4.5 percent and 4.7 percent, respectively, compared with an annual rate of 2.3 percent in 2019, slipping from 2.9 percent in 2018 and 2.4 percent in 2017, for Trump (2021).

Orbán, like Trump, also appears to say and do what he wishes without being concerned about any potential negative consequences of his actions. A vehement critic of the European Union Hungary is a member of, he once compared immigration to a "flu epidemic," and has surrounded himself with "loyal parliamentarians" who ensure that he can "rule by decree indefinitely and without any parliamentary oversight" (Bociurkiw, 2020).

In 2020 Orbán's chief of staff accused the European Commission of applying double standards in the way it treats EU member nations. (Associated Press, 2020). "The latest report of the rule of law by the European Commission highlights that we can't talk about the rule of law but the rule of blackmail," said the chief of staff Associated Press, (2020). The suggestion being that Hungary is mistreated and maligned—a country aggrieved—and its leaders are not going to take it.

When discussing their enemies, Trump and Orbán echo each other in tone and content. In a 2019 *New York Magazine* article, Jonathan Chait observed the methods each uses to attack their proclaimed enemies—people characterized as being part of "a shadowy cabal of globalist financiers." Trump, he writes, casts his enemies as, "these people that don't have your good in mind...It's a global power structure that is responsible for the economic decisions that have robbed us of our working class, stripped our country of its wealth, and put that money into the pockets of a handful of large corporations and political entities." Orbán, Chait asserts, frames his nameless foes similarly, that they:

> "...do not fight directly, but by stealth. They are not honorable, but unprincipled. They are not national, but international. They do not believe in work but speculate with money. They have no homeland but feel that the whole world is theirs."
>
> (Chait, 2019)

In the statements above, both men appear to psychologically split groups of people into two categories and then project aspects of their own ways of being onto their perceived foes: the "global financiers" (Trump could be one of them) and those who "feel that the whole world is theirs," (characteristics that have been attributed to Orbán).

The Use of Social Media and the Obstruction of Truth

Both Trump and Orbán use social media extensively to further their causes, albeit in different ways. Technology companies, along with the Republican election machine, spearheaded Trump's social media campaign in his bid for the presidency prior to the 2016 election. Today, those same tech companies employ algorithms limiting what people see. That means social media algorithms will show users what they "like" rather than what is necessarily the truth. This creates a problem when it comes to learning about objective truth. If users never watch or listen to legitimate news outlets, at best, only a small percentage of the population hears or reads about a range of opinions. In the best-case scenarios, a sliver of real, fact-based news gets in front of people for whom social media is their sole content and news provider.

Orbán's government controls virtually all media outlets in Hungary, so what the prime minister wants posted or reported in the news is what people see and hear. Under the guise of offering objective news, state-controlled media is merely a vehicle for pro-Orbán propaganda (Lendvai, 2017, p. 207).

Some analysts even fear that all factual reports have been eliminated from the Hungarian news diet. Expect to see further tightening of news as the country holds its presidential elections. (Bunyan, 2021).

That said, Orbán finally faced real opposition. To fight back against Orbán's increasingly heavy authoritarian hand, an opposition coalition composed of six parties came together during the summer of 2021 to challenge the Fidesz party in forthcoming parliamentary elections. But, as Amanda Coakley points out in *Foreign Policy*, "the would-be spoilers will have to battle a system stacked against them and dig deep to overcome internal divisions" (Coakley, 2021). Everyone in this coalition would have to put aside their differences and play nice to achieve their common goal. As it turned out, Orbán crushed the opposition, winning his fourth consecutive re-election.

The Radical Anti-Immigration Policies of Orbán and Trump

Viktor Orbán is a different kind of populist leader. Rather than campaigning against the elite, Orbán and his band of longtime friends *became* the elite. Though, to be fair, once in power, plenty of populist leaders often take on the trappings of elitism and remain populists in name only, Orbán quickly dispensed with such notions after he won the election in 2010 and his Fidesz party won a constitutional majority of two-thirds of the vote, which meant he could—and did—rewrite the constitution without opposition.

In 2014 Orbán gave a speech declaring that Hungary would turn away from liberal democracy and follow the time-tested practices of Eastern-style autocracies like Russia and Turkey. His behavior embodied this shift since the Hungarian government controls most news outlets including radio and television channels as well as news websites. According to a source cited in *The New York Times*, the Hungarian media is "beginning to resemble state media under Communism because of the level of control and consolidation" (Kingsley, 2018). Most other institutions in Hungary have been affected as well, including schools and universities, the Hungarian Academy of Science, and cultural institutions. Most industries and enterprises are also increasingly coming under the control of the government.

The declaration renouncing liberal democracy fit Orbán's worldview well, since from an early age he has had a very strong urge to be in control. According to Lendvai, "the absolute will to power has moulded the charter of Viktor Orbán ever since the time as a student leader… (2017, p. 19)." Gabor Fodor, a roommate at Bibo College and close companion until a disagreement damaged their friendship, said Orbán had always been intolerant and brash, but also "sincere and likeable" (Lendvai, 2017, p. 19). In other words, Orbán sounds like he had the ideal personality to evolve into a charismatic populist leader.

Orbán's views are in direct opposition to those of George Soros, a Hungarian-born philanthropist and one-time champion of Orbán and his Fidesz political party. Over several decades, Soros has spent hundreds of millions of dollars on various projects in Hungary. He also founded the Central European University (CEU) in Budapest so that students from all over the globe could get together to study various ideas as well as the concept of freedom. Orbán was one of its early students.

Initially, despite their differences, all seemed to be going well between Soros and Orbán, until a major rift emerged between these two men due, in part, to their different views on immigration. When the feud began, Orbán, who was by then prime minister, demanded that Soros move the CEU to another country. The man who had been his early benefactor who helped his political party a great deal, was suddenly a public enemy. Why did this occur? Why did Hungary's prime minister turn against Soros while attempting to characterize him as someone who should be hated by Hungarians?

Given that Orbán was turning Hungary into an autocracy controlled by one man and his close-knit group of long-time friends—all of whom have accumulated vast sums of money while in positions of power—it is curious that he would vilify his former supporter. What might account for this change of heart? Why did Orbán turn on his early advocate who generously helped him ascend to power?

The answer, at least in part, appears to be connected to his need to maintain control. In addition to the fact that most populists have a disdain for immigrants, Orbán has another agenda when it comes to people from different countries. Since he is popular among the Hungarian people, despite turning Hungary's democracy into a near-autocracy, his popularity could be threatened if Hungary were to become a more globalized nation, embracing people from other parts of the world. Demographic change in the form of immigration could threaten his absolute control.

In order to formulate a plan to become prime minister once again after failing to be re-elected in 2002, a loss that reportedly "deeply wounded him" (Hopkins, 2020), Orbán consulted a pair of veteran Jewish-American political consultants in the United States. George Birnbaum and the late Arthur Finkelstein helped Orbán start a smear campaign against Soros. By doing so, "… the two men - who both worked under Benjamin Netanyahu - are said to have helped to create the world's largest anti-Semitic conspiracy theory" (Bunyan, 2021).

That these two men helped Orbán launch a major campaign against the Jewish community worldwide is most peculiar. In an insightful article, journalist Hannes Grassegger reported on the ways the anti-Soros conspiracy theories have "spawned a new-wave of anti-Semitism" globally and fueled Trump's (and other populist leaders') rise:

> [Birnbaum and Finkelstein] designed a master plan for exploiting these divisions that has worked in many different countries and contexts, and helped create a Jewish enemy that the far right has exploited to devastating effect. In 2016, when Trump ran his final TV ad ahead of the election, it came as no surprise that Soros was featured as a member of "global special interests" who don't have "your good in mind."
>
> (Grassegger, 2019)

Birnbaum and Finkelstein helped win the election for Orbán by vilifying Soros but was the advice he received from the two political consultants the only, reason he launched a major campaign of hatred against his old friend? Presumably, he could have received the advice and chosen to pass it up, given how much Soros had previously helped him personally, and the Hungarian people more generally. But he did not. Instead, he launched a vicious plan to discredit and destroy him.

Is it possible that there is more to the story? I believe there could be a psychological mechanism at play that has not yet been discussed in conjunction with the Orbán/Soros conflict.

One example that supports my hypothesis involves the decision made by the European Court of Human Rights in March 2017 when it determined that the Hungarian government defied provisions established by the European Convention on Human Rights by detaining and then expelling two migrants from Bangladesh. In response to this verdict, Orbán said, "It is a collusion of human traffickers, Brussels bureaucrats and the organizations that work in Hungary financed by foreign money...Let's call a spade a spade, George Soros finances them" (Lendvai, 2017, p. 208). Thereafter, Orbán accused Soros of being a "'demon of the refugee crisis'" as well as the "... 'mastermind behind the campaign against Hungary'" (Lendvai, 2017, p. 208).

Enter splitting and projective identification: two defense mechanisms that could have contributed to the vitriolic attacks launched against Soros. It appears Orbán suppressed the good things that Soros did for him—as well as for the Hungarian people—to launch a major smear campaign against him and by fiercely publicly denouncing him, Lendvai (2017, p. 208) explains: "Orbán personally gave the signal for the attacks on Soros, because of his views on refugees and his assistance to various human rights and refugee organizations worldwide." After failing to integrate the good contributions of Soros with the things he did not like about him, Orbán appeared to project something he cannot tolerate about himself onto this man, "...who has done more for the consolidation of democracy in post-communist Hungary and the other East-European states than perhaps any other private individual (Lendvai, 2017, p. 208)."

It also seems probable that Orbán felt criticized when the Court of Human Rights, in the case mentioned above, found that the Hungarian government violated an EU regulation. Rather than investigating this allegation or accepting responsibility for this offense if it occurred, Orbán might have projected the feelings associated with being found guilty, charges that he could not tolerate, onto Soros, and thereafter blamed him for the Court's decision— since people who use projective identification as a defense always place blame on another person or on other people.

The Connection Between Corruption and Projective Identification

There is also a possible connection between corruption and projective identification as it relates to Orbán and the unscrupulous and dishonest things that have reportedly occurred in Hungary during his rule. While corruption seems to have run rampant in the country under Orbán's administration, public enemy number one, the "most corrupt man in the world" according to Orbán, is George Soros. In the *Columbia Journalism Review*, journalist Esther Kardos printed an interview with a Hungarian economist gleaning the reasoning behind Orbán's hypocrisy:

> Though the 2002 election taught Orbán the power of propaganda, he learned corruption all on his own. "Orbán first smelled money between 2008 and 2012," Zsolt said. "Like I explained earlier, though he grew up poor, he never really had an interest in becoming very rich. This changed when Orbán's father got a hold of a large share of Hungary's stone mines—pretty close to a monopoly, actually—and the Orbán family became very wealthy. This was when greed took hold of Orbán, and luckily for him, his election in 2010 coincided with the E.U. suddenly stockpiling Hungary with billions of forints."
>
> (Kardos, 2019)

Rather than considering the accusations that have been waged against him and his governance in Hungary, Orbán simply railed against Soros. In spite of Orbán's claims, Reuters (2020) came to a different conclusion when it fact-checked a lengthy online post that contained multiple spurious accounts of Soros's activities, debunking claims that Soros via his Open Society Foundation had funded anti-Trump protests following the 2016 election and later during Justice Kavanaugh's confirmation hearings to the Supreme Court of the United States. It appears that Orbán's way of getting rid of internal feelings and thoughts that he cannot tolerate as they relate to accusations of corruption are similar to Trump's way of handling these matters: They both shift blame to others rather than acknowledging their behavior. The same mechanisms seem to apply whenever either of these two men have received criticism about their anti-immigration policies.

In fact, one part of Trump's anti-immigration stance is embedded at the heart of the Make America Great Again slogan used first by his political campaign and later by his presidential administration. On the surface, the message behind this nationalist-promoting mantra to please Trump's base could look positive: emphasizing the importance of giving Americans more jobs, importing fewer goods, exporting more products from the U.S., and a broad plan to create more opportunities for what Trump refers to as "the people." However, beneath the surface is a much more obtuse motive.

The Root of Donald Trump's Dislike for Immigrants

Donald Trump has been accused of a great deal of corruption, yet he never accepts blame for any wrongdoing. Instead, he always points a finger at others. One example that comes to my mind occurred prior to the 2016 presidential election in the United States. During one debate with Hillary Clinton, another candidate vying for the presidency that year, he called the former Secretary of State "crooked Hillary." At this point, that statement seems laughable since the then candidate who became president was attempting to exonerate himself from wrongdoing and accusations of criminality. He did that by projecting feelings associated with corruption accusations that he had faced for much of his life onto Mrs. Clinton.

In terms of immigration, Trump appears to hate people who are not American citizens from birth because he cannot tolerate his mother's own humble immigrant background. While he has claimed that she met his father when on holiday, Mary Ann had emigrated from a remote and impoverished fishing village in Scotland and came to America to be a domestic worker, essentially to escape abject poverty. I wrote about Trump's relationship to the idea of his mother as a vulnerable immigrant, and of himself as her progeny, in *Aftermath: Healing from the Trump Presidency*:

> We should not gloss over or dismiss where she came from and what she was leaving behind when she traveled to the United States. And while it's true that Donald Trump always speaks highly of his mother—when he speaks of her at all, that is—his reluctance to open up about her background and his very humble Scottish roots strikes me as rather odd. It very well may be that he is embarrassed.
>
> Indeed, his treatment of and his attitude toward immigrant minors on the border, who come from similarly impoverished and filthy living conditions, may indicate a deep-seated shame and deeply buried feeling of disgust. And instead of dealing with that feeling directly, I contend that Donald Trump copes by projecting that onto others. In denigrating those who come from similar circumstances, I believe he is attempting to direct attention away from his own family's history.
>
> (Messina, 2021, pp. 63–64)

This is a vivid example of Trump's projective identification, or "blame shifting," in which the truth is never objective or sacred, but rather whatever he makes it out to be.

Orbán notably disdains people living in his country who are not Hungarian. He appears to detest immigrants of all types, heralding his desire and the country's need for "a Hungarian Hungary..." (Lendvai, 2017, p. 217). Consequently, to secure Hungary's borders, he ordered that a fifty-mile fence be erected to keep Serbian and then Croatian refugees out of the country. This commitment to maintaining a homogenized society was also evident at the Trump/Orbán Summit in 2019 when it became clear that, "Orbán and his allies are quite explicit about wanting to preserve that essential Hungarian-ness" (Collins, 2019).

Donald Trump And Viktor Orbán Revise History

Another way Orbán and Trump employ projective identification is by selectively rewriting history and erasing the truth about historical events to suit their visions of the past, the present, and the future as well.

Orbán has used the tactic of ridding himself of things he does not like or cannot tolerate about himself to create a more palatable and advantageous version of reality. He is reported to be literally changing the landscape of parts of Hungary by rearranging public areas—including reconstructing a city square and justifying the action by stating that the aim was to invoke the pre-1945 Soviet occupation appearance of the space—and by removing statues of people from the past he does not like. For example, he decided that Hungarians should forget about the attempted Hungarian Revolution against Russian dominance that occurred in 1956 so he had the statue of Prime Minister Nagy removed, someone he previously admired, claiming Nagy was "...the last responsible Hungarian leader" (Scanish and Eisen, 2019).

Previously, in 1989, in a speech that helped launch his political career, Orbán praised Nagy effusively and argued for the importance of the preservation of his memory in Hungarian society. At that time, as observed in a Brookings Institution publication, "Orbán denounced the hypocrisy of politicians who 'now rush to touch the coffins [of revolutionaries like Nagy] as if they were charms of good luck' despite having once 'made us study from books that falsified the revolution' (Scanish and Eisen, 2019).

Trump is actively rewriting his legacy as the 45th President of the United States while suggesting that he will run again in 2024. He argued for months—without proof—that there is a way for him to be "reinstated" as president via election audits and other efforts to overturn previously certified election results in states where he has strong legislative support (Lahut, 2020). This is one of Trump's ways of employing projective identification as it relates to erasing history. He has also gone beyond telling simple lies and has created what he himself calls, in all-caps, "THE BIG LIE" as he continues to claim that a massive conspiracy robbed him of a second term. The result is that many Republicans now question the election results—and the lie has taken on a life of its own (Wolf, 2021).

While projective identification and blame shifting appear to be mainstays of political strongmen like Orbán and Trump, it is only when we delve into these men's formative and developmental relationships and experiences, exposing the ways in which they themselves have felt shame and self-disgust, that we can truly see the way that they rely on these psychological maneuvers to facilitate the control they wield over others. Pushing back against things they despise about themselves; they choose to attack vulnerable people publicly and vehemently. Recognizing these patterns and seeking out the truth is the only way to overcome them.

References

Associated Press. (2020). *Hungary sharply criticizes EU Commission after report*. October 1. https://apnews.com/article/hungary-europe-archive-viktor-orban-e75fc94e424446ceeaee6 213ef3dde2a.

Belam, M. and agencies. (2021). Donald Trump uses new website to rewrite history of his presidency. *The Guardian*, March 30. www.theguardian.com/us- news/2021/mar/ 30/donald-trump-uses-new-website-rewrite-history-presidency.

Bociurkiw, M. (2020). *Hungarian leader's outrageous power grab*. CNN Opinion, April 3. www.cnn.com/2020/04/03/opinions/hungary-autocrat-covid-19-power-grab- bociurkiw/ index.html.

Bunyan, R. (2021). Hungary prepares 'digital freedom' fight against Facebook and Twitter: PM Viktor Orbán fears he could be banned like Trump. *Daily Mail Online*, January 27. www.dailymail.co.uk/news/article-9192791/Hungary-prepares-digita l-freedom-fight-against-Facebook-Twitter-PM-fears-banned.html.

Bureau of Democracy, Human Rights, and Labor. (2021). 2020 country reports on human rights practices: Hungary. U.S. Department of State. March 30. www.state. gov/reports/2020-country-reports-on-human-rights-practices/hungary.

Centers for Disease Control and Prevention. Covid-19 Data Tracker. https://covid.cdc. gov/covid-data- tracker/#datatracker-home.

Chait, J. (2019). Trump's dream is to become America's Viktor Orbán. *New York Magazine*, December 26. https://nymag.com/intelligencer/2019/12/president-trump s-dream-is-to-become-americas-viktor-Orbán.html.

Coakley, A. (2021). After three straight electoral victories by Viktor Orban, an unlikely coalition senses a chance to halt the country's slide into authoritarianism. *Foreign Policy*, July 16. https://foreignpolicy.com/2021/07/16/hungary-orban-opposi tion-coalition-election.

Collins, W. (2019). In Trump-Orbán summit, populism's critics have a chance to grow up. *The American Conservative*, May 14. www.theamericanconservative.com/articles/ in-trump-OrbánOrbán-summit-populisms-critics-have-a-chance-to-grow-up.

Corum, S. (2021). US reaches grim milestone of 400K COVID deaths days before Trump leaves office. *Truthout.org*, January 19. https://truthout.org/articles/us-rea ches-grim- milestone-of-400k-covid-deaths-days-before-trump-leaves-office.

Dordvec, I. (2020). *Viktor Orban's authoritarian playbook. Atlantic Sentinel*, October 25. https://atlanticsentinel.com/2020/10/viktor-orbans-authoritarian-playbook.

Grassegger, H. (2019). The unbelievable story of the plot against George Soros. *Buzz-Feed news*, January 20. www.buzzfeednews.com/article/hnsgrassegger/george-soros-conspiracy-finkelstein-birnbaum-Orbán-netanyahu.

Herszenhorn, D.M. (2017). Hungary's Freudian political fight: Orbán vs Soros. *Politico*, April 17. www.politico.eu/article/hungarys-freudian-political-fight-Orbán-vs-soros.

Holmes, O. (2020). What Donald Trump has said about Covid-19 – a recap. *The Guardian*, October 2. www.theguardian.com/us-news/2020/oct/02/what-donald-trump-has-said-about-covid-19-a-recap.

Hopkins, V. (2020). How Orbán's decade in power changed Hungary. *Financial Times*, May 21. www.ft.com/content/414f202e-9996-11ea-8b5b-63f7c5c86bef.

Jackson, D. and Shesgreen, D. (2019). Donald Trump says 'controversial' Hungary prime minister Viktor Orban doing 'tremendous job.' *USA Today*, May 13. www.usatoday.com/story/news/politics/2019/05/13/donald-trump-says-hungary-prime-minister-viktor-orban-doing-tremendous-job/1190060001.

Kardos, E. (2020). Living with corruption: An examination of Viktor Orbán's Hungary. *Blog*, December 15. www.cpreview.org/blog/2020/12/living-with-corruption-an-examination-of-viktor-orbns-hungary.

Kessler, G., Rizzo, S., and Kelly, M. (2021). Trump's false or misleading claims total 30,573 over 4 years. *The Washington Post*, January 24. www.washingtonpost.com/politics/2021/01/24/trumps-false-or-misleading-claims-total-30573-over-four-years.

Kingsley, P. (2018) Orbán and his allies cement controls of Hungary news media. *The New York Times*. www.nytimes.com/2018/11/29/world/europe/hungary-Orbán-media.html.

Kruse, M. (2017). The mystery of Mary Trump. *Politico*, November/December, www.politico.com/magazine/story/2017/11/03/mary-macleod-trump-donald-trump-mother-biography-mom-immigrant-scotland-215779.

Lahut, J. (2021). Trump is telling people he thinks he'll be 'reinstated' as president in August, according to a report. *Businessinsider.com*, June 1. www.businessinsider.com/trump-expects-to-be-reinstated-as-president-august-2021-6.

Lendvai, P. (2017). *Orbán: Hungary's Strongman*. Oxford University Press.

Mair, L. (2018). Donald Trump's 'shithole' roots. *US News*, January 17. www.usnews.com/opinion/thomas-jefferson-street/articles/2018-01-17/donald-trump-should-remember-his-family-came-from-a-shithole-too.

Messina, K. (2021). *Aftermath: Healing from the Trump presidency*. Pi Press.

Pilon, M. (2016). Donald Trump's immigrant mother. *The New Yorker*, June 24. www.newyorker.com/news/news-desk/donald-trumps-immigrant-mother.

Reuters. (2020). Factcheck: False claims about George Soros. Reuters, September 29. www.reuters.com/article/uk-factcheck-false-george-soros-claims-idUSKBN23P2XJ.

Reuters. (2021). An official website of Trump launched to stay connected with supporters. Reuters, March 30. www.reuters.com/article/us-usa-trump-website-idUSKBN2BM0FC.

Scanish, M. and Eisen, N. (2019). History in the (un)making: Historical revisionism in Viktor Orbán's Hungary. *Brookings Institution*, November 25. www.brookings.edu/blog/order-from-chaos/2019/11/25/history-in-the-unmaking-historical-revisionism-in-viktor-Orbáns-hungary.

Wasserman, D., Andrews, S., Saenger, L., Cohen, L., Flinn, A., and Tatarsky, G. (2021). 2020 national popular vote tracker. *The Cook Political Report*. https://cookp olitical.com/2020-national-popular-vote-tracker.

Wolf, Z. (2021). *The 5 key elements of Trump's big lie and how it came to be*. CNN, May 19. www.cnn.com/2021/05/19/politics/donald-trump-big-lie-explainer/index.html.

Yu, G. (2020). Trump suggests hydroxychloroquine may protect against Covid-19. Researchers say there's no evidence of that. CNN, April 11. www.cnn.com/2020/04/ 05/health/trump-lupus-hydroxychloroquine-coronavirus-protection/index.html.

Chapter 4

The Forgotten People
Populism in Australia and New Zealand

Prior to livestreaming his murderous rampage on congregants at two mosques in Christchurch, New Zealand, Brenton Tarrant anonymously posted a wild and wide-ranging declaration of intent to the online message board 8chan, a user-generated message board initially frequented by video gamers that became a notorious virtual town square that welcomed white supremacists, ultra-nationalists, and other hate groups. In addition to signaling that he was moving from word to deed, Tarrant railed against Muslims, immigrants, and other "invaders" he argued were responsible for undermining white supremacy. Shortly after posting his appeal to spread the word, white supremacists and sympathizers reposted and shared his message as well as his livestream of the massacres on Facebook and You-Tube, with 1.5 million copies uploaded to Facebook in 24 hours. YouTube representatives told *The Guardian* that at one point there was at least one new upload every second." (Hern, 2019). Facebook said that the original live stream of the attack was viewed around two hundred times and as a recording 4,000 times before the company removed the video from its platform.

The Christchurch Mosque massacres that left 49 people dead and 51 others injured shocked New Zealanders and people throughout the rest of the world. The twenty-eight-year-old transplant from Grafton, Australia who professed ties to alt-right ideology was eventually apprehended and charged with murder. Prime Minister Jacinda Ardern described the attacks as "one of New Zealand's darkest days," and many pointed to the event as a marker in the increasing trend of online hate speech migrating into the real world.

The rise of white supremacy groups in New Zealand and Australia did not materialize unbidden from the depths of the internet, though social media certainly accelerated its recent growth. Violent, ultra-right-wing extremism fueled by populist politicians in Australia and New Zealand might not be as well studied as the kind of populism found in Europe and North America, but this antipodean version is no less potent. This chapter

DOI: 10.4324/9781003202387-5

will look at the populist forces behind the white supremacist movement and other forms of hate against Indigenous Australians, Asians, Jews, and Muslims—surprising, at first blush, considering that Australia is one of the most culturally and linguistically diverse countries on earth. But, just as these countries have both tackled COVID-19 with better results than many Western nations, Australia and, to a greater extent, New Zealand, appear to be better at preventing populist leaders from spreading their messages of xenophobia and hate.

Further, this chapter will examine the theory of radicalization based on motivational, ideological, and social components that are enabled by a populist leader's use of projective identification. Extremism has left an indelible mark on Australia and New Zealand, and though the rate of violence is still much lower than in other democracies, the risk and nature of right-wing extremism has grown, especially since 2000.

A Brief History of Populism in Australia

Australia has served as a breeding ground for right-wing extremism for years, but experts seem to disagree on just how old this issue is. In 2017 the Australian Institute of Criminology issued a paper examining the history of far-right activity in the country, which it traces back to Federation—the date Australia became a nation on January 1, 1901. Other academics point to the origins of the populist movement starting as early as the nineteenth century, when the continent was still under British rule. In a country where over 300 languages are spoken and where worshippers embrace one hundred different faiths, the notion that right-wing extremism could flourish seems far-fetched. And yet, there is precedent. A form of agrarian-based populism took root in Australia in the early 1840s when working class farmers began advocating for independence from the United Kingdom (Lloyd, 2021). This was followed by another movement in the 1890s and 1930s when economic depressions rocked working-class Aussies. In these cases, populist propaganda blamed the banks for ruining the lives of the "little people," and in regions such as Queensland, these ideas formed the social identity of the place that exists to this day (Stokes, 2000).

Queensland: The Cradle of Australian Populism

Since the late 19th century, Queenslanders have viewed themselves as a group apart from their fellow Australians, which helps explain the rise of regional populism in the state. Nicknamed the Sunshine State, Queensland is the second-largest state geographically and is larger than all but fifteen countries worldwide, boasting a diverse ecosystem ranging from tropical rainforests to deserts. Prior to colonization, the northeastern region was the most populated of the entire continent, owing to its welcoming climate and abundant wildlife. By 1770 James Cook had claimed most of the East

Coast in the name of Great Britain, eight years later the colony of New South Wales was founded in what is now Queensland, and Brisbane became a penal colony in 1824 for hardened criminals from Sydney. Queensland was important to Australia, but from the beginning, it was relegated to Wild West status, good for producing foodstuffs and taking prisoners out of the mainstream penal system.

After Federation, populist politics would remain an undeterrable feature in Queensland. Though he was not a Queensland native, Prime Minister Sir Robert Menzies (1894–1978) gave a series of speeches through the 1940s called *The Forgotten People*, in which he addresses, though through a liberal lens, the importance of those left behind by the march of progress. This resonated with Queensland's locals but would pale in comparison to a homegrown populist who rallied the people around a political campaign filled with gaffes and angry outbursts: Joh Bjelke-Petersen (1911–2005).

By the 1980s the more left-leaning, progressive populism championed by Menzies had been supplanted in Queensland by a right-wing brand under the aegis of the National Party. Notably, Bjelke-Petersen, the country's longest-serving state Premier, capitalized on the groundswell of perceived grievances throughout Queensland to maintain his hold on power as well as to provide himself with a mandate to enact sweeping changes across the state. As we saw with President Donald Trump's victory in 2016, Bjelke-Petersen exploited Queenslanders' (Stokes, 2000) mistrust of other states, a strong conservative streak, and pride in rural agrarian provincialism. By 1974 the Labour Prime minister Gough Whitlam labeled Bjelke-Petersen as "a Bible-bashing bastard....a paranoid, a bigot and fanatical" (*The Sydney Morning Herald*, 2005). Another Labor party minister said he "embodied the bewilderment, ignorance, and the simplistic certainty," of his political followers. As an individual, Bjelke-Peterson held greater sway over populist movements than his party—a hallmark of populist leaders—and, like many of the politicians studied throughout this book, he employed blame shifting and projective identification to maintain his control.

Much like his American counterpart would be portrayed in the 21st century, Bjelke-Petersen—also known as "the Hillbilly Dictator"—embodied everything the traditional Australian political apparatus despised: he was an outsider who spoke plainly (if brashly) and railed against the elites whom he charged with ignoring the vast populace (Whitton, 1993). He could be "personally charming" one minute, raging mad the next; a devout Christian who had no qualms about strong-arming political friends and foes when it suited his needs. His government in Queensland maintained power banana-republic-style, through an electoral gerrymander that gave greater weight to votes rom less-populated (and more supportive) rural areas rather than urban ones. Police strongarm tactics became commonplace at any sign of dissent. A single legislative chamber ensured that there were no checks on Bjelke-Petersen running roughshod over Queensland's politics. It was the ideal populist platform, teetering dangerously close to totalitarianism.

When members of his cabinet did not do his bidding, Bjelke-Petersen fired them. His strongarm tactics included clamping down on free speech and public demonstrations, effectively criminalizing any political dissent, as well as implementing laws that banned public protests. Further, Bjelke-Petersen targeted environmentalists, liberals, union members, the LGBTQ community, and Indigenous Australians as responsible for a perceived breakdown in social decorum. These groups represented the antithesis of what he termed to be "good Queenslanders." After his run for Australia's prime minister—which failed—he refused to relinquish his position as Premier until the Queensland governor pressured him to do so (Costar, 2005).

The Queensland Premier lashed out regularly at those who did not live up to his definition of good people, blaming them for bringing the rest of the state down. For example, during the AIDS epidemic of the 1980s, Bjelke-Petersen demonized people suffering from the disease and even quietly opposed HIV screening for Indigenous Australians. Mike Ahern, the man who succeeded Bjelke-Petersen as Queensland Premier, alleged in an interview that his predecessor did not consider the AIDS epidemic a major concern and believed "God was punishing these people and that God alone [could] look after his own" (Caldwell, 2019). Further, sodomy and homosexuality remained a crime in Queensland until 1990, and part of what exacerbated the crisis was that few LGBT Queenslanders felt comfortable getting tested for fear of facing criminal prosecution.

Exploiting unconscious hostilities towards homosexuals is hardly a new weapon in a politician's arsenal and are easy targets for politically conservative forms of projective identification. In this case, Bjelke-Petersen first committed the Kleinian act of "splitting" the people of Queensland into two categories: good (that is, morally conservative, ultra-religious, and White) and bad (homosexuals and Indigenous Australians). Both groups are reduced to their most basic and one-dimensional parts; conservative Queenslanders are good, homosexuals are bad. The groups thus split, Bjelke-Petersen then directed his projections onto homosexuals with impunity. Bigotry and marginalization of homosexuals became part of the mainstream political discourse.

Bjelke-Petersen might have been Queensland's most nationally-recognized populist leader, but he was not the first; in a 1978 presentation at the Royal Historical Society of Queensland, professor Denis Murphy analyzed the political careers of thirty-one Queensland Premiers saying that though "they seem to have been very much like their colleagues in other colonies and States…we have certainly experienced the two ends of the spectrum," citing

Bjelke-Petersen as an avid practitioner of playing dirty for political gain (Murphy, 1978). Bjelke-Petersen might have failed to ascend to the highest position in Australian government, but his strongarm tactics along with a steady drumbeat of populist ideology kept him in power from 1968 to 1987.

One Nation, Under Pauline Hanson

Australia's brand of ultra-right populism embraces a large cohort of religious conservatives, activists, and authoritarians. Since the 1990s, far-right politician Pauline Hanson has corralled deep anti-Asian and Indigenous hatred by creating One Nation, the most successful populist party in Australia, which advocates xenophobic policies targeting primarily Muslims and Asians as responsible for all that ails Australia. In recent years she has branched out to blame the country's "intellectual elite" as being out of touch with the plight of the average Australian. After stepping away from One Nation in the early aughts when the party platform began to decline in popularity, Hanson returned in 2013, and the following year the party was rechristened as "Pauline Hanson's One Nation."

By 2016 Hanson was flying across the continent in her light sport, made-in-Queensland Jabiru J230—festooned with her party logo—as part of her "Fed Up" tour, stumping against "Sharia law, halal tax and Islamisation." After winning a Senate seat that year, her inaugural speech to in September outraged her peers for her inflammatory jabs at a multitude of perceived aggressors. First, that Australia was "in danger of being swamped by Muslims" because the government refused to tell its people how to differentiate between well-wishing Muslims and terrorists: "There is no sign saying, 'good Muslim' or 'bad Muslim.' How many lives will be lost or destroyed trying to determine who is good and who is bad?" (Remeikis, 2006) She then turned to immigrants, saying those who did not "assimilate" could "go back to where you came from," even offering to take them "to the airport and wave you goodbye with sincere best wishes." Then she turned to those on welfare, arguing that "single mums having more children just to maintain their welfare payments.... How many have ever held a job? What would anyone want to work when welfare is so very lucrative?" Asians had "swamped" Australia, too. Hanson's colleagues across the aisle grew so disgusted that they walked out during her tirade.

Throughout her speech, Hanson painted these groups as solely responsible for the rise in organized crime, violence, drug-dealing, and the general collapse of basic social decency. "Never before in Australia's history have we seen civil unrest and terror associated with a so-called religion and followers of that faith.... If we don't make changes now, there will be no hope for the future" (Remeikis, 2006). This speech is a classic example of splitting—reducing entire groups of people to a single stereotype—and then projecting all manner of negative associations onto them. According to Hanson, Australia was on the precipice of being overrun by marauding Muslims whose sole purpose in the country was to impose sharia law and ruin the way of life for "everyday Australians," never mind that the country is one of the most culturally diverse on the planet (Australian Human Rights Commission, 2021). Hanson was no fringe political hack when she laid down this gauntlet; she, along with three fellow One Nation senators, were positing as the most powerful cohort in Australian Parliament. There is no ignoring Hanson. She was elected based on a platform laid out by generations of Queensland populists before her and which she built by employing projective identification targeting Asians, Muslims, and the poor.

Though Hanson provides plenty of fodder for comparison to Trump—her prior business experience consisted of owning a fish and chip hut, and Hanson enjoyed turns on the Australian versions of *The Celebrity Apprentice* and *Dancing with the Stars*—it's worth pointing out that in 2017 the Trump Administration listed the One Nation Party as a "threat to religious freedom" in a country where the federal government is constitutionally banned from making any law that imposes a state religion or establishes a religious test for federal office (U.S. Department of State, 2016). This report did not square with Hanson's assessment of her relationship with the 45th President, of whom she said she could "see in Donald Trump a lot of me and what I stand for in Australia" (Brook, 2017). Referring to her base as "ordinary Australians" creates the faceless, nameless, bureaucratic intellectuals as the ideal receptacle for her projections. Her base, "the people," are aggrieved, disadvantaged, and less educated than those in power—and she's ready to fight for them. As she said in 1996:

> "I am fed up with being told, 'This is our land.' Well, where the hell do I go? I was born here, and so were my parents and children…. Like most Australians I worked for my land; no one gave it to me."
>
> (Leach, Stokes, and Ward, 2000)

Like Trump and even Brazil's Jair Bolsonaro, Hanson has proven quite facile at manipulating the power of social media to amplify her populist message. Like many "outsider" politicians, she benefits when mainstream outlets ridicule her for racist and xenophobic views. Unlike when she first came onto the political scene in the 1990s, Hanson and One Nation are now poised to take advantage of widespread anti-government sentiment, which she actively encourages through her social media accounts. When Hanson is criticized for a particular policy, she turns to Facebook and Twitter to air her grievances to her followers. Though her numbers pale in comparison to Trump's pre-digital exile, they are a formidable, unignorable cohort. Her "Pauline Hanson's Please Explain" Facebook page currently boasts nearly 400,000 followers, and videos are routinely viewed and shared thousands of times.

As demonstrated with other populist leaders throughout this book, projective identification can be rooted in a desire to both expunge deeply held unconscious negative beliefs while also maintaining a grip on power. In this case, Hanson uses her social media platform to target Muslims and the elite while also allowing her adherents to interact with her in real time. Perhaps Hanson is unconsciously trying to rid herself of some deep-seated feelings about her past as a mere fish-and-chip shop owner. She is, like Trump, very much a creation of intense media coverage and derives sustenance from the very derision pointed at her. Hanson's views are hardly unique, but the amount of attention she receives from the media merely amplifies her megaphone. Let's not forget that this relationship is reciprocal, much as the one Trump maintains with the media; the more Hanson inflames the media, the more they cover her, and the more people tune in. Ratings go up, advertising dollars follow. The more journalists try to discredit Hanson, the higher her ratings go (Leach, Stokes, Ward, 2000, p. 123).

Hanson appeals to the people by celebrating their outsider status: anti-elite, anti-immigration, and pro-Australia. Her claims of liberating Australians from the tyranny of government regulation and immigrants while also blaming various societal woes on Muslims, Aboriginals, and homosexuals, are textbook examples of the manifestations of projective identification being employed on a massive scale. Branding these groups as both oppressors and enemies is fundamental to populist power, and projective identification is the glue that holds everything together. Condemning political elitism as a betrayal of "ordinary" (read: ethnically White Anglo-Australians) reached a fever pitch in 2021, when the alt-right group known as the Proud Boys established itself in Australia, exploiting the ecosystem of hate and paranoia created and sustained by Hanson and One Nation.

As recently as January 2021, self-proclaimed Neo-Nazis and members of the Ku Klux Klan were hiking through Australian mountain ranges, chanting racist slogans, and addressing each other with Seig Heil salutes. "They were once widely dismissed as little more than disorganized attention-seeking misfits spruiking racist political manifestos," write Nick McKenzie and Joel Tozer in *The Sydney Morning Herald*, "but Australia's policing and security agencies are increasingly concerned about the capacity of a group adherent or lone wolf feeding off social media posts to commit an act of domestic terrorism" (McKenzie and Tozer, 2021). Racist conspiracy theories such as those that set off the U.S. Capitol riots in January 2021 are being fueled by social media and tacitly endorsed by populist leaders like Hanson, creating a "toxic synergy" of hate that will not be easily eradicated (Barton, 2021).

Those ordinary Australians Hanson extols as the noble downtrodden are now being recruited to darker and more poisonous groups like the Proud Boys, QAnon, and other white supremacist organizations. A March 2021 report by the Hedayah Center revealed that four neo-Nazi groups that have been banned in Europe and North America are thriving in Australia. The organization also listed the various radical right extremist groups currently operating in the country and organized them by narrative, violence level, and whether they had crossed into mainstream social discourse. The sheer number of groups operating in the country is disturbing and merits further examination. This dynamic fuels a form of stochastic terrorism, where aggressive rhetoric inspires acts of terrorism (Braddock, 2020, p. 225).

Bjelke-Petersen and Hanson, and other populist politicians (Clive Palmer is another Australian populist-in-training) have had relatively little success in the country overall, but their influence is growing at an alarming rate, especially for a country as diverse as Australia. That said, there appears to be a movement afoot that recognizes the problems caused by populist rhetoric. Programs such as Tackling Hate have coalesced in recent years to define hate and violent extremism and understand why people engage in hate crimes in the first place. This response to populist dogma is an encouraging step and one that I would categorize as "giving back" the projections, in essence, by refuting the claims made by Hanson and others. This is hardly a miracle cure and will not solve the problem of projective identification quickly. It requires sustained effort and patience. We will examine this in greater detail in a later chapter.

New Zealand: the exception to global populism?

The history of populism in New Zealand traces to at least the start of the twentieth century, when anti-elite Prime Ministers like Dick Seddon, Michael Savage, and Rob Muldoon espoused full-throated endorsements of nationalist and anti-intellectual ideology, and, as we saw in Australia, populism has migrated from fringe groups to major political parties (Moffitt, 2019). But, unlike Australia, those populists who have tried to gain a foothold on national politics have been less successful. In short, their objectives aren't attained as easily. Enter: Winston Peters, founder and leader of New Zealand First, a national and populist political party.

Peters' employment of populist language has a distinctly New Zealand flair. Unlike Trump, Peters has spent his entire career in the political arena and is the country's longest-serving Parliamentarian. He's also a smoother talker than his populist peers, though he hasn't been above harping on immigrants and the elite. In 2012, Peters was kicked out of the House for calling fellow politician Gerry Brownlee "an illiterate woodwork teacher" (Magone, 2012). In 2014, Peters told this joke at a campaign launch: "As they say in Beijing, two Wongs don't make a white" (Agence France-Presse, 2014). He maintains that no one truly understands him, especially the media covering him. "It is our sort of lot to be constantly berated by the media," he said in 2020. "Why? Because we don't fit their narrative." The "we" to whom Peters is referring is unclear, but most likely it is to himself (Graham-McLay, 2020). Were he more adept at unconsciously projecting his biases onto targeted groups, perhaps we could theorize that the "we" in the above statement is about Peters' populist base.

And though Peters has been in politics for decades, he is not your typical populist. Prior to founding New Zealand First, he was a member of the National Party—in other words, his narrative starts off as too mainstream to fit the typical populist "outsider" mold. Further, his stand on certain policies doesn't exactly square with what it means to be an ideological right-leaning politician. But there's no mistake that Peters belongs among the populists mentioned in this book because he does mix the cult of personality with politics while advocating for "New Zealand first" policies. As far as projective identification goes, he just doesn't appear to exhibit it in the same way Trump and Hanson do. Recall that projective identification is a primitive defense mechanism and employed by people with deep psychological trouble.

A Rejection of Populism?

Further deterring Peters' populist ambitions, the country's Labour Party delivered a massive win in the 2020 elections, taking 62 of 120 parliament seats and returning Ardern to the position of prime minister. Unlike in countries like Brazil and the United States, New Zealanders have mostly rejected conspiracy theories regarding immigrants and COVID-19. It helps that the people have been reasonably satisfied with how their government has functioned for the past 20 years—which has enacted mostly moderate policies. In a poll conducted every year since 1999 by research firm UMR, respondents have been asked whether they were happy with the direction their government was going. And for 21 years, the overwhelming response—even during the 2008 financial crisis and COVID-19—has been positive. However, these polls are not shared publicly and are used for the Labour Party's internal strategy sessions, and when they are leaked, only the most salient elements see daylight, however the proof of these polls can be found in the voting record which reflects these findings.

Major right-wing media outlets don't have the same presence as they do in other countries. Rupert Murdoch's News Corp does air Sky News Australia on the independently owned Sky News New Zealand, but the lack of a dedicated media outlet sucks the oxygen out of any major populist rhetoric. Peters is also a lackluster Tweeter; with only about 46,800 followers, his last tweet appeared on October 27, 2020, when he shared pictures of him meeting with U.S. Senator Scott Brown and Ambassador Hiroyasu Kobayashi from Japan. It was shared 13 times. By contrast, Trump's most popular tweet from his now-deleted Twitter account got 1.8 million likes and nearly 400,000 retweets. That tweet announced that the president and his wife Melania had contracted coronavirus (Madhani and Colvin, 2021).

This chapter concludes on the note that populist leaders in New Zealand do not currently have the same kind of power as they do in other countries—a fact that I attribute, in part, to the fact that Peters doesn't split individuals into "good" and "bad" and then project various grievances onto his intended targets. In sum, Peters doesn't appear to employ splitting and projective identification as mechanisms of defense. Tarrant felt compelled to murder innocent worshipers in Christchurch, it can be argued, because of influences that reached him from all corners of the world, thanks in large part to the internet.

Conspiracy theorists are active in New Zealand. At the time of the massacres, they claimed that no one was taking up the mantle and scrubbing out those "invaders" responsible for Tarrant's and others' perceived grievances. His manifesto reveals just how insidious white supremacist rhetoric has become, and although New Zealand might not be a fertile cradle for such behavior, it is not immune from the consistent mainstreaming of white supremacist ideology. Tarrant's manifesto was written to be shared, which it was, and widely. From a psychological standpoint, as a hypothesis, I believe it is worth thinking about whether the shooter was both a recipient of projective identification and an unconscious projector. His seventy-four-page rant appears to speak for a group of people who have used raw aggression and directed it towards immigrants and Muslims, turning it into a deadly projection.

As an avowed white supremacist, Tarrant and others like him do more than give voice to their hate, they encourage others to join them. White supremacists here and elsewhere around the globe act on what they are hearing from populist leaders. In other words, the projective identification that may have been foisted on Tarrant and others like him from populist leaders could be succeeding to the point where the next logical step for these people might be to act on their feelings. As anti-immigration and anti-globalist sentiment circulates across social media channels courtesy of populists as far away as the United States, these messages serve as virulent projections that could lead people like Tarrant to believe that violence is the only recourse. The Christchurch manifesto is not meant to be factual but to portray Tarrant as a man standing up for the vast maligned and ignored populace.

In a cruel twist of irony, white nationalism has gone global, owing in large part to social media's near-immediate ability to transmit information. Though various groups claim to be waging an ideological war on their home turf, they are unified in their international mission to save the white race from extinction.

References

Agence France-Presse (2014, August 11). New Zealand mp Winston Peters accuse of racism over Wong 'joke.' *South China Morning Post.* www.scmp.com/news/asia/article/1571185/new-zealand-lawmaker-blasted-racist-joke-about-chinese.

Australian Human Rights Commission (2021). Face the facts: cultural diversity. https://humanrights.gov.au/our-work/education/face-facts-cultural-diversity#:~:text=Australia%20is%20a%20vibrant%2C%20multicultural,people%20have%20migrated%20to%20Australia.

Barton, G. (2021). To shut down far-right extremism in Australia, we must confront the ecosystem of hate. *The Conversation,* February 7. https://theconversation.com/to-shut-down-far-right-extremism-in-australia-we-must-confront-the-ecosystem-of-hate-154269.

Braddock, K. (2020). *Weaponized Words: The Strategic Role of Persuasion in Violent Radicalization and Counter-Radicalization*. Cambridge University Press.

Brook, B. (2017). Trump administration report singles out Pauline Hanson's rhetoric on Muslims. *News Com AU*, August 16. www.news.com.au/finance/work/leaders/trump-adm inistration-report-singles-out-pauline-hansons-rhetoric-on-muslims/news-story/f82b52b5 76b1dcfe5f2bfba86054ed52.

Caldwell, F. (2019). Queensland attempted to tackle AIDS while sodomy remained a crime. *Brisbane Times*, January 1. www.brisbanetimes.com.au/politics/queensland/queen sland-attempted-to-tackle-aids-while-sodomy-remained-a-crime-20181220-p50ngv.html.

Costar, B. (2005). *Queensland's authoritarian populist*. Australian Policy Online, April 26. https://apo.org.au/node/4859.

Graham-McLay, C. (2020). 'I'm going nowhere but up': Winston Peters on populism, politics, and the polls. *The Guardian*, August 2. www.theguardian.com/world/2020/a ug/03/im-going-nowhere-but-up-winston-peters-on-populism-politics-and-the-polls.

Hern, A. (2019). Facebook and YouTube defend response to Christchurch videos. *The Guardian*, March 19. www.theguardian.com/world/2019/mar/19/facebook-and-you tube-defend-response-to-christchurch-videos.

Leach, M., Stokes, G., and Ward, I., eds (2000). *The Rise and Fall of One Nation*. St. Lucia, Brisbane: University of Queensland Press, p. 28.

Lloyd, C. (2021). *The 1840s depression and the origins of Australian capitalism*. School of Economics, University of New England and Research School of Social Sciences, Austrian National University. www.researchgate.net/profile/Christopher-Lloyd-12/p ublication/268433889_The_1840s_Depression_and_the_Origins_of_Australian_Cap italism/links/56c6600908ae03b93dda54d6/The-1840s-Depression-and-the-Or igins-of-Australian-Capitalism.pdf.

Madhani, A. and Colvin, J. (2021). A farewell to @realDonaldTrump, gone after 57,000 tweets. AP News, January 8. https://apnews.com/article/twitter-donald-trump -ban-cea450b1f12f4ceb8984972a120018d5.

Magone, P. (2012). Peters booted out for 'illiterate Brownlee' insult. Stuff, March 1. www. stuff.co.nz/national/politics/6507688/Peters-booted-out-for-illiterate-Brownlee-insult.

McKenzie, N. and Tozer, N. (2021). Neo-Nazis go bush: Grampians gathering highlights rise of Australia's far right. *The Sydney Morning Herald*, January 27. www.smh.com. au/politics/federal/neo-nazis-go-bush-grampians-gathering-highlights-rise-of-australia- s-far-right-20210127-p56xbf.html.

Moffitt, B. (2019). Populism in Australia and New Zealand. *The Oxford Handbook of Populism*. New York: Oxford University Press, pp. 128.

Murphy, D. (1978). The premiers of Queensland. The 1978 Clem Lack oration of the Royal Historical Society of Queensland. www.researchgate.net/profile/Rae-Wear/p ublication/43456575_The_Premiers_of_Queensland/links/56bae73d08ae2567351ee14e/ The-Premiers-of-Queensland.pdf.

Remeikis, A. (2006). One Nation leader Pauline Hanson delivers incendiary maiden speech to Senate. *The Sydney Morning Herald*, September 14. www.smh.com.au/p olitics/federal/one-nation-leader-pauline-hanson-delivers-incendiary-maiden-speech- to-senate-20160914-grg60g.html.

Stokes, G. (2000). One nation and Australian populism. In: *The Rise and Fall of One Nation*. St. Lucia, Brisbane: University of Queensland Press, p. 25.

The Sydney Morning Herald. (2005). "Don't you worry about that:" Obituary for Joh-Bjelke-Peterson. *The Sydney Morning Herald,* April 25. www.smh.com.au/national/dont-you-worry-about-that-20050425-gdl6zb.html.

U.S. Department of State. (2016). 2016 Report on international religious freedom: Australia. www.state.gov/reports/2016-report-on-international-religious-freedom/australia.

Whitton, E. (1993). *The Hillbilly Dictator: Australia's Police State.* Sydney: ABC Books.

Chapter 5

Populism in Poland

Populism in various forms has existed in Poland since at least 1918, when it was reestablished as an independent country as part of the Allied States post-World War I Armistice terms. Along with other countries like Ukraine, Latvia, and Lithuania, Poland began the long struggle for sovereignty. It would not be until 2001 when the term "populism" would describe the markedly right-leaning political shift within Poland following the formation of the Law and Justice Party (PiS) and that party's shift away from the center-right through an increasingly important emphasis on Christianity, nationalism, and populism by 2007. In 2015 PiS gained a majority in the Polish parliament for the first time, which it retains to this day. As scholar Daniel Stockemer notes in *Populism Around the World,* "...those aspects of populism that existed during the interwar period (1918–39) and during the period of communism (1946–89) are relevant to the varieties of populist that developed after Poland's transition to democracy in 1989" (Stockemer, 2019, p. 68).

The shift towards contemporary Polish populism began around 1989, when the Communist party of Poland began to lose its grip on Poles who were quickly tiring of being controlled by one elite group after another. At the same time, a major opposition movement emerged backed by Solidarity, a trade union federation. As tension between pro-democracy organizers and the communist government mounted, the country held a semi-open election which Solidarity won overwhelmingly, "taking almost all the seats in the Senate and all of the 169 seats they were allowed to contest in the Sejm or parliament" (CNN, 2008), displacing the Polish United Worker's Party and effectively putting an end to communism in Poland.

Following years of economic chaos under the communist regime, Poland's leaders were now faced with the task of developing an infrastructure that would permit the country to prosper. The newly elected leaders Tadeusz Mazowiecki, an activist and journalist who had been appointed prime minister, and later, shipyard worker-turned-president Lech Walesa, tackled this much needed restructuring through what became known as the Balcerowicz Plan. Moving away from, "...the inefficient

DOI: 10.4324/9781003202387-6

state-controlled system of economic planning," finance minister Leszek Balcerowicz imposed punishing economic reforms across Polish industrial sectors (CNN, 2008).

While rapid change seemed the only way to turn antiquated financial systems into programs that could compete with the rest of the free world, Poland ultimately transformed into an investment-friendly market economy: trade reopened with the rest of the world during this period, and the zloty became convertible to other currencies. The Polish government also embraced globalism during this time by joining the North American Treaty Organization in 1999 and the European Union in 2004. "Over a relatively short period of time, Poland had become one of the most dynamically developing economies in Europe and by the mid-1990s, it became known as the 'Tiger of Europe'" (CNN, 2008).

Economic progress aside, the country endured years of social turmoil following the end of communism, punctuated by tremendous instability due in part to the numerous and varied transition groups that came into power in rapid succession, each for short periods—at one point there were 29 parties or electoral committees vying for power. Notwithstanding the setbacks that ensued, Poland made many gains. As leaders worked on transforming the country, discontent among the working class increased, owing to dishonest dealings and what seemed to be an endless stream of corruption scandals among political elites. The Polish people, understandably, grew tired of the hypocrisy and greed, and subsequently, "PiS became the most credible party voicing populist anti-establishment rhetoric" (van Kessel, 2015).

While it appeared as though Poland had made a full transformation into a democratic country with four presidential elections under its belt, each punctuated by smooth transitions of power, the reality of the political situation is knottier. Today, as in the past, Polish politics remain complex. To some extent, the complexity derives from the competing factions within parliament; however, despite the existence of a range of ideologically distinct political parties, right-wing populists have retained a tight grip on political control in Poland—a common characteristic of many other Eastern European countries today, as well.

The Current Leadership in Poland

In 2017 Mateusz Morawiecki was elected Prime Minister of Poland on a social and political platform committed to deregulation, private entrepreneurship, and the development of smart technologies. But that has come with a particularly undemocratic price of limiting press freedoms and controlling the flow of money into and out of the country. In addition, according to a mission report prepared by the International Press Institute (IPI) at the end of

2020, the media in Poland has faced increasing restrictions since Morawiecki came to power.

Poland's laws significantly restrict foreign ownership of companies in "strategic sectors, and limits acquisition of real estate, especially agricultural and forest land" (US Department of State, 2020). The Broadcasting Law states that:

> "a television broadcasting company may only receive a license if the voting share of foreign owners does not exceed 49 percent and if the majority of the members of the management and supervisory boards are Polish citizens and hold permanent residence in Poland."
>
> (US Department of State, 2020)

An amendment was proposed in 2017 to place further restrictions on foreign ownership of media outlets. As expected, in the summer of 2021, the government which is controlled by the PiS party, enacted legislation that severely restricts how broadcasting entities can operate (Suroweic and Lundholm, 2021).

Government appointed executives and reporters limit freedom of the press. Efforts to control media mirror those put in place in the last decade by Hungary's populist leader Viktor Orbán, including "antimonopoly investigations to block unfavoured mergers, licensing changes and the use of retroactive tax penalties and discretionary fines." (Wiseman, 2021). Not even advertising agencies or printing presses and newsstands are free from scrutiny and interference.

How Poland Differs from Other Eastern European Populist Countries

On the topic of immigration, Poland stands apart from Hungary's fervent anti-immigration legal and policy position and other populist-leaning countries in Eastern Europe–at least, theory differs from practice. According to 2019 *Politico* reporting, Poland's immigration policy is two-faced. While the ruling PiS claims to have an anti-immigration focus, their desire to act on these claims changes dramatically when there are jobs open which Poles have no desire to fill. In this version of Poland's economic reality, which is particularly à propos in the case of Ukrainian migrant workers, (predating the Russian invasion of Ukraine), the government turns a blind eye to its policies on immigration (Eyre and Goillandeau, 2021). Discernible labor shortages, especially in the service economy, seem to be throwing the doors open ever wider to the migrant laborers from countries in South Asia and North Africa, as well as the Balkans, who choose Poland as their new home and place of employment.

The Uncertain Future of Poland's Leadership

Despite right-wing dominance of Poland's government, the country's political future remains uncertain. Part of this instability comes from the overwhelming feelings of suspicion and distrust that exist among Poles when it comes to trusting their leaders with political power. As to be expected, the right-wing parties in Poland—which include PiS, the Labour Party, and the National Movement, are aligned with conservative-leaning values: Catholicism, traditional families, Euroscepticism, and centralized government. They are also aligned in their opposition to Middle Eastern and African refugees. A fear of Islam and Islamization in Poland can be traced as far back as 1683, when the Polish-Austrian army defeated the Turks in the Battle of Vienna in 1683 (Finkel, 2006).

Because of the acrimonious and protracted history between Poland and Islamic countries as well as the cultural differences that exist between these two groups of people, Polish right-wing leaders do not think it is possible for immigrants from Muslim-majority countries to assimilate into Polish culture, which is overwhelmingly Catholic. PiS members regularly voice concern over what they perceive as a growing community of Muslim fundamentalists that could potentially lead to jihadist uprising. Others believe that unchecked, Muslim population growth could lead to a Muslim majority within Poland. Ironically, while the worry about an Islamic take-over is a big topic in Poland, the facts are quite different. Poland has a lower number of Muslim immigrants than any other European country. Like nearly everyone on the planet these days who has access to WiFi and a social media account, many Poles are influenced by propaganda and fake news that spread across the internet, including all kinds of stories about Muslims taking over the country. These fears are particularly curious since the Muslim population in Poland is low (less than .01 percent of the total) and only a very small number of people from Islamic countries are interested in emigrating to Poland. Nevertheless, some right-wing Poles have all kinds of unfounded perceptions (Dudzińaka and Kotnarowski, 2019).

A 2019 Brookings Institution study explored the ways that Polish right-wing parties frame Muslim's place in the country. Some of their Polish participants in the study had, "developed relatively common stereotypes based on rumors and media coverage, including unverified information about crimes committed by Muslims" (Dudzińaka and Kotnarowski, 2019). Further, "Muslims are Poland's least accepted ethnic or religious group," and with so few actual Muslims living in the country, right-wing leaders feel liberated to frame that community as one to be feared. This targeted attack on Muslims, though long-standing, does stand in stark contrast to a centuries-old tradition of welcoming other ethnic and religious groups; in addition to welcoming expelled Protestants, Poland became home to one of the largest Jewish diasporas anywhere in the world, numbering three million by 1918—sadly, a statistic that would be nearly wiped out during the Holocaust (Zamoyski, 2015). We now have an ideal petri dish for wide-reaching, community-targeted projective identification to occur (Dudzińaka and Kotnarowski, 2019).

Psychoanalytic Concepts that May Have Impacted Widespread Views of Muslim Immigrants in Poland

As is the case with Hungary, Poland's populism emerged as a result of two significant psychoanalytic defense mechanisms, splitting and projective identification, which were employed with ever greater frequency by leaders who are incapable of integrating both good and bad qualities in the lives of others.

As discussed in previous chapters, the first psychological mechanism is splitting. It causes people to separate and manage positive and negative qualities in themselves and others. The second defense mechanism that supports the development of populism is projective identification, which enables people to get rid of the "bad" aspects of themselves by projecting these intolerable qualities or characteristics onto another person or other people. Thereafter the projector believes the unwanted qualities reside in the other person. As demonstrated above, Muslims are the unwitting recipients of this sustained behavior.

Anti-Semitism and Projective Identification in Poland Today

Though Jews lived peacefully in Poland for nearly 800 years, that changed during World War II, when only about 380,000 of the nearly 3.3 million Polish Jews survived. Following the war, the Polish government established monuments, museums, and other annual events dedicated to Holocaust remembrance. The running line was that the Nazis were the only ones who perpetrated these atrocities, but it has become clear through members of the Polish intelligentsia that other Poles committed violent acts against Jews. A 2018 *Atlantic* article entitled "The Truth About Poland's Role in the Holocaust," refers to these attacks:

> Perhaps the most infamous of these episodes was a massacre in the town of Jedwabne in summer 1941 when several hundred Jews were burned alive by their neighbors. More difficult to unpack is the tangled history of the southeastern village of Gniewczyna Łańcucka. In May 1942, non-Jewish residents of the town held hostage some two to three dozen local Jews. Over the course of several days, they tortured and raped their hostages before finally murdering them.
>
> (Friedberg, 2018)

The idea that Poles were complicit in the Holocaust does not sit well. In February 2018, President Andrzej Duda signed a memory law that made it illegal to accuse the Polish nation of complicity in the Holocaust. "There was no participation by Poland or the Polish people as a nation in the Holocaust," Duda said (Gunter, 2018). The new law criminalizes the phrase, "Polish death camp," as well as expressing the sentiment that the Polish nation was not, "responsible or complicit in the Nazi crimes committed by the Third German Reich" (John, 2018). Opponents fear this law will stifle free speech and whitewash the historical record, which does reveal that, though Poland was occupied in 1939 by Nazi Germany (who killed an estimated 1.9 million non-Jewish Poles), and some Poles helped hide Jews, other atrocities like the 1941 massacre of some 400 Jews in the town of Jedwabne were perpetrated by ethnic Poles (Jewish Virtual Library, 2022). Now it is illegal to even recognize the totality of this brutal historical record.

Modern Anti-Semitic Sentiment in Poland: An Example

Recent visitors to Poland have reported that anti-Semitism appears to be on the rise. A former reporter, traveling with a group of students, recounted harrowing experiences that she felt were different from others she had previously experienced. She had never expected discrimination of the type she witnessed to be so blatantly displayed on street corners in Poland. Despite her awareness that anti-Semitism in Poland had been a reality before the Holocaust, she had not realized it had reappeared (Okun, 2019).

The former reporter recounted receiving a Nazi salute from local Poles who learned the group was Jewish. Another visitor was punched in the head for wearing a Jewish head covering. In another incident, the group visited a market where they were shocked at the wares on display: a full product line of anti-Semitic items. Among the pieces available were Jewish good luck charms, "small wooden signs you can hang on a wall of a house, which feature a Jewish money lender sporting a stereotypically large nose and holding a bag of money which is decorated with the Jewish 'Star of David'" (2019). The reporter learned that "hanging a Jew" in a house would bring money and prosperity. Other figurines featured money lenders with stereotypical "Jewish" noses and holding money sacks. It is not surprising to learn that these items were accompanied by swastika-adorned pins.

Appalled at this display of anti-Semitism, the reporter approached the owner and expressed her objections to the figurines he was selling. She was told that it was important to preserve Polish history of World War II—Polish history that includes the killing of potentially hundreds of thousands of Jews by Poles during World War II and after the war was over, when armed conflict had ceased. Of course, the Polish vendor was selling memorabilia of the Holocaust to make a profit. Yet the statues themselves depicted Jews as being greedy men with large noses. In this case, the vendor appears to be projecting greediness onto inanimate objects that depict Jews as being ugly, money-grubbing people who were the *victims* of heinous acts committed by the Poles (Lipshiz, 2021).

Safely home, this traveler reported her experiences to the Polish Embassy. The reply she received shocked her. It indicated that they were sorry she had encountered problems but was asked to remember the fact that so many Polish people had also been victims of the Holocaust. The letter added that German Holocaust paraphernalia was not allowed. This was a curious response. One might wonder what the figurines had to do with the Poles who lost their lives in the 1940s.

On the surface, the Polish Embassy's response makes little sense, since millions of German Jews were massacred during the Holocaust, far more than the non-Jewish people from Poland. With this information in mind, what might the embassy personnel have been trying to communicate? If you consider splitting and projective identification, the possibilities of understanding increase. If the Polish people as a nation want to rid themselves of the guilt that accompanied the killing of Jews during WW II at the hands of their forebears, they might initially be dividing people into different categories: the "good" group that deserves respect—the Polish people who died in the Holocaust; and the "bad" group that has become the subject of mockery as depicted in the Jewish figurines.

The Germans considered the Poles to be inferior, something they clearly communicated to the Polish people. Now, the Poles could be trying to rid themselves of the sense of being inferior by projecting this second-class status onto the Jews. In this way, they can get rid of the feeling or thought of being "less than" by putting it onto the Jews. They take it a step further by making figurines that are meant to be laughed at and mocked. They then watch people react to make sure Jews are still the subject of ridicule instead of having to feel inferior themselves.

The Rise of Populism in Europe: A Case Example

In 1999 Atlantic staff writer Anne Applebaum was living in Poland with her husband and had plans to throw a New Year's Eve party in the northwest corner of the country. It was to be a celebration of sorts: Poland, after many years of oppression, appeared to be on the verge of becoming a true democracy. Unfortunately, since that time things have turned a precarious corner. Applebaum writes in her book, *Twilight of Democracy: The Failure of Politics and the Parting of Friends* how, two decades after that party, she still crosses the street:

> to avoid some of the people who were at my New Year's Eve party. They, in turn, would not only refuse to enter my house, they would be embarrassed to admit they had ever been there. In fact, about half of the people who were at that party would no longer speak to the other half.
>
> (Applebaum, 2020)

Applebaum goes on to address a new concept—a "profound divide" that has emerged among her friends living in various parts of the world. Her guests—mostly Poles, included a smattering of friends and colleagues from London, Moscow, and New York—are experiencing a deep and observable split.

It is one which, albeit with local variations, has splintered European and American politics. Some constituents, such as Applebaum and her husband, have remained loyal to their center-right roots. But others have taken a very different turn and embraced the hard-right populist and authoritarian parties which now dominate Hungary and Poland, compete for power in France, Italy and Spain, and have reshaped the political landscape in Britain and the US (Philpot, 2020).

The "split" Applebaum appears to be talking about is a version of the psychological splitting I have addressed throughout this book: the behavior of dividing a group or groups of people or countries into "good" and "bad." She is also talking about projective identification since the people about whom she is referring are attempting to get rid of something; I would suggest that this "something" is the need to expel guilt, either in the true sense of the word or through association with what others do or have done.

Applebaum is familiar with Eastern European politics and knows her way around the post-communist world, having served in the 1990s as deputy editor of The Spectator, the official publication of the British Conservative Party. She wrote about Russian and Eastern European politics and worked for US-based magazines for many years. She also is seeing what has begun to emerge in this new era of anti-Semitism; a political climate she finds to be disturbing. As much as Poland has started to reflect the right-wing sentiment frequently adopted by other Eastern European countries—or the United States for that matter—Applebaum acknowledges that Poland until recently has proactively educated its people about the atrocities that occurred during the Holocaust. This changed when PiS took over, however. Now, in a new twist, the shroud of suspicion that was cast over Jewish communities continues—but has expanded to include Muslim communities as well.

Unfortunately, many of the former liberal democratically minded Polish partygoers now have taken firmly anti-Semitic and anti-other positions. These shifts suggest that splitting and projective identification have entered the landscape of European politics where people are divided into good and bad categories. Following these divisions, those people who cannot tolerate the truth—which commonly reflects aspects of themselves—project internal unwanted feelings and thoughts about Jews onto others, who then become the "bad" or tainted people. Unmistakably, this is the "It's not me, it's you" thinking of Donald Trump, Viktor Orbán, and other like-minded political figures.

References

Applebaum, A. (2020). *Twilight of Democracy*, New York: Doubleday.

CNN (2008). Life after communism. CNN, October 10. http://edition.cnn.com/2008/WORLD/europe/09/29/poland.profile/index.html.

Dudzińska, A. and Kotnarowski, M. (2019). Imaginary Muslims: How the Polish right frames Islam. Brookings Institution, July 24. www.brookings.edu/research/imaginary-muslims-how-polands- populists-frame-islam/#footnote-61.

Eyre, M. and Goillandeau, M. (2019). Poland's two-faced immigration strategy. Politico, January 6. www.politico.eu/article/poland-two-faced- immigration-strategy-ukraine-migrants.

Finkel, C. (2006) *Osman's dream: The story of the Ottoman Empire, 1300–1923*. Basic Books, pp. 286–287.

Friedberg, E. (2018). The Truth About Poland's Role in the Holocaust. *The Atlantic.* February 6. www.theatlantic.com/international/archive/2018/02/poland-holocaust-death-camps/552455.

Grabowshi, Jan. (2013). *Hunt for the Jews.* Bloomington and Indianapolis, IN: Indiana University Press.

Gunter, J. (2018). Holocaust law wields a 'blunt instrument' against Poland's past. BBC News, February 3. www.bbc.com/news/world-europe-42920934.

Jewish Virtual Library (2022). Jews in occupied Poland: The massacre in Jedwabne. Jewish Virtual Library. www.jewishvirtuallibrary.org/the-massacre-in-jedwabne.

John, T. (2018). Poland just passed a Holocaust bill that is causing outrage. Here's what you need to know. *Time*, February 10. https://time.com/5128341/poland-holocaust-law.

Liphshiz, C. (2021). The latest 'Lucky Jew' figurines in Poland: Scented candles that are 'good for financial success.' Jewish Telegraphic Agency, March 15. www.jta.org/2021/03/15/global/the-latest-lucky-jew-figurines-in-poland-scented-candles-that-are-good-for-financial-success.

Okun, G. (2019). Confronting anti-Semitism in Poland today: A memoir. Libertarianism.org, January 29. www.libertarianism.org/columns/confronting-anti-semitism-in-poland-today-memoir.

Philpot, R. (2020). Rise of European populists today echoes dark Dreyfus era, Jewish historian warns. *The Times of Israel*, August 27. www.timesofisrael.com/rise-of-european- populists-today-echoes-dark-dreyfus-era-jewish-historian-warns.

Stockemer, D. (Ed.) (2019). *Populism Around the World: A Comparative Perspective.* Chams: Springer.

Surowiec, P. and Lundholm, M. (2021). Poland: why is a new media law prompting street protests and outrage from the US? *The Conversation*, August 13. https://theconversation.com/poland-why-is-a-new-media-law-prompting-street-protests-and-outrage-from-the-us-166061.

U.S. Department of State (2020). Limits on foreign control and right to private ownership and establishment. 2020 Investment climate statements: Poland. www.state.gov/reports/2020-investment-climate-statements/poland.

Van Kessel, S. (2015). *Populist parties in Poland. In: Populist Parties in Europe.* London: Palgrave Macmillan, p. 121. https://doi.org/10.1057.97811374113_5.

Wiseman, J. (2021). Democracy declining: Erosion of media freedom in Poland. Mission Report. Media Freedom Rapid Response, February 11. https://ipi.media/wp-content/uploads/2021/02/20210211_Poland_PF_Mission_Report_ENG_final.pdf.

Zamoyski, A. (2015). *Poland: A History*. William Collins.

Chapter 6

Austrian Populism in the 21st Century

In 1938 Adolf Hitler ordered the resignation of the Austrian Chancellor, whom he promptly replaced with a pro-Nazi Chancellor and who, in turn, invited German troops into the country to "maintain law and order." The "Anschluss," as it is known, resulted in the annexation of Austria into Germany, and though many people were in favor of this reunion after the fall of the Austrian Hungarian Empire, the union proved to be devastating for many, especially Austrian Jews who were the victims of horrific violence.

Austria has undergone many profound changes since then, notably joining the EU—an organization of 27 member countries that are committed to promoting democratic ideals as well as monitoring anti-Semitism. That notwithstanding, questions remain about Austrians in leadership positions who appear to be tied to ideas that reflect the past. In something of a balancing act, those same leaders claim to denounce anti-Semitism, yet there are plenty of situations where it seems they believe otherwise.

Perhaps old beliefs linger despite attempts that have been made to distance the country from its past. A study published in *The Economic Journal* (Oechsner, 2020), claims that extremists who migrate to another country can influence its politics for years. The researchers conducting this work studied Austrians living in the occupation zones in 1945 who were subsequently relocated to either the United States or Russia. The study found that local institutions and family ties perpetuated generational anti-Semitism, while political affiliations and preferences can be transmitted for up to four generations: "Descendants of migrating extremists together with local party institutions are continuously spreading their beliefs to residents through active engagement in local politics" (Ochner and Roesel, 2020).

A member of the People's Party (ÖVP), Sebastian Kurz led the Austrian government for two terms in office until October 2021, when a corruption inquiry forced him to resign, and shortly thereafter he accepted a position as a "global strategist" for PayPal co-founder Peter Thiel. Kurz's first term was only slightly less rocky: he held the position of Prime Minister in 2017 but was ousted in the spring of 2019 following a vote of no confidence by the Austrian Parliament. However, in an election that took place in September of the same

DOI: 10.4324/9781003202387-7

year, the ÖVP won the majority of votes, and he was reinstated. Interestingly, the Green Party won 14 percent of the votes in the same election, leading to the formation of an unlikely coalition government between the conservative right-wing party and the Greens. Kurz, who is in favor of anti-immigration policies, capitalized on this unlikely development and declared he would defend both the border and the environment (Petrik, 2020).

Bucking the stereotype of older politicians leading conservative political groups, as a savvy 35-year-old, Kurz mobilized young people in Austria to go to the polls. Yet, the ability to turn out the young vote did not guarante loyalty to Kurz: His popularity among millennials was split. Some found him to be far too conservative and wondered how he got into office. One young voter who initially thought he would back Kurz explained his change of heart as he learned more about Kurz's actual policies, finding him unacceptably con-servative—an old-time hard-liner with outdated views on homosexuals and immigrants (Vice, 2020).

Another young person thought that the ÖVP was using Kurz to appeal to younger voters and who believed that Kurz was merely a tool being employed by the party to curry favor among younger voters (Vice, 2020).

While these two millennials do not approve of Kurz, others do. For example, Anna-Maria, a 25-year-old woman, was a "big fan" of Kurz and his policies because, "I think he really speaks to my views on society. That's why I'm a member of the ÖVP's youth wing." She believed that Kurz would find a way to assimilate refugees. (Vice, 2020).

Anti-Muslim Sentiment Doubled in 2021

In 2020, while Kurz was Chancellor, anti-Muslim racism increased in Austria, aided, in no small part, by COVID-19 conspiracy theories. In May 2021 the government published an "Islam Map" online that showed the locations of over 600 mosques throughout Austria, ostensibly to "fight political ideologies," but critics fear the map will be used to attack Muslims (Farzan, 2021).

Increased public negativity towards Muslims in Austria comes at a time when the government is launching a new measure to further curtail Muslim lives. The latest agency to be formed for this purpose, the Documentation Centre for Political Islam, will audit activities of *certain* members of Austrian society, i.e., Muslim members of the community. Susann Raab, the Austrian Minister of Integration, is determined to excise political Islam from public spheres, calling it a "poison" for the Austrian community (McElroy, 2020).

Nevertheless, Austrian officials claim they are monitoring the social media activities of Muslims so they can be certain what is shared is not going to extreme, political Islamic groups. However, this seems like a slippery slope. If this new development is not questionable enough, the Austrian government now in power is taking the restrictions of Muslims a step further by regulating the activities of children when they are not in class:

One area of focus is thought to be after-school groups or weekend clubs that are targeted by the ideologically extreme activists. Austrian newspapers warned of the dangers of "playground controllers." That is when pupils and youths are inculcated into networks that control their outlook and lifestyle.

(McElroy, 2020)

This action seems to be extreme. If government or school officials are worried about their children being on the playground with questionable people, the "playground controllers," perhaps they should not allow their children to be in the presence of unknown people in the first place. This is as opposed to assuming there are unsavory types associating with the youth in their country who must be watched. It would be like a family with young children allowing their kids to play with people they suspect of wrongdoing while watching these "others" closely. This type of issue can be handled by permitting children to be around people who are known to be safe and respectful.

Assuming respect begets trust, if Kurz and his government officials were to be straightforward and direct instead of using the tactics of disguise they employ to cover up their actual intentions, which appear to be to separate Muslims from Austrians, perhaps suspicion from those who question their intentions would dissipate. In addition to his lack of transparency when it comes to monitoring Muslims on playgrounds, Kurz's banning of head coverings for girls starting in kindergarten is discriminatory (Oltermann, 2019).

It also illustrates how Kurz uses projective identification as a mechanism of defense. In his case, while he appears to try to make himself look like a good leader, he also demonstrates the ways in which he discriminates against *some* people in his country but not all. He has also shifted his position, apparently for political gain.

Kurz began his political career as Austria's youngest foreign minister at the age of just 27 with one set of ideas but later dramatically changed his stance. His willingness to work with Muslims and Turks shifted when it became clear that an anti-Turkey policy was more popular. As prime minister he changed the country's Islamic Law, which had been on the books since 1912 (Nasralla, 2015).

As for his ban against the wearing of headscarves for young Muslim girls that starts at a very young age, he might well be projecting his own dangerous feeling of hatred towards Muslim onto the heads of these young, female children. By claiming these young girls can be targeted if people know their religious backgrounds, he appears to be creating the perception that he is shielding them from danger. However, for these girls he may be harming them by "othering" them and taking away their dignity. In so doing, Kurz claimed there is external danger when it is danger that is within his own mind; danger that he can direct towards them at any time.

Kurz also created a problem for the Muslim community which could be by design: These children are likely to feel ashamed, disrespected and generally devalued as human beings if they hear about such a law. This problem is complex. Wearing head scarves has many meanings. In some conservative Islamic countries this custom is a symbol of male dominance. However, in the West, it has many different meanings including the perspective that many women and young girls feel that wearing a hijab gives them the opportunity to identify with other Muslim women.

Muslim women in the West also say covering their hair has little to do with men. It is a choice some make to let people know they are Muslim. It is something that many are proud of; something that Kurz took away from young Muslim girls. In the example below, a Muslim American woman decided to start wearing her head covering after not wearing it for a certain period of time. Coincidently, her husband, who thought it was her decision to make, preferred that she not wear a head covering, yet she decided to do what she felt was in her best interest. "Clothing is a language. We communicate who we are and what we believe and many other subtle details through what we choose to wear. As Muslims, our clothing tells the world in Whom and what we believe. We are standing up for our beliefs, our way of life, the *Quran*, and *Allah*" (Sylaj, 2019).

Another example of choosing to wear a headscarf was told by an American teenager who indicated that she is a typical young girl who plays tennis, reads Harry Potter books, and listens to music like her friends. She also wears make-up and watches Netflix. She said that no one forced her to wear her hijab but instead said it represents who she is as a person. She also likes to let people know she is a Muslim; something that makes her feel good. While none of her friends are Muslim, she feels supported by them. No one criticizes her or bullies her about the choice she made. She is proud to let people in her world know she is a Muslim.

However, not all young women enjoy the same autonomy as those described here. For every woman who says she can choose whether to wear a head covering is another who does not have a say about whether she can wear one or not; some ultra-conservative families require it, placing these girls under the double burden of projective identification from their parents and from the Austrian government.

Kurz does not know why Muslim women or girls wear head scarves or he knows and does not care. While he seems to believe this tradition is only a form of oppression and is harmful to young girls, that banning head coverings is in keeping with child protection laws, it would be interesting to know if he has spoken to any Muslim women or girls about why they wear head scarves. If he listened and if he cared about what they had to say, he might have a different perspective.

Rather than being mired in paranoia and conspiracy theories, perhaps Kurz and his hand-selected Ministers could quell their anxiety if they *listened* to women and girls about the reasons behind wearing a head covering. Instead, Kurz discriminated against women and young girls, some as young as five years old are subject to the new Austrian law.

To add insult to injury, Kurz and his associates did not outlaw anything boys wear on their heads, such as Jewish yarmulke and Sikh patka because the law only refers to garments covering all of the hair on a person's head (DW, 2019).

Not only were Kurz and members of his government guilty of discrimination, they also exhibited misogynistic behavior. Why ban head coverings for girls and not boys? How can that be justified? Furthermore, if in fact there is a safety issue to girls in Austrian schools who wear head coverings, the government could easily come up with laws that would make it a criminal offense to harm these young people. Had he considered this type of action? If not, why not? Instead of hiding behind child protection laws that do not seem to apply in this case, why not make Austria a safe place for all the people who live in his country?

At the very least, banning headscarves is an example of "othering" which is a way of splitting people into categories; those who fit in with the accepted group and those who do not. This way of labeling people also affects how individuals within each group are perceived and treated by members of the community.

The debate over wearing head coverings for Muslim women is an ongoing topic of discussion in Islamic countries. It is for Muslims to decide the fate of head coverings, particularly Muslim women. Kurz had no business making decisions about something that he does not understand as a Christian male world leader in Western Europe. It would be like Muslims making important decisions about banning crucifixes. What sense would that make since the crucifixion of Jesus is not part of their religion?

At the end of the day, racism and xenophobia appear to reside in the minds of those who feel hatred towards Muslims; people who believe it is their right to make laws about various customs of other cultures without having adequate knowledge. This behavior was unacceptable for a world leader.

Sebastian Kurz's Connection to Radical Right in Austria

Sebastian Kurz, unlike other European leaders who are members of the EU, did not oppose to the radical right-wing party that is on the rise in Austria (The Freedom Party, FPÖ). This was illustrated when he allowed members of the Freedom Party to join his government.

At first glance, it seems problematic because the FPÖ has reportedly gone against various EU regulations. According to Time magazine interview, Kurz took a different view:

"Unlike many of his peers in Germany, he does not want to dismiss Europe's new nationalists as a bunch of neo-Nazis in disguise. Further, he claims the "decision was a democratic necessity – the Freedom Party won more than a quarter of the vote in those elections. His critics say he made a Faustian bargain, sanitizing some of the most odious figures on the right-wing fringe and bringing them into the mainstream."

(Shuster, 2018)

Kurz, meanwhile, defended his decision in that same *Time* interview, arguing that:

"The Freedom Party has changed a lot. And in Europe we have many right-wing or far-right parties winning elections. There is also a greater understanding in Europe that the E.U. is made up of 28 democracies. And in a democracy, whether you like it or not, it's the people who decide. It's the decision of the people."

(Shuster, 2018)

The Curious Media Award Honoring Chancellor Kurz: Is It Another Odd Austrian Juxtaposition in 2021?

Though he suppressed the media in Austria, Kurz received the Freedom Prize award by Weimer Media Group. Yet in ratings given to countries by *Reporters without Borders*, Austria is ranked 18th, which appears to be related to several moves Kurz made to stifle independent journalism. For one thing, his party initiated a lawsuit with the liberal newspaper, *Der Falter*, for writing that Kurz violated campaign finance rules. Kurz lost the lawsuit in 2019, but that did not stop him from criticizing media outlets for promoting what he considers to be fake news (Nostlinger and Karnitschnig, 2021).

As of 2021, Austria had moved up one place on the Reporters without Borders World Freedom Index. Meanwhile, Kurz restricted freedom of the press and attacked many news outlets but promoted any press offering a pro-government focus. The German award, therefore, negates the reality in Austria. Kurz did not expand media freedom in Austria but restricted it through direct message control, the preferential treatment of pro-government media and most recently through attacks on critical media outlets. Further, Kurz has been accused of interfering and undermining the work of media outlets, largely by withholding funding from those groups that do not play ball—meaning, that do not cover him or his politics favorably. For example, over €210 million was set aside by Kurz's political groups for media spending, most of which goes to advertising. Critics say this money directly fueled tabloids and Kurz, which, in turn, undermined more independent-minded journalism (Nostlinger and

Karnitschnig, 2021). Awarding Kurz a prize for fighting for media freedom is, therefore, more than absurd (Lahodynsky, 2021).

Kurz was a popular politician but resigned due to a corruption scandal in October 2021. (Lamparski and Schwab, 2017). Karl Nehammer is now the Chancellor of Austria. Since he is from the same party as Kurz, it is unclear whether or not populism will flourish under his leadership.

References

DW (2019). *Austria bans Muslim headscarf in primary schools.* May 16. www.dw.com/en/austria-bans-muslim-headscarf-in-primary-schools/a-48756057.

Farzan, A. (2021). Muslim groups in Austria fear attacks after government published map of mosques. *The Washington Post*, May 29. www.washingtonpost.com/world/2021/05/29/austria-islam-map.

Lambarski, N. and Schwab, P. (2017). Austrian far-right: History of a 'pact with the devil.' *The Times of Israel*, October 24. www.timesofisrael.com/austrian-far-right-history-of-a-pact-with-the-devil.

Lahodynsky, O. (2021). The varnish is peeling off for Kurz. *New Europe*, April 16. www.neweurope.eu/article/the-varnish-is-peeling-off-for-kurz.

McElroy, Damien. (2020). Austria takes 'pioneering' approach to tackle influence of political Islam. *The National News*, July 16. www.thenationalnews.com/world/austria- takes-pioneering-approach-to-tackle-influence-of-political-islam-1.1049772.

Nasralla, Shadia. (2015). Austria passes 'law on Islam' banning foreign money for Muslim groups. Reuters, February 25. www.reuters.com/article/us-austria-muslims/austria-passes-law-on-islam-banning-foreign-money-for-muslim-groups-idUSKBN0LT28420150225.

Nostlinger, N. and Karnitschnig, M. (2021). *Sebastian Kurz's media war.* Politico, May 11. www.politico.eu/article/sebastian-kurz-media-war-austria-press-freedom.

Oechsner, R. (2020). Migrating Extremists. *The Economic Journal*, Vol. 130, issue 628, pp. 1135–1172. https://doi.org/10.1093/ej/ueaa017.

Oltermann, P. (2019). Austria approves headscarf ban in primary schools. *The Guardian*, May 16. www.theguardian.com/world/2019/may/16/austria-approves-headscarf- ban-in-primary-schools.

Petrik, T. (2020). How Austria's greens became the right's best ally. *Jacobin Magazine*, January 22. https://jacobinmag.com/2020/01/austria-greens-peoples-party-sebastion-kurz- coalition.

Shuster, S. (2018). Sebastian Kurz on governing alongside the far right. *Time*, November 29. https://time.com/collection/next-generation-leaders/5466680/sebastian-kurz-interview- chancellor-austria.

Sylaj, H. (2019). Why do Muslim women wear hijab? Interfaith Now. *Medium*, November 6. https://medium.com/interfaith-now/why-do-muslim-women-wear-hijab-8d0cd811e2b1.

Vice. (2017). Austrian millennials React to a millennial becoming their country's leader. October 17. www.vice.com/en/article/mb7mx3/austrian-millennials-react-to-a- millennial-becoming-their-countrys-leader.

Chapter 7

Populism in India

Populist rhetoric in India can be traced back to when Indira Gandhi and Charan Singh encouraged people to rise beyond their caste and buck the establishment. Meanwhile, Hindu nationalism has existed in India since the 1920s, but in the past 40 years the country has witnessed a strategic push to reframe "Indian" making it synonymous with "Hindu." It is the largest religion in the country—80 percent of all Indians are Hindu—but this nationalist movement exists in stark contrast to the founding principle that it is stronger because of its diversity. Hindu nationalists have wanted a Hindu state since the beginning, and when they did not get one in 1947, they took out their anger on Mahatma Gandhi: Hindu nationalist Nathuram Vinayak Godse assassinated him in 1948. The nationalist fervor died down for a while, but it is back. Narendra Modi is largely responsible for that, in part by casting non-Hindus (primarily Muslims) as unworthy of being Indian—a classic case of projective identification. This is more than likely an attempt to get rid of the negative feeling associated with his own low cast status.

First, it is worth examining the political system, even in brief, so that we understand the various players and how populism in India has blossomed. Modi will serve as our subject of discussion when it comes to projective identification.

India's leadership is shared by a president and a prime minister; the president often deals with issues related to protocol—ceremonial duties, mostly— and affairs of state. He also oversees the military while the prime minister often deals with the day-to-day of running the country and the government.

The President of India is Ram Nath Kovind, who came into power in 2017 as a member of the BJP (the Indian People's Association). Most of the Indian people did not know much about him before he became president, even though he previously served as the governor of a state.

How Kovind Rose to Power

As the son of a grocer, President Kovind came from humble beginnings. He earned a degree in commerce and law before moving to Delhi to

DOI: 10.4324/9781003202387-8

embark on a career in civil service. Prior to becoming president, he assisted members of the Koli community, a sub-caste of the Dalit (formerly known as the Untouchables) caste, of which his family is a member. Even though the Kolis are at the bottom of the caste system, they enjoy certain benefits that some members of the higher castes think should be revoked, and Kovind fought for those rights. He also was a union government advocate and became an advocate-on-record for India's Supreme Court. Thereafter, he served as the executive assistant to the Prime Minister, Morarji Desai. In 1980 he was appointed to the union government's standing council in the Supreme Court.

In 1994, he was elected to the "Rajya Sabha" (the upper parliament in India) and served for twelve years on different committees. Kovind was appointed as the Governor of Bihar in 2015, which led to a period of his career where allies and adversaries routinely praised his non-confrontational approach to the political problems at hand. In 2017 he was named the BJP's (Bhartiya Janata Party) candidate for the presidency and was sworn in as the country's fourteenth president on July 25 of that year. A career politician and civil servant dedicated to enriching the lives of his people—that is Kovind. By all accounts, he is a compassionate leader who has invoked a message of empathy on various occasions. But a nationalist? No. Nothing like Modi.

The Role of Prime Minister Modi

The real leadership in India resides with Modi, an unlikely candidate for the job since he is from a lower caste. However, his rise to power began with his appointment to the General Secretary position for the Gujarat Branch in 1988, a year after he joined the BJP. There, he worked towards strengthening his political party. Members from the higher castes support the group, but it has focused on expanding its base by attracting and retaining people from the lower castes by putting them in high profile positions in the BJP.

Modi enjoyed electoral success in 1989 after calling for a Hindu temple to be built in a sacred area called Ayodhya. Modi gained greater prominence two years later by earning 117 seats for the BJP in the lower portion of parliament and, as a result, increased his party's power in four states.

After finishing his work in Gujarat, he went to Delhi for nearly a decade to work for the party but returned to Gujarat in 2001 to help the community deal with the aftermath of a massive earthquake. Soon after he was elected as the state's chief minister. Up to this point, it appeared that Modi's work had been solidly in the service of all those in his charge, regardless of religion, but that changed.

Modi's Tarnished Record with Muslims

On February 27, 2002, while Modi was serving as Chief Minister of Gujarat, rioters attacked a train carrying Hindu pilgrims. Modi blamed Muslims for the deaths of 58 passengers who burned to death after the train was set on fire. Some argued that Modi had sent armed forces to the area to attack the train and then blame the Pakistani secret services, though that charge was never proven. After the attacks, Modi ordered the charred bodies of the victims dragged through the streets of the nearby city of Ahmedabad, which in turn incited the killings of an estimated 1,000 Muslims. Unofficial tallies place the Muslim casualty count closer to 2,000.

Other disturbing accounts emerged from the event: mobs of men dragged women and young girls from their homes and raped them. A mob leader even boasted to a local magazine about how he slit open the abdomen of a pregnant woman (Chakrabortty, 2014). Modi's overwhelming response to the train fire was a savage wedge meant to further polarize religious groups in India and a way for him to secure political power, and it would not be the last time. Denying Muslims rights would become a hallmark of Modi's politics.

According to one source, Modi claimed the arson was caused by Islamic terrorists before anyone knew who committed the atrocities that occurred on the train. This led to a bloodbath where, "...5,000 Hindus meticulously worked its way through a slum: ninety-seven Hindus were hacked to death... Across the road from the scene of the carnage stood a reserve police quarter. Nobody lifted a finger (Komireddi, 2019, p. 99)." It seems that nobody was spared. Even a former parliamentarian was killed after he tried to shelter 250 people from his town. He was "...dragged out of his house by a mob of Hindus and sliced open with a sword and torched alive. Jafri had spent the day making desperate calls to Modi's office" (2019, p. 100).

Modi Minimizes the Massacre in Lead-Up to 2014 Election

The massacres seemed to fade into the background as the days and years passed. When asked about the situation, Modi and his associates downplayed it. According to a story in The Guardian, Modi's team employed a standard comeback: They argued that the 2002 carnage was "a long time ago," and that their goal leading up to the elections was to make nice and move forward (Chakrabortty, 2014). Although there was at times some vague sense swirling about that Modi had something to do with the incident, it was often followed by a question and a couple of statements about the prosperous economy in Gujarat. While "supporters were quick to "dismiss the pogrom of 2002 as ancient and contested history, what they are trying to erase is that epic, shameful violence" (2014). I argue that the massacre serves as a touchstone for when Modi reintroduced Hindu nationalism on a broad scale. Muslims would continue to be perceived as inherently bad and the root of all Indian ills. This is a form of splitting that often accompanies projective identification.

Narendra Modi's Communication Style

Like many charismatic leaders, Modi knows how to draw a crowd and keep people engaged. Whether stumping for votes or giving a speech before cabinet members, Modi considers his audience. Language is a particularly important vehicle for him. Though Hindi is the most spoken language in India, it is only one of twenty-two official languages. According to a 2019 report in *The Indian Express*, Modi can speak—or at least recite—eight regional languages, as demonstrated during a community summit in Houston, Texas, that was also attended by then-president Donald Trump (Express Desk, 2019). Modi has been known to incorporate local languages into his speeches around India to ensure he can effectively communicate with people. Even if he cannot speak each language fluently, he understands how important it is to be perceived as a man of the people.

As we've seen throughout this book, populist leaders like to control their own media, and Modi is no exception. Plus, someone who uses projective identification as a defense mechanism can increase the pressure on his or her victims. It also allows the diffusion of projective identification on a grand scale.

Despite boasting some 47 million Twitter followers and another 15 million on Instagram, Modi wanted a dedicated television channel to promote his initiatives. In 2019, a few weeks before the Indian general elections were due to take place, Modi started his own television channel called NaMo. This station grew out of NaMo Gujarat, which he launched as an addition to his YouTube Channel in the lead-up to the 2014 elections, (Price, 2015, loc 904). Though ostensibly an abbreviation of Modi's name, some observers noted that the word *namo* in Gujarati means "to bow down." This is an interesting coincidence, if nothing else (Price, 2015), though it would be surprising if the play on words were lost on Modi.

Interestingly, in 2019 NaMo channel operators never applied for a broadcast license and the station lacked the required security clearances to act as a television station, rendering NaMo an illegal broadcast station. As such, since the company never applied for a license, it is unclear who owns it, muddying the lines between news and potential propaganda (Dutta, 2019). A service provider later said that NaMo TV is being offered as a "special service" and so does not need any government license to operate (Kumar, 2019). The NaMo TV channel broadcasts, among other things, speeches by Modi, real-time election tracking, rallies, and interviews with fellow BJP top brass. You would be hard pressed to find anything critical about Modi or the BJP on NaMo.

Modi has harnessed the power of technology to appear, almost like a deity, anywhere around the country as a 3D hologram. Hologram Modi has streamed into villages and rallies across the country. At a cost of over £150,000—something observers chastised as "morally reprehensible" when so many Indians live in poverty—this technology was not cheap. But from the outset, Modi claimed that he was delivering these speeches in 3D, "to show you that India is not being left behind" in the technology race (Price, 2015, loc 930). Each virtually assisted rally grew, eventually beaming into some 1,400 villages, where most residents do not even have television sets (2015).

Modi also connects with the people of India directly through monthly radio addresses called "Moan ki baat" which means conversation of the month. By addressing people in this way, he avoids difficult and confrontational questions from the press. This, for someone who uses projective identification and/or blame shifting as control mechanisms, become, are powerful tools he can use to keep tabs on those receiving the projections and those whose support he needs. Additionally, by splitting Indian Muslims into a negative category, his ability to share that message so rapidly creates a population of adherents who believe his message.

Ever attentive to his audience, Modi pays close attention to the way people dress in each part of India and alters his attire to reflect the dress of the local people he is visiting in an attempt to make sure they feel similar to him.

Narendra Modi's Caste

During the 2014 election, members of Congress alleged that Modi was a "Fake OBC" (OBC stands for Other Backward Castes, it represents low castes but not the lowest), that he was not a tea vendor in his youth, as he claimed (PTI, 2014). It turned out that he hails from the Modh-Ghanchi-Tel (oilpresser) caste which is an OBC category. Modi's humble roots are an important element of his public narrative. According to Price:

> [He] used his own transformation through hard work and dedication to tell a story of what India itself could achieve if it chose to do so. His family with no special privileges, and his refusal to use his position of power to benefit them, was a positive asset on the campaign trail. It showed not only that he understood poverty, but also that he was personally incorruptible.
>
> (Price, 2015, loc 326)

Successful populists often cultivate an outsider personality, someone who is not cut from the same elite political cloth. Modi claims to profoundly understands the needs of the vast populace because he too, is like them.

Did Modi Turn Over a New Leaf, or Were His Promises a Ruse?

After the train incident and prior to the 2014 election, Modi seemed poised to turn over a new leaf. He appeared to have a desire to work towards unifying India. He began saying he did not think one group of people should thrive at the expense of another; something that was a different type of message from Modi's past statements. At that point, he seemed to be describing a different kind of India; one without divisions and fighting between Hindus and Muslims. Instead, he talked about people working together to fight poverty.

After he became Prime Minister, his behavior and mindset seemed to change in many ways, most notably to reflect a surge in Hindu nationalism, one of which involved rewriting Indian textbooks, focusing primarily on the contributions of Indian Muslims (Gettleman, Schultz, Raj, and Kumar, 2019).

First, Modi placed other Hindu nationalist allies at the heads of important universities and cultural institutions. Place names of Muslim origin were changed—so, too, were textbooks—to de-emphasize Muslims' contribution to India and play up Hindu teachings. Many Muslim Indians, who make up one of the world's largest Muslim populations, at some 200 million, said they had never felt so marginalized (Gettleman, 2019).

Modi's government also gathered up many Muslims in Kashmir and forced them to follow his new citizenship law that excludes Muslims from certain countries. But the move that really put India on edge, and cleaved it even more deeply between Hindus and Muslims, came when Modi's government passed a new citizenship law that paved a special path to Indian citizenship for migrants of nearly every prominent South Asian faith, bar one: Islam (Gettleman and Ali-Habib, 2019).

There have also been violent incidences that have occurred throughout India where Muslims have been taunted, harassed, and killed. In 2020 Muslim sections of New Delhi were burned in an apparent attempt to drive Indian Muslims out of the city. That Modi went from, "Together for all, development for all," to chanting "Shoot the traitors," seems to solidify the fact that he has serious problems with Muslims (Gettleman and Abi-Habib, 2020).

Changing the Caste System: Is Such a Thing Possible?

Since India became an independent nation, some of its leaders have suggested doing away with caste-based discrimination, and Modi owes his 2014 and 2019 elections to a groundswell of underclass support. Though caste-based discrimination was outlawed in 1950 as part of the Indian constitution, many Dalits are still shunned, forced to live in segregated communities and denied opportunities to ascend the social strata.

This shift turned out to be a positive move for the BJP since it enjoys significant OBC support. Strategically, the BJP has focused on dismantling the caste-based parties' monopoly over lower-caste votes. The tactic of painting other parties as corrupt bastions of single-caste politics worked wonders, as did an effort to compress the existing 2,479 lower castes into a smaller unit of individualized caste identity to diminish their collective heft (New Indian Express, 2016).

The BJP supported the aspirations of lower castes' leaders through either finance or political alliance, accommodating OBC leaders in the party or ministerial portfolios at the local, state and national level. At the same time, the party is building a network of lower castes cadres in both rural and urban areas, as well as among young people and women. To penetrate the lower castes' social base, the BJP formed an OBC Morcha or "special wing" in July 2015 (Alam, 2015).

Narendra Modi's Personality Style and Mechanisms of Defense

To better understand Narendra Modi, it is important to consider his personality and ways he defends against internal as well as external threats. According to Komireddi (2019), Modi's carefully constructed world view ensures he remains emotionally distant from other people, even though much of his outreach (holograms visits, vast rallies, etc.) attempts are to cement his presence in the lives of average Indians.

Modi gave an interview to a well-known trained clinical psychologist and social theorist, Ashis Nandy, who said, "…he met all of the criteria that psychiatrists, psycho-analysts and psychologist had set up after years of empirical work on authoritarian personality. He had the same mix of puritanical rigidity, narrowing of emotional life, massive use of the ego defense of projection, denial and fear of his own passions combined with fantasies of violence—all set within the matrix of clear paranoid and obsessive personality traits. I still remember the cool, measured tone in which he elaborated a theory of cosmic conspiracy against India that painted every Muslim as a suspected traitor and a potential terrorist." Nandy emerged from the interview "shaken": he "had met a textbook case of a fascist and a prospective killer, perhaps even a future mass murderer" (Komireddi, 2019, pp. 105–106).

The Use of Splitting, Blame Shifting, and Projective Identification

It appears that Modi uses splitting and projective identification as mechanisms of defense in addition to the those mentioned above in part because of the way he treats Muslims for reasons that are not totally clear.

By separating them from Hindus in his mind—Muslims being the "bad" group while Hindus are in the "good" group–he demonizes an entire group of people with a different cultural history: some of whom are citizens of his country. It is as if he is symbolically trying to turn them into the lowest caste of all people in India; a system he is trying to eliminate.

As a hypothesis, it might be that Modi projects aspects of himself and his life experiences that most likely have been humiliating or shameful to him—things he does not like and cannot tolerate about himself—onto Muslims who he appears to hate.

As a young boy and then as a man, it is likely that he was exposed to situations that made him feel marginalized, in part because of his low caste. Because his mother washed dishes to make money and his father sold tea on a cart at a train station, it seems quite likely that he encountered people who talked down to him or caused him to feel inferior. Assuming he had difficulty tolerating these feelings, he might have projected them onto Muslims making them feel their status in India is inferior to Hindus. This mechanism could also lessen Modi's feeling of being inferior to others that he most likely experienced at various times in his life. By casting off this sense of himself and attributing it to Muslims, he can relieve himself, at least temporarily, of feeling like a second-class person.

Modi seems to continuously monitor the behavior of Muslims, something that occurs when projective identification is employed, i.e., when the projector keeps tabs on the actions of the recipient(s) to make sure the undesirable characteristics still are present in the other. In this case, Modi's vigilant observations of Muslims would fulfil this need.

For the most part, populist leaders project aspects of themselves onto "others" making them the bad, unacceptable people. A second hypothesis encompasses the possibility that this practice might well be particularly exemplified in India's caste system which by its nature instills a sense of inferiority in those that are in lower castes. Assuming this is the case, those hailing from lower castes, like Modi, will be familiar with being marginalized. Modi shows no signs of relinquishing his persecution of Muslims and will likely continue to push them out of the public sphere. A country for all in Modi's India seems to be coded language for "all Hindus." A third hypothesis is that Modi also defends himself when criticized by using blame-shifting, which is a conscious process that the user incorporates to exonerate him or herself from blame. This most likely occurred in the Gujarat massacre where between 1000 and 2000 Muslims were murdered.

References

Alam, A. (2017). The caste politics curse that India just can't shake off. *The Conversation*, October 6. https://theconversation.com/the-caste-politics-curse-that-india-just-cant- shake-off-84216.

Chakrabortty, A. (2014). Narendra Modi, a man with a massacre on his hands, is not the reasonable choice for India. *The Guardian*, April 7. www.theguardian.com/commentisfree/2014/apr/07/narendra-modi-massacre-next- prime-minister-india.

Express Web Desk (2019). Video: OM Modi speaks in eight regional languages to say 'everything is fine' in India. *The Indian Express*, September 23. https://indianexpress. com/article/india/video-pm-modi-speaks-in-eight-regional-languages-to-say-everything-is -fine-in-india-6019081.

Gettleman, J. and Abi-Habib, M. (2019). As protests rage on citizenship bill, is India becoming a Hindu nation? *The New York Times*, December 16. www.nytimes.com/ 2019/12/16/world/asia/india-citizenship-protests.html.

Gettleman, J., Schultz, K., Raj, S., and Kumar, H., (2019). Under Modi, a Hindu nationalist surge has further divided India. *The New York Times*, April 11. www. nytimes.com/2019/04/11/world/asia/modi-india-elections.html.

Gettleman, J. and Abi-Habib, M. (2020). In India, Modi's policies have lit a fuse. *The New York Times*, March 1. www.nytimes.com/2020/03/01/world/asia/india-mod i-hindus.html.

Komireddi, K. (2019). *Malevolent republic: A shorth history of the new India*. Hurst.

New Indian Express. (2016, December 8). *Central OBC list to include 15 new casts*. New Indian Express. www.newindianexpress.com/nation/2016/dec/08/central-obc-list-to-include-15-new-castes-1547010.html.

Price, L. (2015). *The Modi Effect: Inside Narendra Modi's Campaign to Transform India*. London: Hodder & Stoughton.

PTI. (2014). Narendra Modi a 'fake OBC', claims Congress. *India Today*, May 8. www.indiatoday.in/elections/highlights/story/narendra-modi-a-fake-obc-claim s-congress-192146-2014-05-08.

Chapter 8

Slow Erosion

Populist Leaders in Western Europe

There is no single approach when it comes to populist politics. Leaders borrow methods and tactics from others and fashion them to the tastes and temperament of their homeland in hopes of securing power. Underpinning them is the employment of projective identification, and most populists—at least, the most successful ones—shake the hornets' nest that is deep-seated discontent by demonizing their opponents and welcoming those who feel aggrieved and persecuted by the political status quo. The process involved in this dynamic largely hinges on splitting and projective identification.

Western Europe is not immune from the advent of Trumpist nationalism; charismatic leaders in Germany, France, and the United Kingdom are channeling widespread feelings of frustration and rejection among the so-called silent working-class majorities into successful bids for political power. Just as many pundits and poll-watchers initially dismissed Donald Trump as a showboat jokester, they similarly regarded Le Pen, Johnson, and the leaders of Germany's Alternative für Deutschland (AfD) as political actors, indulging fringe voters with no serious chance of election.

But it has become clear that after years of effort and incremental increases in power that populism is gaining traction. In the 2022 presidential elections, Le Pen came within striking distance of the presidency, something her father, the founder of the French ultra-right Front National (FN) party (now rebranded as the National Rally, or RN), could never fully achieve. And yet, it appeared that her ascent was threatened (for a while) by a last-minute run for the presidency by Éric Zemmour, an ultra-right, first-generation son of Jewish Berber immigrants. The former journalist turned media pundit's unprecedented rise in popularity caught everyone off guard. Johnson, meanwhile, elicits comparisons to Trump—both described as loud, crude, and flamboyant—but the prime minister followed a different path to gain and secure power that relied on an anti-European narrative honed and refined over a thirty-year period. His determination to finalize Brexit is every nationalist's dream fulfilled, and Johnson's various crusades leading up to and after the referendum to leave the EU were frequently framed as epic battles

DOI: 10.4324/9781003202387-9

between "us" and "the elite"—a surprising tactic for an Oxford-educated classicist but one in line with Johnson's modus operandi.

In Germany, the 2017 elections secured Angela Merkel a fourth term as chancellor, but voters also sent members of the anti-immigrant AfD to parliament, forming the largest political bloc in the Bundestag. The AfD remains more powerful than any one leader—for the moment—but one regional party representative, Björn Höcke, is fast becoming the face and voice of the "Germany First" party. As for reckoning with his country's Nazi past with remarks like "we need nothing other than a 180-degree reversal on the politics of remembrance" (referring to Germany's annual commemoration of the Holocaust), it appears he's over it. The 48-year-old former history teacher might not lead the entire AfD, but his stance on immigration, Jews, and reviving nationalist pride has attracted international attention, and his approach to securing political power is classic projective identification. Le Pen's unconscious employment of projective identification stems from a tumultuous upbringing with a polarizing father figure which morphed into a desire to right the wrongs of contemporary French society. In an attempt to rid herself of the sins of her father, Le Pen has taken a different route. AfD party leaders, have long split Jews (and now, Muslims) into a "bad" category and thus blame them for the downfall of German supremacy.

Höcke and Le Pen claim to be different kinds of leaders—kinder, respectable—than the fascists who ruled Europe in the 1930s and 40s. The AfD and the RN are not neo-Nazi parties, but they have successfully integrated ultra-nationalist politics into mainstream media and conversations. Johnson, meanwhile, proves more challenging a populist to peg, at least from a psychoanalytical perspective. These three leaders use projective identification in their rhetoric, blaming immigrants, elite cosmopolitans, and intellectuals for one-sided globalism that, they argue, has negatively affected the vast aggrieved citizenry. This chapter offers a descriptive analysis of Le Pen, Johnson, and Höcke, and how they psychologically split people into categories, blaming those in the "other" group for poverty, tax hikes, and an overall decline in living standards. Projective identification and the shifting of blame contribute to the manipulation of their political adherents and helps them maintain their grip on power. As I hope to demonstrate, however, each leader has a different approach, leadership style, and way of using mechanisms of defense.

Like Father, Like Daughter? Understanding Marine's Rise to Power

Before Trump began musing a presidential run, Marine Le Pen was carefully and thoughtfully rebuilding a political party mired in controversy nearly since its creation concerning overt anti-Semitism and bigotry. Why maintain allegiance to such a party? Marine Le Pen's father, Jean-Marie, founded the

National Front in 1972 as a corrective response for what he believed was a decline in French society, and in the half-decade since, his inflammatory rhetoric has slowly become part of the French mainstream conversation. However, to understand Marine, I believe we must examine her father's role in laying the groundwork for her current political success.

So, what did Le Pen *père* despise so much about the direction of his beloved France?

Part of this societal collapse, in Le Pen's view, was due to the decline of the Catholic Church's influence and a "demographic depression" caused by "the professional promotion of women outside the family." He also asserted that "although men and women are profoundly different, and although nature has programmed women to assure the reproduction of the species as their essential task, the feminization of society has encouraged women's independence and turned them away from the vital function of reproduction (Eltchaninoff, 2018)." The decline of French civilization is due to this sense of loss. Women have allowed themselves to be swept up in this revolution that is not really in their best interests, and, poor things, those modern women do not realize they are being had. It was up to Jean-Marie to lead them to salvation.

Jean-Marie also blamed foreigners, Jews (frequent indirect and direct targets of anti-elite rhetoric throughout Europe), and immigrants for French society's debauchery. In addition to the profound negative consequences of women working outside the home, Le Pen blamed an unending influx of immigrants, mostly of non-European origin, whose presence threatened to undermine the stability of the French Republic (Eltchaninoff, 2018). To further illustrate the difference between the "pure" French and these interlopers, he suggests that Muslims are incapable of higher education because they begin masturbating at age eleven or twelve, whereas "Europeans...are not prone to this sexual obsession because of our religion, which controls such impulses" (2018). Le Pen's political party, therefore, responded directly to these socio-cultural incursions on basic French values, armor for an apocalyptical showdown between French survivalists and invading migrants.

For some 30 years Jean-Marie Le Pen championed strict controls on immigration and questioned the reality of the Holocaust. His support primarily drew from a fringe cohort of fascists left over from World War II. Through the eighties and nineties, Le Pen slowly gained political credibility, due in no small part to his unwavering persistence and undeniable charisma. Slow and steady pays off: Each election cycle brought more legislative seats to the FN. Le Pen always eyed the Elysée Palace and in 1995 ran for president. He won only 15 percent of the vote, but the electorate did send FN party members into mayoral seats in cities like Orange and Nice (Encyclopaedia Britannica, 2021). The party claimed power in chunks but was never considered a contender for major power grabs.

That all changed in 2002, when the presidential elections jolted the French out of their political *ennui* as Jean-Marie Le Pen advanced to the final election round. This astonished pundits and the voting public, but it was not some silent wave that pushed Le Pen. Voter apathy proved a major component. Sixteen politicians threw their names into the presidential ring, and an embarrassment of choice, along with insipid campaigns, kept many voters at home, assuming "their" candidate would make it to the final round. A misplaced, naïve confidence ruled the political theater, and an historic 28 percent of eligible voters stayed home. Le Pen squeaked into the final round with 17 percent of the total vote—roughly 234,000 more votes than he received in 1995, enough to put him one round away from the top job in the land. Realizing they were improbably close to electing a fascist racist misogynist to the highest office in the country, the French electorate overwhelmingly rallied behind the 83-year-old conservative Jacques Chirac—not so much because he was popular, but because he remained the only suitable alternative.

April 21, 2002—the date of the French presidential elections—serves as contemporary political shorthand for French politicians who might be tempted to underestimate the might of the ultra-right electorate. And forecasters did not discount that Marine Le Pen had more than a chance at winning the presidency in 2022. This father-daughter pair proved to be proficient projective identifiers, and their persistence in sowing the seeds of populist discontent are bearing fruit now.

Marine Le Pen: A "Brutal" Upbringing Forms a Desire for Power

Marine Le Pen's upbringing has been described by her biographers and historians as "brutal" and "politically violent," but none of the turbulence of late-night parties thrown by her father or her mother's prolonged absence could have prepared her for a cold November night in 1976, when the apartment building inhabited by the Le Pens was bombed with dynamite explosives that ripped off the entire front of the building. A baby in a neighboring apartment fell five floors, saved from likely death by getting stuck in tree branches. Marine, then eight years old, and her sisters, "were on our knees shivering, holding hands, praying with the fervor of despair," she writes in her autobiography *Against the Flow*. The case remains unsolved, but Marine saw it as a turning point in her life. "That night I went to sleep like all little girls my age. But when I woke, I was no longer a little girl like the others" (Beardsley, 2017). The bombing traumatized Marine, but it also served as the moment she created a shell around herself—one that permitted her to cultivate a certain toughness necessary for a career in the French political arena. In addition, that the perpetrator was never caught creates a nebulous "other" for Le Pen, an ideal narrative vessel into which she can channel her populist rhetoric and project her innermost emotions and feelings.

Since assuming control of her father's party, Marine Le Pen has undertaken the Herculean task of reforming the FN to appeal to a wider electorate. Her rebranding of the FN (renamed in 2018 as the Rassemblement National (National Rally, or RN) is the latest effort to normalize the populist rhetoric and ideology introduced by her father. The tact appears to be working: her popularity has grown among all social groups, perhaps none more than among—no surprise here—white working-class communities long felt ignored by the national government. Trump's election in 2016 legitimized Le Pen's strategy of cultivating blue-collar resentment of the intellectual elite. In parts of France, such as in the northeast where unemployment is stratospheric—even by French standards—Le Pen held a rally against rampant immigration made permissible, she claimed, by out-of-touch politicians interested in lining their pockets. It hit a nerve. Her call to restore France to its "authentic roots" has appeal.

Unlike her father, who targeted Jews as the primary scourge on French values, Marine tailors her outrage at immigrants hailing from predominantly Muslim-majority countries. Enemies must always be present in a populist's bid for power, and Marine exploits a latent Islamic xenophobia for political gain, and not without controversy; in 2015 she appeared in court to face charges of incitement to discrimination, based on comments she made at a rally in Lyon in 2010. During that speech, Le Pen compared Muslims worshipping in the streets to Nazi occupation:

> "I'm sorry, but some people are very fond of talking about the Second World War and about occupation, so let's talk about occupation," she said. "It's an occupation of swaths of territory, of areas in which religious laws apply. There are no tanks, no soldiers, but there is an occupation, and it weighs on people.
>
> (Willsher, 2015)

The trial recalled Jean-Marie's 2012 conviction for contesting crimes against humanity for saying that the Nazi occupation was not "particularly inhumane (Sciolino, 2005)." Unlike her father, who served a three-month suspended prison sentence and paid a $10,000 fine, Marine was found not guilty and well within her right to exercise free speech. During the trial, Marine Le Pen, also a lawyer and defending herself during the proceedings, described her comments from 2010 as "an exhortation to respect the law" for "those who have been abandoned, the forgotten ones." She seemed totally at ease in the courtroom and did not seem bothered by the accusations made against her. Indeed, rather than turn her into a social pariah, the trial provided Marine with fresh ammunition to launch against the French government, accusing justice minister Christiane Taubira of orchestrating "a real judicial persecution" of her and her political party (Breeden, 2015). Marine Le Pen consistently shifts blame for society's woes on corrupt government, and this trail served to prove her point, cementing her status as an outsider champion—a latter-day Joan of Arc, but armed with a law degree and no plans on being burned at the stake.

As the leader of the RN, Marine Le Pen's populist proposal for France is unsurprising: it includes a plan to reclaim control over the country's borders and laws. At one point she advocated a return to the franc but abandoned that in 2017. In an interview with NPR's Eleanor Beardsley, Le Pen threatened that, were she president of France and her demands for increased French autonomy were not met by the EU, then she would not hesitate to seek a referendum on pulling her country out of that body, akin to Brexit. "The EU knows the people do not believe in it anymore, so it functions through threat, intimidation, and blackmail. The way the EU reacted to Brexit was very revealing, especially for anyone who thought it had an ounce of democracy left in it (Beardsley, 2017)." In this example, splitting occurred when Le Pen doubled down on the notion that the faraway, disinterested members of the EU are unequivocally uninterested in France's concerns and are, therefore, bad. The EU then serves as the target of Le Pen's projections.

Though Le Pen no doubt felt galvanized by Trump's presidential victory, she cannot employ the same crass rhetorical style as him (or, for that matter, her father) because contemporary Frenchmen and women, on the whole, do not respond to that type of politicking. The fringe ultra-nationalists do not represent a large enough cohort to demand such speech. To legitimize the RN required condemning her father's anti-Semitic slant and even exiling him from the party he founded. Her public rebuke of her father minced no words: "The French have been witnesses for several months to an escalation of provocations and personal remarks by Jean-Marie Le Pen that are in complete contradiction with the National Front's political thinking, and with our commitment" (Eltchaninoff, 2018).

And although she has vociferously denied that anti-Semitism remains a core RN value, her choice of language employed to describe the out-of-touch intellectuals recalls similar depictions leveled at supposed secret cabals of French Jewish bankers at the dawn of the 20th century:

> "In their arrogance, they thought they could turn up their noses at the slow and laborious construction of our Nation, in order to create an exclusively virtual world in which their main goal would be the coming of a new man, severed from his roots, nomadic, dispensable, a slave to the order of the market."
>
> (Eltchaninoff, 2018)

Compare that to Eduard Drumont's two-volume bestselling *La France juive* (*The French Jew*), in which the author attacks Jews for nearly every ill beset upon humanity and for profiting off the backs of the hard-working French. "Homeland as a word has no meaning for the Semite," Drumont writes in volume one of his *magnum opus*. "Perpetually nomadic, can the Semite ever experience such depth of feeling? (Drumont, 1887)." The target of populist hatred might have shifted towards Muslims, but the undercurrent of anti-establishment rhetoric retains those ancient dog whistles. This narrative is carefully constructed and scattered like breadcrumbs on a trail to lead people to derive hidden symbolic meaning (Braddock, 2020). As a result, Le Pen strengthens her position against Muslims, and the French base happily follows along. This coded vocabulary serves two purposes: to broaden the RN's appeal to a population possibly unfamiliar or ignorant of its anti-Semitic undertones while signaling to old-line party members that little has changed. Nowadays, the overt projective identification and blame shifting channeled by Jean-Marie for some 40 years has been redirected towards Muslims. These statements form the language of anxiety. Denigrating others is part and parcel of the populist rulebook.

As the country looked to the 2022 presidential elections, polls consistently showned Le Pen gaining in popularity against President Emmanuel Macron. Decades of relentless projective identification and blame shifting brought her tantalizingly close to the presidency. Her ability to split people into unequivocal, almost immutable groups of good versus bad stems from deep-seated splitting and projective identification. As a hypothesis, it is quite possible that she identified with her father's use of projective identification.

Éric Zemmour

Éric Zemmour has participated in public debate on hot issues ranging from immigration to feminism for decades. His gift for crafting elegant prose belies the contents of his work. His 2006 book, *The First Sex*, for example—the title a clear reference to Simone de Beauvoir's seminal treatise on feminism, *The Second Sex*—analyzes the "devirilization" of French society. "Man is intelligence, woman is substance," he writes, offering his book as a sort of treatise for those younger Frenchmen he diagnoses as victims of feminism on how to reassert their dominance over women. Misogyny is not Zemmour's only talent; he's anti-Muslim and anti-immigrant, too. It is anti-French to be openly Muslim, according to Zemmour; to assimilate is the only way to make it in France. In 2014 he even suggested that the roughly 5 million French Muslims be removed from the country. When asked by a reporter if that were even possible, he replied, "it's unrealistic, I know, but history can surprise us" (*Le Parisien*, 2014). He openly supports the so-called "great replacement" conspiracy theory wherein white Frenchmen and women will soon be "replaced" by Muslims (Obaidi, Kunst, and Ozer, 2021). This ethnic cleansing, according to the theory, is being orchestrated globally by cabals of Jewish elites.

Zemmour did run for presidential office and lost in the first round,, but more relevant is understanding his meteoric rise in popularity among the French people, garnering a startling amount of enthusiasm with his unwaveringly ultra-right rhetoric. RN acolytes feared that his presence among the candidates could have pulled votes away from Le Pen and undermine the conservative push. Most importantly, at this point in time, Zemmour's rhetoric, although inflammatory, reveals just how far Le Pen and the RN have come in legitimizing ultra-right content.

Among his many concerning viewpoints, his rewriting of World War II and the role of the Vichy government is startling. In his book *The Suicide of France: 40 years that defeated France*, Zemmour argues that the Vichy government is misunderstood, victimized by woke historical revisionists, and in fact "sacrificed foreign Jews in order to save French Jews," crediting Marshal Petain with this supposedly savvy political maneuver. Never mind that Petain was tried and convicted of treason after World War II, a partial penance for the approximately 76,000 French Jews deported to concentration camps. His sentence carried the death penalty but was commuted to life in prison.

Zemmour also cast doubt on the Dreyfus Affair of 1894, wherein an Alsatian French officer of Jewish descent was falsely convicted and sentenced to life in prison for espionage. His retrial and subsequent conviction in 1899 would be overturned in 1906, when Dreyfus was fully exonerated and reinstated in the French Army. Zemmour's take on this affair? "Lots of people were ready to clear Dreyfus, but this affair is murky. We will never know," adding that Dreyfus's innocence was "not obvious" (Henley, 2021).

Why all the excitement with Zemmour's revisiting of historical events? He's hardly the first ultra-right-wing nationalist (exhibit A: Jean-Marie le Pen) to condemn Dreyfus's exoneration or whitewash the Vichy government's collaboration with the Nazis (Knobel, 2021). To cast even the slightest doubt on supposedly settled affairs, especially those that stir up complex emotions, is part of a calculated strategy to rewrite history and to sow doubt among the people—eventually, as we have seen with other populist leaders, relentless revisionist and misinformation campaigns erode public confidence in truth and facts. Undermining facts weakens democracies, as we have seen play out in the United States as orchestrated by Trump. Unlike Trump, Zemmour has a written track record of his beliefs; you can say a lot of things about Éric Zemmour, but you cannot say he flip-flops on issues. And it is that stalwart adherence that has propelled him upward in the French polls.

But is Zemmour France's answer to Trump? Both have been accused of sexual misconduct and both incite hatred towards Muslims; Zemmour, in fact, is on trial for calling unaccompanied child migrants "thieves, killers, and rapists" (Chrisafis, 2021), which he has categorized as essentially a witch-hunt. This is Zemmour's third such trial; he was previously convicted for incitement of racial hatred in 2011 and in 2016 (Chrisafis, 2011).

Where does all this animosity and desire to rewrite history come from? In other words, where's the projective identification? Zemmour, the Parisian-born Berber-Jewish son of a paramedic and a housewife, seems to deeply disavow some element of his Jewish heritage. A paradox, no doubt; his wife, Mylene Chichportich, is also the daughter of North African Jewish immigrants. On boards such as 4chan, Zemmour has been described as "100%/our/jew," and that "despite being Jewish, seems to truly love France"

(Rose, 2021). It appears that he is attempting to cast off his Jewish heritage by supporting ideologies such as the great replacement conspiracy and harboring deep hatred towards Muslims. Like Jean-Marie Le Pen, Zemmour shifts blame for perceived French grievances onto Muslim immigrant populations and reinforces those beliefs at every turn—in speeches, in print, and on the debate stage. Decades of such rhetoric has both solidified his relationship with his political base and perhaps provided a sort of unconscious relief of his perceived inherent wickedness for being born a Jew.

Boris Johnson

Anti-elite, anti-intellectualism fuels populist sentiment, assisted, surprisingly, by the very people and institutions under siege. A common claim among populists is that the elite believe that there is no such thing as class or privilege, that differences do not exist, and that "professionals supposedly owe success to their 'human capital,' not to having been born, overwhelmingly, into the educated middle class" (Lind, 2020). These thoughts fester among populists, sowing animosity and bitterness among the vast working-class who feel their government abandoned them in the march towards an automated, globalized future.

People in various countries share these sentiments, but the British successfully aired their simmering grievances via Boris Johnson, a leader whose populist bona fides do not perfectly align with other leaders discussed in this book, but he does shift blame to specific groups to suit his populist purposes.

The Johnson origin story reads almost too Trumpian; bullied and rejected as a child, Johnson's unusual trajectory offers ample comparison to POTUS 45 and supports the hypothesis that the underpinnings of Johnson's use of projective identification were established during his childhood years.

Alexander Boris de Pfeffel Johnson was born in New York City to Charlotte, a twenty-two-year-old college dropout and painter, and Stanley, author, environmentalist, and womanizer whose frequent job changes moved the family thirty-two times over fourteen years and across two continents. Boris's trademark white-blond hair is not Celtic in origin, but Turkish: Stanley's grandfather, Ali Kemal, hailed from a village in Anatolia known for its blond hair and blue-eyed inhabitants, and the genes clearly made their way to Boris (Purnell, 2011, p. 19.).

Stanley—much like Donald's father, Fred Trump—encouraged a win-at-all-costs, hyper-competitive temperament among his children, and was especially tough on Boris, who was deaf until his eighth birthday (Purnell, 2011). Stanley set high expectations for his children, and Boris strived to meet those expectations, no matter how trivial the pursuit: "If Boris, as the eldest, did not secure his rightful place by winning, he would erupt in anger. He once took his frustration out on a wall after losing a point to sister Rachel at table tennis, kicking it and breaking a toe in the process," explains his unauthorized biography (2011). This competitive streak remains a major element of Johnson's personality: At a charity rugby event in 2015 in Japan, Johnson tackled a ten-year-old schoolboy to the ground (Bhunjun, 2015).

That mentality extended to scholarly endeavors as well: His biographer recounts that "Boris soon scooped up academic prizes like rosettes at a gymkhana but he himself admits probably the single most galvanizing event of his life—and the incident to install the formidable driving ambition we know today—was when Rachel, his younger sister by 15 months, learned to read before him." On the eve of her fortieth birthday, Rachel recalled that "'Al [Boris] had one friend, Carl, and he once went to Carl's house, but I think that was it. We never, ever went to play with other children. We didn't need friends'" (Purnell, 2011. p. 29). Mother Charlotte suffered a mental breakdown in 1974 when the family was living in Brussels. During her stay in the hospital, Charlotte received a Parkinson's Disease diagnosis. The children learned to fend for themselves during her recovery, and when she and Stanley divorced in 1979, Boris and Rachel were sent to boarding school in England.

Away from his parents, the young man transformed from the reserved "Al" his family knew to the eccentric, flaxen-haired Boris who relished being the center of attention. This outward, over-exuberant personality hid a deep, almost cutthroat desire for power and fame, according to friends and acquaintances, both of which would be his in equal measure.

After completing secondary school at Eton, Boris enrolled in Oxford where he joined various social clubs and developed the ability to seduce for personal and political gain, skills that he would employ throughout his career as a journalist, game show host, and politician. In one early example, he failed to be elected president of Oxford Union, an exclusive social club on campus; he reinvented his personality, enlisted friends to glad-hand for him, and won in the following election cycle.

With his university degree in hand, Johnson joined The Daily Telegraph in 1989 as its Brussels correspondent, where rather than subsist on the tedium of daily reportage, he developed and polished his brand of Britain-first politics with stories brimming with Euroscepticism. His pieces created a narrative around how the European Union would ultimately threaten British sovereignty, and his natural flair for flamboyance often landed his stories on the front page, especially when blaring headlines like "Delors plans to rule Europe," "Euro headquarters to be blown up," (which never happened and still serves as the European Commission's base of operations) and "Brussels recruits sniffers to ensure that Euro manure smells the same." Additionally, it is no wonder that Johnson harbored such animosity for Brussels: recall that this was the same city where his mother spiraled towards a psychological breakdown. The Johnson home in Brussels was not a happy one, and as an adult, it appears those feelings did not change much.

What set Johnson apart from his tabloid cousins was how well he mixed fact with exaggeration. As Kurt Braddock explains in *Weaponized Words*, leaders like Johnson engage in psychological manipulation by tailoring their messages to persuade followers that their way is the only way to ensure the continued well-being of the country. And these early pieces articulated nationalist grievances while entertaining readers—did Johnson think he might run for political office at the time? That's unclear, but he is hardly the first journalist to parlay headlines into political power: Winston Churchill, Benito Mussolini, even Sarah Palin once covered the news. Additionally, Johnson's stories made him a star in the U.K. and fueled his rise to power—first, as bumbling two-term mayor of London and then as prime minister.

Johnson's decades-long attacks on "Brussels bureaucrats" built and sustained a loyal base of Britain-first supporters. In the leadup to his eventual run for president of the Conservative Party in 2018, Johnson wrote a piece for his old employer, *The Daily Telegraph*, about a forthcoming ban in Denmark on wearing burkas in public. It compared women who wore the full-face veil to "bank robbers" and "letterboxes" (Johnson, 2018). A local watchdog group reported that anti-Muslim incidents increased significantly in Britain in the week following Johnson's, column, and 42 percent of those who said they engaged in anti-Muslim acts cited Johnson or his recent article as inspiration. Though he might argue otherwise—that he's pro-Muslim but anti-Conservative Islam—that column cemented his position with the populist movement against immigrants from Muslim-majority countries.

In an essay accompanying an update to his 2006 book, *The Dream of Rome*, Johnson walks a fine line between calling for a reconciliation between Islam and Christianity, saying, "It is time we all grew up and made peace." But not before outlining the atrocities caused by Muslims and the Ottoman Empire (Johnson, 2007, p. 242). This chapter attempts to appeal to readers at two ends of the ideological spectrum: those who, like Johnson, prize Roman contributions to Western Europe and those who might look at extending an olive branch as not worth the effort. As for the modern-day relationship between Europe and Turkey, he writes, "It is very easy for politicians to wind people up against Turkish accession to the EU, for instance, because we are dealing with a very pungent stereotype" (Johnson, 2007). In other words, Johnson's not against the average Turk—he's against the religion of Islam when practiced as militant conservatism. It is a distinction, but how many of his followers are going to bother with that level of nuance?

On January 31, 2020 the United Kingdom withdrew from the EU—the only country to ever formally do so. After 47 years of membership of the EU and its predecessor, the European Community, this rupture seemed sudden, but increasing skepticism in a common market dates to the 1980s when Conservative Prime Minister Margaret Thatcher opposed the creation of a "superstate" that would strip countries of their sovereign rights. The concept of Euroscepticism materialized from this era and coincided with Johnson's time in Brussels as a *Daily Telegraph* journalist. Although he was not the only prominent critic of the EU, Johnson was one of the most vocal.

When the 2016 referendum for the U.K. to leave the EU came up for a vote, 51.89 percent of the electorate agreed that it was time "to have our country back," which Johnson exploited in his run for office in 2019. Phrases like "Unleash Britain's potential" filled his speeches, as did numerous untruths pulled straight from the Trump playbook, leading some journalists to dub 2019 the U.K.'s "first post-truth election," and blamed the turn of events on American influence—namely, the 2016 election of Trump.

Like Trump, when Johnson faced media and public scrutiny, he deflected tough questions and banished journalists who refused to play nice. A journalist attempted to show the Prime Minister a photograph of a boy suspected of suffering from pneumonia forced to lie on the floor of an emergency room while waiting for a bed. Flustered, Johnson took the journalist's phone. He later apologized but refused to examine or discuss those disturbing images (Woodyatt, 2019). When Johnson writes or talks about others, he can be crude and demeaning, and, like Trump, has a long history of misogynistic comments towards women. In 2016 *Journal I.E.* put together a list of "people, places and things Boris Johnson has insulted or knocked over." In one example, he called former president Barack Obama "part Kenyan" and said, prior to Trump becoming president, that he "wouldn't visit some parts of New York [for the] real risk of meeting Donald Trump." There is no filter—physical or verbal.

Johnson, like Trump, uses projective identification as a bullying tactic, to intimidate his adversaries and to curry support among his followers. Johnson attacks the EU as antithetical to British interests, and as too distant to understand what the people of Britain really need. However, Johnson stands apart from the other leaders discussed in this book. Although most populist leaders examined here do not appear to employ projective identification in the same way as Trump, Johnson is an exception. He is among the more divisive leaders the U.K. has elected in modern history. By one token, he's crass, boorish, pugilistic—it is his way or the highway—and by another, nurtures a deep desire to be loved and adored. Being wrong—wrong about Brexit, wrong about handling the pandemic—could be related to hidden feelings of shame that were initially experienced in childhood.

A profile of Johnson in *The New Yorker* defined the "Johnsonian" way as one that included "lies, the performative phrases, the layers of persona—they accrete, one on top of another, flecked here and there with Latin, until everyone has forgotten what the big deal was (Knight, 2019)." Johnson does not fit squarely into one mold of populist, nor does he appear to always employ projective identification to disarm and disavow feelings he cannot process or acknowledge. As described in the *New Yorker* profile: "the jolly eel around Johnson enables him to air sinister ideas and dodge the consequences" (Knight, 2019). Muslims and faceless bureaucrats, however, are frequently blamed for the downfall of British civilization, and he regularly projects blame onto these groups.

Germany

Germany's history with populists is excruciatingly documented, and rather than revisit Hitler and his rise to power, which is done elsewhere in great detail, I will focus on contemporary populist leaders who have steadily gained power and influence among German voters by exploiting a sense of collective misunderstanding. In Germany, those feelings are represented by the Alternative für Deutschland (AfD) party, led by Bernd Luck and Alexander Gauland, who, since 2013, have pushed populist rhetoric into common conversation. Populist leaders share certain psychological traits, projective identification among them, and in Germany, the blame shifting that usually occurs between one charismatic leader and the population is replaced by a charismatic party whose various representatives work collectively to gain power and legitimize ultra-nationalist policies.

Heimat

Founded in 2009 in response to the Eurozone debt crisis, Germany's right-wing AfD lost its fleeting position as the country's largest opposition party in the Bundestag in 2021, but there is little doubt that this group is now an established member of Germany's political arena. Chief among the group's arguments to abandon Eurozone policies was the financial rescue of poor southern European member states, like Greece. AfD leaders reasoned that the Eurozone would stop functioning properly if rich countries kept bailing out poor ones. Restricting immigration remains another major concern of the AfD. For a few years, party leaders tried to maintain voter support among both moderates and ultra-right nationalists in an attempt to attract as many warm bodies to the party as possible; interestingly, a spokesperson described AfD as "the last truly liberal party in Germany" (Lochocki, 2015). This might sound contradictory, however the Brookings Institution categorizes the AfD and other populist groups as "Left-Right" parties, meaning they "favor a strong role for the state in social and economic affairs, while holding staunch pronationalist, anti-immigrant views" (Gedmin, 2019). Such parties function—and, these days, flourish—because their leaders capitalize on grievances and economic concerns that are blamed on outsiders: in this case, non-ethnic Germans and Muslims.

Perhaps one of the party's most charismatic leaders is Björn Höcke, the leader of the Thuringian state wing of the AfD and considered by political insiders as the future of the far-right in Germany. As such, he is not without controversy: a German court declared the former history teacher to be a fascist based on what it called "verifiable fact"—he opposes Germany's migrant asylum policies, the euro, sex education, and favors what he calls "Prussian values" which lean towards traditional family models (Oltermann, 2020). Like Jean-Marie Le Pen, Höcke blames the demise of "good" German values on the influx of immigrants and promiscuity. In his book, *Nie zwei in denselben Fluss*, Höcke calls for ridding Germany of "culturally alien" people to avoid "death through population exchange." Which, clearly, can only be achieved through "well-tempered cruelty (Funke, 2019)." So laced is this book with neo-Nazi language that excerpts read from his book to lawmakers from his own party could not tell if they were by Höcke or Hitler.

These arguments all feed a sense among a growing cohort of Germans that outside forces are at work corrupting and stealing their beloved "Heimat," the German term for "homeland." Some of this is based on when ethnic Germans were forced from their homes in what is now Poland, the Czech Republic, and Russia. After World War II, approximately 14 million ethnic Germans retreated into Germany to flee the Red Army—refugees and "expellees" forced to create new lives in a strange land. Though these events are not often studied, if at all, outside Germany, history teacher Höcke drilled his students on this concept. Sources reveal that he regularly taught this lesson in front of a map created before World War I, when Germany's borders were much larger than they are today. This visual served to remind his pupils of what he calls "their European roots."

Until the early 2000s "expellees'" marked their flight into Germany with annual "Day of the Homeland" celebrations, but in recent years, social media has made it easier for disparate groups of "expellees" to find each other and commiserate on their collective grievances. The AfD, with Höcke at the helm, recognized an opportunity among this cohort, and in 2017 created a Facebook group just for "Expellees, Returnees and German Minorities," where participants could commiserate. By aligning themselves with a controversial group, the AfD is signaling that it is committed to the aggrieved. A spokesperson for the AfD-sponsored Facebook group said that "we saw the expellees weren't a relevant topic…anymore. We know it's emotional topic and when every fourth German has a family member who was expelled, it can really speak to people." Even three or four generations after being forced to leave their homes, descendants still feel aggrieved and victimized (Jackson, 2019). These "forgotten people" are believed to make up 25 percent of the current German population—a sizeable demographic that could easily sway the balance of power if they voted en bloc, and the AfD is working every angle to demonstrate that it understands them and will fight for them.

If there's been a common thread among these three examples, it is that feelings of sovereignty and identity are incredibly important to citizens and leaders trying to secure power. These group leaders are manipulating those feelings to create paranoid voters who mistrust their government.

How a narrative is presented is often just as important as the type of story in question. Studies have shown that exposure to certain narratives can have positive effects. In "Narrative and Framing: A Test of an Integrated Message in the Exercise Context," authors Jennifer Gray and Nancy Harrington found that "gain framed messages are significantly more successful in promoting positive exercise variables" (Gray and Harrington, 2011). In contrast, other studies show that certain persuasive narratives can have the opposite of their intended effect. The best narratives—the ones that get readers or viewers to adopt certain viewpoints or even act on them—engage in successful psychological transportation, wherein the readers feel as though they have been transported into another world (Braddock, 2020, p. 78). "The experience of psychological transportation opens the door to several mechanisms of persuasion," writes Braddock. Furthermore, content becomes secondary to the pleasure factor: if a video, book, or podcast elicits feelings of happiness, acceptance, or comfort, the narrative has established a bond with its audience, breaking barriers to persuasion and making it easier for content creators to manipulate end users.

References

Beardsley, E. (2017). France's Marine Le Pen contends populism is the future. NPR, January 6. www.npr.org/2017/01/06/508587559/frances-marine-le-pen-contends-populism- is-the-future.

Beardsley, E. (2017). Marine le Pen's 'brutal' upbringing shaped her worldview. NPR, April 21. www.npr.org/2017/04/21/525110143/marine-le-pens-brutal-upbringing-shaped- her-worldview.

Bennhold, K. and Eddy, M. (2020). 'Hitler or Hocke?' Germany's far-right party radicalizes. *The New York Times*, February 20. www.nytimes.com/2019/10/26/world/europe/afd-election-east-germany- hoecke.html.

Bhunjin, A. (2015). KO: Boris Johnson knocks over boy during rugby game in Japan. *Rugby World*, October 15. www.rugbyworld.com/countries/rest-of-the-world/ko-boris- johnson-knocks-over-boy-during-rugby-game-in-japan-51103.

Braddock, K. (2020). Chapter Three, "Extremist Narratives and Counter-Narratives." *Weaponized Words: The Strategic Role of Persuasion in Violent Radicalization and Counter-Radicalization*. Cambridge University Press.

Breeden, A. (2015). French court acquits Marine Le Pen of hate speech. *The New York Times*, December 15. www.nytimes.com/2015/12/16/world/europe/french-court-acquits- marine-le-pen-of-hate-speech.html.

Chrisafis, A. (2021). French presidential hopeful Eric Zemmour begins race hate trial. *The Guardian*, November 17. www.theguardian.com/world/2021/nov/17/french-presidential-hopeful-eric-zemmour-race-hate-trial-far-right.

Chrisafis, A. (2011). *French journalist convicted on racism charge over drug dealer comment*. *The Guardian*, February 18. www.theguardian.com/world/2011/feb/18/french-journalist-racism-drug-dealer.

Drumont, E. (1887). *La France Juive: essai d'histoire contemporaine*. vol. 1. Paris: C. Marpon & E. Flammarion, p. 60. https://babel.hathitrust.org/cgi/pt?id=mdp.39015000627854&view=1up&seq=110&q1=n omade.

Eltchaninoff, M. (2018). *Inside the Mind of Marine le Pen*. Oxford University Press, Kindle Edition, Location 345, 1364. p. 111.

Encyclopaedia Britannica (2021). Jean-Marie Le Pen. www.britannica.com/biography/Jean-Marie-Le-Pen.

Funke, Hajo. (2019). Hocke wants the civil war. Zeit Online, October 24. www.zeit.de/politik/deutschland/2019-10/rechtsextremismus-bjoern-hoecke-afd-fluegel-rechte-gewalt-faschismus?utm_referrer=https%3A%2F%2Fomelas.co.uk%2F.

Gedmin, J. (2019). How 'populist' is the AfD? A 'Muslims in the West' reaction essay. Brookings Institution, December 4. www.brookings.edu/articles/how-populist-is-the-afd.

Gray, J. and Harrington, N. (2011). Narrative and framing: A test of an integrated message strategy in the exercise context. *Journal of Health Communication*. 16:3, 264–281, doi:10.1080/10810730.2010.529490.

Henley, J. (2021). Rise of far right puts Dreyfus affair into spotlight in French election race. *The Guardian*, October 30. www.theguardian.com/global/2021/oct/30/rise-of-far-right-puts-dreyfus-affair-into-spotlight-in-french-election-race.

Jackson, J. (2019). Germany's far-right AfD aims at a forgotten demographic. DW.com, October 27. https://p.dw.com/p/3RxnR.

Johnson, B. (2007). *The Dream of Rome*. Second edition. HarperPress, p.242.

Johnson, B. (2018). Denmark has got it wrong. Yes, the burka is oppressive and ridiculous. *The Daily Telegraph*, August 5. www.telegraph.co.uk/news/2018/08/05/denmark-has-got-wrong-yes-burka-oppressive-ridiculous-still.

Knight, S. (2019). The empty promise of Boris Johnson. *The New Yorker*, June 13. www.newyorker.com/magazine/2019/06/24/the-empty-promise-of-boris-johnson.

Knobel, M. (2021). Lorsqu' Éric Zemmour jette le soupçon sur l'innocence d'Alfred Dreyfus. *Revue des deux mondes*, October 22. www.revuedesdeuxmondes.fr/lorsqueric-zemmour-jette-le-soupcon-sur-linnocence-dalfred-dreyfus.

Le Parisien (2014). Ce qu'Eric Zemmour a vraiment dit au "Corriere."December 21. www.leparisien.fr/culture-loisirs/tv/polemique-ce-qu-eric-zemmour-a-vraiment-dit-au-corriere-21-12-2014-4391411.php.

Lind, M. (2020). What's behind the west's populist wave. *Prospect Magazine*, March 5. www.prospectmagazine.co.uk/magazine/whats-behind-the-wests-populist-wave-immigration-brexit-boris-johnson-class-divide.

Lochocki, T. (2015). *Countering right-wing populism: The AfD and the strategic dilemma for Germany's moderate parties. JSTOR*, February 1. www.jstor.org/stable/resrep18838?seq=1#metadata_info_tab_contents.

Obadi, M., Kunst, J., Ozer, S. et al. (2021). The "great replacement" conspiracy theory: How the perceived ousting of Whites can evoke violent extremism and Islamophobia. Group Processes & Intergroup Relations, August 6. https://doi.org/10.1177/13684302211028293.

Oltermann, P. (2020). Outrage as German centre-right votes with AfD to oust Thuringia premier. *The Guardian*, February 5. www.theguardian.com/world/2020/feb/05/centre-right-german-parties-vote-with-afd-to-oust-thuringia-premier-bodo-ramelow.

Purnell, S. (2011). *Just Boris: A Tale of Blond Ambition*. Aurum.

Rose, H. (2021). Eric Zemmour: Jewish heritage is a useful tool for the French far right. *The Conversation*, November 11. https://theconversation.com/eric-zemmour-jewish-heritage-is-a-useful-tool-for-the-french-far-right-170838.

Sciolino, E. (2005). Le Pen calls Nazis not so 'inhumane.' *The New York Times*, January 14. www.nytimes.com/2005/01/14/world/europe/le-pen-calls-nazis-not-so-inhumane.

Willsher, K. (2015). Marine le Pen faces court on charge of inciting racial hatred. *The Guardian*, September 22. www.theguardian.com/world/2015/sep/22/marine-le-pen-fa ces- court-on-charge-of-inciting-racial-hatred.

Woodyatt, A. (2019). Boris Johnson takes reporter's phone and dodges questions on shocking emergency room picture. CNN, December 9. www.cnn.com/2019/12/09/ uk/boris- johnson-refuses-look-at-phone-intl-scli-gbr/index.html.

Chapter 9

Cincinnatus, Deferred

Hugo Chávez, Daniel Ortega, and When Unchecked Populism Turns to Authoritarianism

Various dictatorships that dominated South American politics from the 1970s to the 1990s were washed away by a democratic tidal wave, leaving only communist Cuba and Mexico's civilian one-state party. Multiple factors led to this dismantling of dictatorships—the end of the Cold War, economic disaster, and democracy simply proved too powerful to ignore. However, much has changed in the past thirty years; revolutionaries who successfully toppled authoritarian regimes in the name of democracy were eventually freely elected by their people, but soon some of these leaders decided that total authority was more in line with what they wanted. Given this shift in priorities, they consolidated power and changed laws to secure themselves permanently in their presidential posts. Rather than follow in the noble footsteps of the Roman military leader Cincinnatus, who, after serving 15 days as a dictator, resigned his post and returned to his plow, Hugo Chávez and Daniel Ortega threw the plow away and remained at the helm of their countries.

Not all populist leaders become authoritarian dictators, but left unchecked, many do move in that direction. Much of the success enjoyed by these men is due to the fact that they have used splitting projective identification and blame shifting successfully as they unconsciously rid themselves of intolerable internal qualities. Conscious shifting of blame also helped them seek and gain control of others. With that in mind, I believe the example of the late Chávez of Venezuela serves as a prime example of how populist power can quickly erode a democracy, especially in the hands of someone using these defense mechanisms to shift blame and retain power. Nicaragua's Ortega still runs his country, but clearly not according to some populist mandate: he has readily abandoned any pretense of serving his citizens in a ruthless bid to remain president.

A hallmark of populist discourse is purposefully vague rhetoric coupled with laser-sharp accusations against specific oppressors, and it is a tactic that served Chávez well and that Ortega continues to exhibit. Both men balanced their relationship with their respective countrymen by stoking feelings of persecution, and, especially in Chávez's case, legitimizing their positions by cultivating relationships with high-profile international supporters. Ortega,

DOI: 10.4324/9781003202387-10

meanwhile, has spent the past two decades engaging in verbal warfare and convincing the populace that his various deadly moves to consolidate power and eliminate dissent are part of a greater purpose—to save the people of Nicaragua from outside influence (notably, of the United States).

As a member of the socialist Sandinista National Liberation Front, Ortega, like Chávez, spent his political career cultivating a proletariat image of himself, though once elected president in 2007, he has done nearly everything in his power to topple Nicaragua's democracy in favor of an autocratic government led, naturally, by him.

Though their style of populism differs tremendously from other world leaders discussed in this book, specifically in that they have taken populism to the authoritarian extreme, Ortega and Chávez share projective identification in common, as I will demonstrate in the following pages. Further, though Chávez has been dead since March 2013—and controversially succeeded by his vice-president Nicolás Maduro—his ascent to power, aided in no small part by his wizardry with words, serves, I believe, as a cautionary tale for what could happen in other countries where populism has taken root. Unchecked, what at first blush might appear to be a fringe actor asserting a democratic right to free speech could, under the right conditions, become the next authoritarian demagogue. With the passage of time, we can see that Chávez was not merely a democratic leader interested in lifting his countrymen out of poverty; his interest in sustaining power moved him to become the type of supreme leader he claimed to have fought all his adult life to remove.

The various social and economic policies of both leaders are rooted in projective identification, worsening preexisting social division and unrest. Both men, but Chávez in particular, are hard to pin down. Chávez was by turns idolized and demonized, his gift of oratory and deft understanding of the human condition propelled him to power and to global recognition that few South American leaders ever attain. But by 2002 his people began to turn against him, believing he had created such a chasm between the rich and the poor that class warfare was unavoidable. By sustaining a decades-long war against corruption, injustice, and inequality fueled by a booming oil industry, Chávez positioned himself as a "man of the people," as someone who claimed to understand the pain of the impoverished and would move heaven and earth to raise them up from poverty.

Much ink has been spilled elsewhere regarding the politics of Chávez, and this chapter will not attempt to examine the totality of his career, however I will attempt to piece together his uncanny ability to manipulate language to transform existing social problems into demands for change. Successful populists forge bonds between them and their followers by claiming that they speak for the people, and they convince their citizens of their ability through charisma, magnetic speaking, strategic blame shifting, and, sometimes, brute force.

The Land of the People, Mud Huts, and Maternal Separation

For populists, there is perhaps no better demonstration that they understand poverty than having lived it themselves. The destitute of Latin America might have the same rights as their middle- and upper-class brethren, but often rely on "brokers" or grease-palmed politicians who will ensure access to necessities like food and electricity. In return, politicians hope that the people will vote to keep them in power. This kind of system is ripe for corruption, and though the impoverished do not always get what they need, smart populists will ensure that their needs are attended to at least some of the time (De la Torre, 2017, p. 205).

Chávez legitimately knew the bitter taste of deprivation like many of his fellow Venezuelans. As the second of six surviving sons, Chávez was born on July 28, 1954, to parents who barely made ends meet as primary school teachers. The Chávez origin story figured prominently in the leader's frequent personal accounts. He often said that he envisioned his retirement as a return to his childhood home where he would enjoy his golden years communing with nature—Cincinnatus by way of Venezuela. The reality of his upbringing, however, might have been less idyllic. Nestled in Los Llanos ("the plains"), Chávez's hometown of Sabaneta was largely known for its sugar production. More importantly, however, the land surrounding Sabaneta is a dusty frontier land populated by tough cowboys who even today still roam the grassy flatlands covered by cattle ranches and dotted with wilderness filled with jaguars, giant guinea pigs known as capybaras, and anacondas. The staggering beauty of the land starkly contrasted with those scraping to get by, and it left a mark on Chávez, who would refer to this land as the authentic, honest Venezuela where the impoverished might as well have lived on another planet when compared to the oil-driven wealthy enclaves found in the capital city of Caracas. The people of the plains were the people of Chávez, and he never forgot them.

Young Hugo's parents lived in an even more remote corner of the Plains, in a village called Los Rastrojos. After giving birth to her first child in this backwater without even a midwife to assist her through labor, Elena Frias de Chávez trekked to Sabaneta for her subsequent deliveries where she gave birth to Hugo in the home of her mother-in-law. With a roof of palm leaves and a mud floor, the Chávez dwelling was typical of those in Sabaneta, which, during the 1950s numbered perhaps 1,000 residents. Childhood friend Efren Jimenez recalled that Sabaneta "was made up of about four streets....We all knew each other, we were all like one big family." But regular electricity was still elusive; if they were lucky, a single communal generator illuminated the homes of Sabaneta's residents for four hours or so a night.

Though both parents were educators, money was tight, and with five other mouths to feed, Hugo was sent to live with his paternal grandmother, Rosa

Ines Chávez, who also had no running water or indoor toilet, but her home was a step up from the truly sorry accommodations out in Los Rastrojos, if only by virtue of location. Biographer Bart Jones paints an image of a region that had seen little discernible change since Thomas Edison invented the lightbulb:

> Rosa cooked over a wood fire, fetched water from a well, and utilized an outhouse. Her single luxury was a small radio run by batteries. She was lucky to get a few hours of electricity at night from the village's small gas-oil-fueled power plant. Vehicles were rare. People got around on bicycle or walked, often making the hour-long trek to Los Rastrojos by foot. Half a century later, the streets of Sabaneta still teemed with bicycles.
>
> (Jones, 2007, p. 22)

Further, as a devout Roman Catholic, Rosa ran a tight ship and encouraged Hugo to be willing to help those even less fortunate than them.

Possessed with a quick mind—Hugo could memorize and recite entire passages from books—he eventually joined a government-run literacy group called *cadenas abajo*—"off with the chains"—and as a plucky ten-year-old paid it forward by teaching adults in Sabaneta to read.

Like many origin stories, there are a few versions of Chávez's childhood. Some argue that Chávez's strained relationship with his mother fueled deep resentment. A former lover of Chávez named Herma Marksman said she believed that "he [Chávez] loved his father more than his mother. I think that he really missed the warmth of his mother during those early years" (Marcano and Tyszka, 2007). This statement appears to be at odds with other evidence we've seen about Chávez's relationship with his mother. Perhaps this was a ruse to convince people he did care for her? It certainly would not have been a good look for Chávez to publicly disavow his mother, a poor country girl trying to scrape out a living. Marksman also claimed that Chávez told her that he did not speak to his mother for two years. However, in a 2007 interview, Chávez's brother, Adan, refuted the assertion of maternal discord (Jones, 2007, p. 25). Was Elena Frias de Chávez as cold as Marksman claimed? In an interview in 1999 with a Venezuelan magazine, Elena asserted that as an 18-year-old, the last thing she wanted was to become a mother:

> I didn't want to have children...I don't know, I didn't like them, it didn't seem appealing, but since God told me, 'That is what you are going to do,' I got married and a month later I was pregnant.
>
> (Marcano and Tyszka, 2007, loc 394)

Elena's lack of enthusiasm might have accounted for her frosty early relationship with her son, who, prior to moving in with his grandmother, would run away and hide when his mother attempted to beat him as a corrective measure. Rosa, by contrast, might have been stern, but there does not seem to be a record of Chávez attempting to escape her. Chávez addressed his grandmother as "mama" or "mamita" in his correspondence during his imprisonment (Marcano and Tyszka, 2007, loc 370). He also wrote to his mother, but with less frequency.

On Chávez's live television show, "Aló Presidente," the lynchpin of his media outreach program that ran from 2006 through 2012, the president often recalled his youth as "poor but happy" and never publicly referred to the early years as anything less than charmed. Yet, there were moments of humiliation: On the first day of school, Chávez was not allowed into the building because he lacked shoes. His grandmother "cried and cried because she couldn't afford to buy him shoes," recounted an aunt. Yet she found a way to procure the necessary footwear to ensure Chávez could attend class. A single such slight would not have shaped Chávez into the man he became, but it and other situations like it could easily have helped Chávez form his life-long alliance with the country's poor and downtrodden.

Roots of Resistance in Attachment Trauma

A critical component to a full and rewarding life originates from a secure attachment with another person or group. Humans thrive when these close relationships are healthy and established early in life. Without them, we become withdrawn and depressed. Learning how to form these bonds of trust begins soon after a baby is born. Interestingly, whether children form such bonds does not always become clear until later in life. When such feelings are in flux—perhaps, in some cases, owing to neglect or abuse—a child becomes unable to form loving or caring bonds, which can lead to attachment trauma. Feeling a loss of one's dignity can lead to intense feelings of shame and closes off the victim from being able to form long-lasting and meaningful relationships. It seems to me that Chávez suffered some amount of attachment trauma with his mother but managed to, at least on some level, substitute that maternal relationship for one with his grandmother.

Venezuelan psychiatrist Edmundo Chirinos met Chávez in prison after the latter's failed coup attempt in 1992 to depose Carlos Andres Perez. Chirinos said Chávez wanted to address various personal issues. During their conversations, Chirinos noted connections between Chávez's adulthood and events of his childhood:

> Chávez feels genuine scorn for oligarchic people, not only in the sense of possessing money but of affectation, through gestures, language…and so in that respect, he exhibits an evident bipolarity, of an affinity for the humble and a rejection of the all-powerful.
>
> (Marcano and Tyszka, 2007, p. 411)

In public, Chávez affirmed the positive influence his grandmother had on his life: he named one child Rosa and another Rosines, both in her honor. Of his relationship with Rosa Ines, he said that though he loved his parents:

> "I have to recognize that the education Rosa gave me was very important for me. She was a pure human being...pure love, pure kindness...At Rosa's side I got to know humility, poverty, pain, sometimes not having anything to eat. I saw the injustices of the world...I learned with her the principles and the values of the humble Venezuelan, those that never had anything and who constitute the soul of my country."
>
> (Jones, 2007, pp. 25–26)

Tough, humble, devoted to a fault, Rosa Ines and what she represented served to propel the narrative that Chávez understood the plight of the aggrieved because he was one of them. No one would understand the difficult position that 80 percent of the Venezuelan population endured better than he. Populist leaders, especially those who employ projective identification as a defense mechanism, often have difficult early relationships with their mothers.

Charisma

Chávez liked to compare himself to Simon Bolivar, the aristocratic Venezuelan soldier and politician who led revolutions against the Spanish Empire in a bid to unite Latin America. To invoke the name Bolivar in South America is akin to claiming some affinity with George Washington in the United States. Chávez branded his form of socialism as "Bolivarian" in a direct attempt to align himself with the "Great Liberator" and to give Chávez's outsider status legitimacy. Invoking the spirit of Bolivar positioned Chávez to align himself with a centuries-old revolutionary zeal, providing legitimacy to his cause. In another twist, with his mixed heritage, Chávez looked like most Venezuelans. Fusing outsider status with the legitimacy of a revolutionary leader proved irresistible to the voting public. At his 1999 inauguration speech, Chávez invoked the Great Liberator multiple times, in a direct attempt to align himself with the myth of Bolivar, even opening his speech with a direct quote:

> 'Fortunate is the citizen, who, under the emblem of his command, has convoked this assembly of the national sovereignty so that it may exercise its absolute will!' In one thousand cities, on one thousand roads, during thousands of days touring the country during these last almost five years, I've repeated before countless Venezuelans that phrase first uttered by our Infinite Father, the *Libertador*....I've repeated that phrase many times, and in the last few months of 1998 during my unusual electoral

campaign—because it was truly unusual—I said so, inspired by the certainty of Walt Whitman's 'sure as the most certain sure.' I was brought here by a tide....We must find a way to regulate these crises....

(Chávez, 1999)

After taking office, Chávez renamed his country the Bolivarian Republic of Venezuela and called his government Bolivarian. In 2010, he exhumed the remains of his idol—during which Chávez reportedly "wept with emotion," to confirm his suspicions that Bolivar was murdered. As it happened, forensic scientists could not determine conclusively one way or another if his early death was due to illness or malfeasance (Gupta, 2011).

Meanwhile, the Chávez propaganda machine exploited the fears of the Venezuelan people regarding safety (organized crime, street violence, and drug trafficking increased dramatically during Chávez's presidency) and perceived threats:

"Ample evidence exists that Chávez-controlled media are using emotional arguments to gain attention, exploit real and imagined fears of the population and create outside enemies as scapegoats for internal failings, and to inculcate the notion that opposition to the regime equates to betrayal of the country."

(Manwaring, 2005, p. 11)

The Revolution Will Be Televised

In a 2012 article for *The New York Times Magazine*, reporter Rachel Nolan described the title sequence of Chávez's live broadcast of *Alo Presidente* (Hello President) as "the realest reality show in the world." A drum roll and tooting trumpet ushered the words "humanity," "struggle," and "socialism" across the screen, which Nolan likened to a parody on par with the "Daily Show" on Comedy Network. But this program, hosted by the Venezuelan president every Sunday from 11am until "Chávez is done talking," was no joke. "It is the only television show in the world in which a head of state regularly invites cameras to follow him as he governs," Nolan explained (Nolan, 2012). During the show's run from 1999 to 2011, the President was notorious for making significant policy decisions on the spot, to the point that members of his cabinet had to attend tapings so they would be able to react as quickly as possible. The show also provided a regular outlet through which Chávez could target his enemies. By consistently labeling adversaries as "bad," "evil," and "against Venezuela," Chávez subjected his opponents to splitting and projective identification on a weekly basis. Further, the people watching *Alo Presidente!* accepted these projections about their perceived enemies as truth. Those who did not accept the pronouncements found themselves in jail or fleeing the country; indeed, in the 36 months after

Chávez took office in 1999, an estimated 200,000 upper and middle-class Venezuelans left the country, taking some $8 billion with them (Anderson, 2001).

Until as late as 2014 over 20,000 pages of transcripts and several hundred hours of video recordings of *Alo Presidente!* were available on the website of the Venezuelan Ministerio del Poder Popular para la Communicacion y la Informacion at www.alopresidente.gob.ve, but I was unable to access the site in 2021, when I encountered connection time out messages after multiple attempts. For this project, I had to rely on researchers who were able to access those transcripts prior to the website going dark. Eduardo Frajman, for example, examined the entire collection of material for his study entitled "Broadcast Populist Leadership: Hugo Chavez and *Alo Presidente!*" for the August 2014 issue of *Journal of Latin American Studies,* and to which I will refer here. Frajman says that the program "was a unique creation of Chavismo, designed to balance Chávez's knack for improvisation with a structure designed to curb his excesses and keep him on message."

The show originated with a call-in format, where viewers could speak directly to Chávez on pressing issues. This allowed Chávez to develop direct lines of communication with the people while also permitting him to tout various government initiatives. According to Frajman, the format shifted after a coup attempt in 2002 to emphasize Chávez's role as the great leader. This duality inherent in populism—that the leader is at once "just like you" but also special—can be difficult to maintain, but this television show permitted Chávez to have the ability to connect and make people feel like he heard them. Frajman writes that "*Alo Presidente!* relied on Chávez's facility with the spotlight, his 'gift of gab,' his extensive knowledge of Venezuelan folk culture, songs and food" (Frajman, 2014, p. 505). Blessed with an outsize persona and a willingness to indulge in plebian songs and language, Chávez was tailor-made for starring in his propaganda.

Like fellow populists Donald Trump and Jair Bolsonaro, Chávez understood that an effective media strategy was critical to promote his ideology and to reach the masses. Being a political outsider has its advantages when trying to make the case that you are against the "elite," but it is not so helpful when you are trying to convey your own philosophy. Chávez's television show gave him the platform to assert his dominance in the political world while also letting Venezuelans feel as though they were in contact with the most powerful person in the country.

Chávez also did more than just host his own television show; eventually, he silenced any competition and his critics in Venezuelan media by closing over two hundred radio stations in 2009. After his brief removal from power in 2002, Chávez clamped down on dissent and in the intervening years introduced a series of bills that eroded media freedom and censored any journalistic outlet that criticized his policies (Open Source Center, 2009). This is projective identification at its apex: Chávez said the media was out to destroy the good he was doing for the country, and rather than merely using words to attack the media, he closed them down and jailed journalists. In this case, I believe Chávez was projecting inner feelings of self-doubt about his governance by shifting blame for Venezuela's political descent onto journalists who he claimed were misguided and antagonistic.

The creation of Twitter in 2006 provided a virtual megaphone to anyone with a computer and an ability to distill their thoughts into 140 characters or less. Chávez was a natural tweeter and found the forum to be a seamless extension of his efforts on *Alo Presidente!* Via his Twitter account @ChávezCandanga, which translates to mischievous Chávez (but also suggests a reference to the devil), Chávez announced meetings and policies to his followers—if you did not follow his feed, you might miss a major news story. It also served as a conduit through which Chávez could blame others he felt were responsible for his country's descent into chaos. And though he's been dead for nearly a decade, the account has not been deleted and still boasts 3.8 million followers. By 2011—one year after joining the platform—Chávez earned the moniker of the "Twitter President" and turned more frequently to the medium after his cancer surgery and chemo treatments (Ghitis, 2011).

Some of Chávez's greatest Tweets included those aimed at other countries and which aligned him with foes of the United States. To then Russian Prime Minister Vladimir Putin, he agreed that "The United States is a true parasite of the world economy!" Perhaps more than *Alo Presidente!*, Twitter served as the best mechanism through which supplicants could directly petition the leader for assistance. Chávez claimed he had a team of 200 people whose sole role was to read and respond to pleas for help. According to a report by *The Guardian* in 2010, shortly after Chávez launched his Twitter account, he received "more than 287,921 pleas for help, including some 19,000 for a job, 17,000 for a house, 12,000 for credit, and 7,000 for legal aid" (Carroll, 2010). In Chávez's case, part of the successful employment of projective identification centered around the creation of a bond between "us" and "them." With Twitter and *Alo Presidente*, Chávez was able to lash out at adversaries "on behalf" of his people. Massive corruption? Poverty? Unemployment? Staggering rates of violent crime? Not his fault—Chávez blamed previous inept governments and American involvement in destabilizing his country. Fine, but how would he fix these issues? "Have patience," was a standing Chávez response.

By 2001 Chávez had already called and won eight referendums, allowing him to refashion the constitution and extend his term in office. He appointed new judges to the Supreme Court and abolished the old Senate, replacing it with a National Assembly filled with Chávez loyalists, while members of the Venezuelan military filled top government posts. If anyone thought about challenging his position, they'd have been ill-advised to act. The shift from populist but democratically elected leader to dictator was complete.

Daniel Ortega: Nicaragua's Presential Dictator

Constitutional democracy might be an anomaly in Nicaragua's tumultuous history, but it did appear to have a chance of success during the last decades of the twentieth century. Today, the populist-turned autocrat Daniel Ortega is scrapping a fledgling democracy in favor of authoritarianism by amending the constitution to favor nearly unlimited terms in office. After leading the overthrow of the Somoza family in Nicaragua in 1979, Ortega shot to power, first as a member of the post-revolutionary five-member council, then as president of the country from 1985 to 1990.

In 2006, following a 16-year absence from the political arena, Ortega was reelected as president under what some observers considered to be dubious circumstances. By 2011 Ortega violated the constitution by running for—and then winning—a third term. As of publication, Ortega has secured a fifth term as president, but not by enacting favorable policies for the people of Nicaragua. As of June 2021, four opposition leaders (among them an economist, sociologist, and former ambassador) were arrested and accused of money laundering and treason. Two of those arrested were considered by observers to be likely presidential candidates. With the path now largely clear of competition, Ortega is all but assured a victory.

How did Ortega, a shoemaker's son, go from the left-wing revolutionary Sandinista Liberation Front to being compared to Zimbabwe's infamous dictator, Robert Mugabe? Ronald Reagan called Ortega a "little dictator" in the 1980s, while the Obama administration considered him a necessary but not altogether trustworthy force against rising violence. The days of waging guerilla warfare against an unrelenting dictatorship seem to have been waged by another man entirely, as Ortega today suppresses oppositions, imprisons dissidents, and stifles free speech. In fact, as of publication, Ortega is among the longest non-royal rulers in the world. As we've seen in other countries, Ortega carefully manipulated words and deeds to convince people that his way is the only way to secure sovereignty for Nicaragua.

Any country can devolve into a populist autocracy: In 2009, Latin America specialists at the Woodrow Wilson International Center for Scholars identified Ortega's brand of populism on the heels of his narrow 2006 presidential victory not as:

> "evidence of a general leftist turn among Nicaragua's electorate; rather, a new electoral rule combined with the schism of the right-wing anti-Sandinista bloc—the Nicaraguan Liberal Alliance (ALN), which won 28.3 percent of the vote, and the Constitutionalist Liberal Party (PLC), which won 27.1 percent of the vote."
>
> (Chamorro, 2009)

Further, unlike Chávez, who actively courted poor voters in Venezuela by creating massive stimulus programs, Ortega has alienated most poor Nicaraguans and relies on a well-greased political machine instead. That he once extolled power for the people is almost laughable; Ortega has recreated a family dynasty of his own, with his wife as Vice-President.

Dictators merely want power—whether they are "left" or "right" is often irrelevant. Ortega promised the people of Nicaragua back in 1990 that he would continue to "rule from below" despite a resounding electoral loss to Violeta Chamorro—a not-so-veiled threat that his party would undermine the democratically elected president at every turn, which he did. Ultimately, Ortega has become the very thing he seemed to spend a lifetime fighting: a demagogue. Projective identification and strongarm tactics played significant roles in securing his position: shifting blame for Nicaragua's ills onto the Chamorros and outside influences has let Ortega feel that he bears no responsibility for the current predicament of his people.

Daniel Ortega was born in 1945 to working-class, politically active parents who openly opposed the regime of Anastasio Somoza Debayle. His mother, Lidia, was arrested and imprisoned for possession of "love letters" suspected of being underground political texts, while Daniel's father had also long opposed the Somoza family. By his teenage years, Ortega had taken up the family passion and joined the resistance to topple the Somoza regime. In 1967 Ortega robbed a bank in the city of Managua, hoping to use those stolen funds to finance the resistance movement. He was captured and imprisoned for seven years, during which time he underwent "severe" torture, described in the book *Unfinished Revolution:*

> "You lose your shyness a bit," quipped Ortega about the experience of having to wait in line to use a single prison toilet so filthy that no one dared sit down on it, and then to have those waiting for their turn cheer you on if your business was accomplished quickly. It was the same with the single shower....
> After the initial torture—which in addition to the usual kicks and beatings, sometimes while hooded, included electric shocks directly to the testicles— prison life mostly settled down into a blur of animalistic monotony.
>
> (Morris, 2010, p. 46)

The Prison Poetry of Daniel Ortega

During his seven years at the Modelo prison in Tipitapa, Ortega kept his mind alert by reading widely—Greco-Roman classics and Proust, among others—and wrote poetry. Humberto Ortega claims that his brother wrote ten poems while incarcerated, but only four have been published. Crude and clearly composed by a 20-something man isolated from general society, the poems also reveal the hidden hell of prison life. Below is the opening stanza of "In the Prison."

In the Prison

      Kick him like that, like that
      In his balls, in his face,
      In his ribs.
      Pass the stick, the bully club,
      Talk, talk son of a bitch,
      let's see, get the salt water,
      taaaalk, we don't want to fuck you...
      —Most Honorable and Reverend
      Archbishop,
      —Most Excellent and Illustrious
      Ambassador.
      Peace, respect for others,
      Wealth, democracy.
      Handcuff him
      put him in Tiny
      you're going to eat your own
      shit bastard,
      —*La cucaracha, la cucaracha*
      No longer can he travel
      Since he's missing, since he's missing
      a leg to walk on
                   (Morris, 2010, p. 51)

This excerpt suggests unspeakable torture likely meted out over Ortega's seven years in prison. That he suffered psychological trauma in addition to physical harm is undoubted. Whether he has ever sought treatment to understand or work though this trauma is unknown, though based on his political maneuvering over the past 40 years, I suspect that he has not. This most toxic mental conflict surely manifested itself via Ortega's outward projections onto political foes and dissidents.

In many cases of projective identification, normal psychological development is impeded when someone feels unsafe or has experienced physical and emotional pain. Upon his release from prison in 1974, Ortega was a changed man. Nicaraguan novelist and former Ortega administration official Sergio Ramirez remarked that this experience, understandably, influenced his personality. "He has always been an isolated man," Ramirez told *The Washington Post* in 2018. He was "not someone with a lot of friends" (Parlow, 2018). The "pragmatic consensus-builder" was never described as particularly charismatic or dogmatic, but genuinely appeared to want the best for his people. That would eventually erode into a raw desire for power.

During his run for president in 1984, Ortega leveled his charges of anti-democratic maneuvers at the perennial foe, the United States: "They say we're anti-democratic, but we know what real democracy means. Democracy is literacy, democracy is land reform, democracy is education and public health" (Kinzer, 1991, p. 246). Projective identification, as we've seen, can affect groups as much as individuals. When exhibited by populist leaders, projection onto a group can turn far more vicious and ruthless, owing perhaps to the public nature of these types of projections (Messina, 2019).

During that same speech, Ortrega presented land titles to poor Nicaraguan peasants—specifically trucked in for the accompanying photo-op—and continued to rail against the United States and then-President Reagan. And to be fair, Reagan had decided that the Sandinista government posed a threat to American security and armed various right-wing rebel groups known as the Contras in a bid to overthrow the Marxist Sandinistas. In 1985 *Newsweek* ran a scathing photo documentary entitled "Execution in the Jungle," which illustrated the brutality with which Contras tracked and killed anyone in their way, often soft targets like unarmed women and children. The Contra-backed civil war provided Ortega plenty of grist for years beyond the actual conflict.

People who have been traumatized, whether by spending time in war zones, prison, or enduring physical, emotional, or sexual abuse, often have tremendous difficulty cultivating any self-awareness. In the case of Ortega, I believe that his early prison trauma fundamentally changed his psychological outlook and solidified his desire to attain and maintain power at all costs. In 1985, Ortega restricted the freedom of the press, saying that it was necessary to control the flow of information during wartime. "Censorship is an instrument to defend our revolution," Captain Nelba Blandon said in 1986, "We can't permit the press to become a destabilizing force in our society simply out of fear of the reaction from abroad" (Kinzer, 1991, p. 296). Fast-forward to Ortega's current term as president, and we see further reductions in journalistic freedom. Following protests in 2018 against Ortega's plan to reform the country's social security benefits, government authorities shot and killed investigative journalist Angel Gahona while he live-streamed a demonstration (Rivas, 2021). That was only the beginning:

> Months later, the government placed a blockage on materials needed to print newspapers....In December of 2018, national police ransacked the newsrooms of *Confidencial* (a news site), *Esta Semana*, and *Esta Noche* (TV news programs), which are all run by one of the country's most prominent journalists, Carlos Fernando Chamorro....By the middle of 2019, more than ninety Nicaraguan journalists...had gone into exile in Costa Rica.
>
> (Rivas, 2021)

It seems like more than a coincidence that Carlos Chamorro and Cristiana Chamorro are the children of Violeta Barrios de Chamorro, the woman who beat Ortega for the presidency in 1990. That defeat appears to haunt Ortega and after spending two decades clawing back to power, he is determined to stay there no matter the cost to his countrymen.

References

Anderson, J.L. (2001). The revolutionary: The president of Venezuela has a vision, and Washington has a headache. *The New Yorker*, September 10. www.newyorker.com/magazine/2001/09/10/the-revolutionary.

Carroll, R. (2010). Hugo Chávez's twitter habit proves a popular success. *The Guardian*, August 10. www.theguardian.com/world/2010/aug/10/hugo-Chávez-twitter- venezuela.

Chamorro, C. (2009). Ortega's 'citizens of power' in Nicaragua: Democratic participation or authoritarian populism? Understanding populism and political participation: The Case of Nicaragua. Woodrow Wilson Center for Scholars. www.wilsoncenter.org/sites/default/files/media/documents/publication/Nicaragua. pdf.

Chávez, H. (1999). *Inauguration speech of Hugo Chávez*. Federal Legislative Palace, February 2. https://tellingstoriesofthestoryteller.com/translation-of-Chavezs-inauguration-speech.

De la Torre, C. (2017). Populism in Latin America. *The Oxford Handbook of Populism*. Oxford University Press, p. 205.

Frajman, E. (2014). Broadcasting populist leadership: Hugo Chávez and "alo presidente." *Journal of Latin American Studies*. Vol. 46. No. 3, p. 505. doi:10.1017/S00222.16X14.

Ghitis, F. (2011). World citizen: Hugo Chávez, the twitter president. *World Politics Review*, July 28. www.worldpoliticsreview.com/articles/9615/world-citizen-hugo-Chávez-the-twitter-president.

Gupta, G. (2011). Venezuela unable to determine cause of Bolivar's death. *The Christian Science Monitor*, July 26. www.csmonitor.com/World/Americas/Latin-America- Monitor/2011/0726/Venezuela-unable-to-determine-cause-of-Bolivar-s-death.

Jones, B. (2007). *Hugo! The Hugo Chávez story: From mud hit to perpetual revolution*. New Hampshire: Steerforth Press, pp. 22, 25.

Kinzer, S. (1991). *Blood of brothers: Life and war in Nicaragua*. Putnam, p. 246.

Kinzer, S. (2021). Daniel Ortega: from revolutionary to absolute overlord. Responsible Statecraft. https://responsiblestatecraft.org/2021/06/16/daniel-ortega-from-revolutionary- to-absolute-overlord.

Manwaring, M. (2005). Venezuela's Hugo Chávez, Bolivarian socialism, and asymmetric warfare. Defense Technical Information Center, p. 11. https://archive.org/details/DTIC_ADA439743/page/n17/mode/2up?q=enemies.

Marcano, C. and Tyszka, A. (2007). *Hugo Chávez: The definitive biography of Venezuela's controversial president*. Random House. Epub. Loc. 370, 394, 396.

Messina, K. (2019). *Misogyny, Projective Identification, and Mentalization: Psychoanalytic, Social and Institutional Manifestations*. Routledge, p. 99.

Morris, K. (2010). *Unfinished Revolution: Daniel Ortega and Nicaragua's struggle for liberation*. Chicago Review Press, pp. 46, 51.

Nolan, R. (2012). The realest reality show in the world. *The New York Times Magazine*, May 4. www.nytimes.com/2012/05/06/magazine/hugo-Chávezs-totally-bizarre-talk-show.html.

Open Source Center (2009). *Venezuela: Chávez moves to silence opposition media*. Director of National Intelligence. https://fas.org/irp/dni/osc/Chávez.pdf.

Parlow, J. (2018). From rebel to strongman: How Daniel Ortega became the thing he fought against. *The Washington Post*, August 24. www.washingtonpost.com/world/

the_americas/from-rebel-to-strongman-how-daniel-ortega-became-the-thing-he-foug ht-against/2018/08/24/117d000a-97fe-11e8- 818b-e9b7348cd87d_story.html.

Rivas, O. (2021). Three years of deteriorating press freedom in Nicaragua. *Columbia Journalism Review*, June 22. www.cjr.org/analysis/press-freedom-nicaragua-daniel-ortega.php.

Chapter 10

Killer Savior

Populism in the Philippines

The populism currently gripping the Philippines differs significantly from the populism seen throughout contemporary Europe in several notable ways. Perhaps the most striking difference has to do with its political provenance: While many modern-day populists who emerge are from within the ranks of the far right, the 16th president of the Philippines, Rodrigo Duterte, is an avowed leftist and socialist. For comparison, Hugo Chávez and Daniel Ortega certainly started out as left-leaning socialists but changed tune once they cemented their grip on power. Duterte has remained solidly left leaning.

Another distinction between Duterte and other populist leaders is intimately related to their respective goals. In most populist-led countries, particularly in Europe and to some extent in the United States, the nationalist turn is rooted in the identification of an "in" group (often characterized as the country's elite) and an "out" group (the populace) which is placed in opposition to the establishment. In this case, most Filipinos describe themselves as "underdogs" against a vague "other"; Duterte positions himself as taking up the entire country's cause.

While he is condemned throughout the world for his regime's brutality towards drug dealers, specific cohorts of women, and anyone else who opposes or threatens his authority, in the Philippines itself, large crowds enthusiastically cheer him on in a way reminiscent of the Trump base endorsing their hero. Unlike Trump, Duterte has spent decades burnishing an image of a violent overlord, claiming to have personally killed drug dealers and criminals while also sanctioning police and vigilantes to kill enemies of the state. Like fellow populists, Duterte is a man of contradictions, as we will see.

Why Duterte is Popular Despite his Ruthlessness

President Duterte enjoys a remarkable level of popularity among Filipinos. In 2020 Pulse Asia reported an approval rating of 91 percent, although it is worth noting that Pulse Asia has come under scrutiny for being politically biased. Other polls reflect popular support from around two-thirds of the

DOI: 10.4324/9781003202387-11

population (Clara Ferreria, 2021). Duterte's popularity as a president remains elevated because many Filipinos are tired of a liberal democracy that has failed them. He is also well-liked by people among various social classes, albeit for different reasons—an unusual characteristic for populist leaders. Most often, a populist leader will strategically pit members of particular social classes against others to gain and keep power. In Duterte's case, though, the widespread understanding is that every Filipino, with Duterte's support, must together ward off nefarious people from elsewhere in the world, making national in-fighting much less of a problem than we've seen in other populist-led countries.

There is, however, one marked exception to the idea that Filipinos must band together to ward off outsiders: Filipino nationals who deal drugs or are in any way involved in the drug trade are soundly (and often viciously) excluded from Duterte's big tent. An army of people are charged with getting rid of them—another reason many Filipinos like their President.

Duterte's Early Life and the Years Before he Became the President of the Philippines

Violence appears to be a trait of the Duterte family. From an early age, Rodrigo Duterte was considered by his peers and the adults around him to be a tough guy, frequently mixing it up in street fights and involved in other disruptive behavior which led to his expulsion from two schools. His parents, notably his mother, Soledad, punished him severely for his behavior with regular beatings. Rodrigo's father Vicente, a mayor and then provincial governor, was reported to be absent a fair amount of the time when Rodrigo was young. [There was]"violence in the house, violence in the school and violence in the neighborhood," said Rodrigo's brother Emmanuel in an interview with *The New York Times*. "That is why he is always angry. Because if you have pain when you are young, you are angry all the time" (Paddock, 2017). Emmanuel also claimed in that story that at one point their mother wore out her horsewhip from correcting Rodrigo.

The children attended a Catholic school, where Rodrigo claims to have been molested as a teenager by an American priest (Bulent, 2020). Assuming this incident is accurate, how might it have contributed to his way of dealing with people who act in ways he considers to be unethical or predatory? How might it be related to the way he operates as a leader? This molestation could remain a trauma that was never addressed.

This incident might have affected Duterte's early association with the tough guys he liked to hang around. Did he like to see himself as one of them? Did these men contribute to his early use of aggressive language? Or was he seeking their protection or drawing strength from them? It is hard to know the specific consequences of the trauma he experienced or of the harsh treatment he received from his parents, particularly from his mother. Even though he has claimed that his father's bodyguards taught him about life on the streets in the Philippines and implied such "lessons" were positive events in his childhood and adolescence, is it also possible that he had to toughen up to protect himself. The ancillary evidence seems to point in that direction.

The men who were employed to protect Vicente also taught Rodrigo to drink, shoot guns, and perhaps engage in other illicit or illegal activities. As mayor of Davao City, and then later as president, the ferocity and swiftness of Duterte's official punishments for any criminal involved directly and peripherally in the drug trade is well documented.

While the behavior Duterte endorses and orders he gives appear to be unconscionable to many people throughout the world, he might have held a strong early identification with the aggressors in his life. It is easy to imagine how the tough street behavior he learned as a youth led him to shoot a fellow student in high school who was bullying him. In his official capacity as mayor, Duterte shot three people as a statement to his police department: If he could be tough and kill people with his own gun, they certainly could do what was demanded of them by their mayor in the war against local drug dealers (Goldman, 2016).

Early in his career, though, Duterte took a less aggressive approach to his fellow Filipinos. Prior to making a bid for the presidency, Duterte was a successful attorney. During his tenure as mayor, he fought for the rights of women and supported gay and lesbian rights to such an extent that Davao City was considered an LGBTQ+-friendly city. Though he has flip-flopped on his support of gay rights in the past and at one point claimed he had "cured" himself of homosexuality, at this point, it appears he supports gay rights (Gutierrez and Jett, 2019). These stances diverge substantially from anything most far right leader's support.

Duterte's Curious View of Women

While, on a personal level, Duterte claims to be fond of women, his behavior towards and policies concerning them is disjointed and reveals a brutal misogynist (Santos, 2018). On the one hand, he supports women's access to healthcare, having signed Executive Order No. 12, which requires the Filipino government to fully implement the Reproductive Health Act. Additionally, the Committee on Decorum and Investigation to receive and probe complaints on sexual harassment was reinstated in his presidential term (Ranada, 2017). He called women "heroes" on International Women's Day in 2017. The pro-women program he instituted in Davao City led many of his followers to appreciate his progressive style of leadership as it pertains to the establishment of policies for women. "Both his supporters and some women's rights advocates laud pro-women programs in Davao City as proof that Duterte is a progressive leader when it comes to women empowerment," read one news story in 2017 (2017).

These official policies are quite different from Duterte's behavior towards women. He has made disparaging remarks about women on a regular basis; an occurrence which appears to be connected, at least on the surface, with his generally reckless use of language. No single group is spared from Duterte's foul mouth, public figures from Barack Obama to Pope Francis, both of whom he has called sons of "whores," have been the subject of Duterte's impudence. Notably, in a 2018 speech to former communist soldiers, Duterte issued a clear directive on how they should handle women guerrilla fighters: "We will not kill you. We will shoot you in the vagina." Duterte's theory being, as he said later in the speech, that women relieved of their reproductive organs would be "useless" (Ellis-Petersen, 2018). In 2016 he joked about the death of 36-year-old Jacqueline Hamill, an Australian missionary who, in 1989, was gang raped and killed by inmates during a siege in a jail in Davao City while Duterte was the city's mayor. As one of the first to see her body after the siege ended, Duterte recalled his first thoughts. "I looked at her face—son of a bitch—what a waste. What came to mind was, they raped her, they lined up. I was angry because she was raped, that's one thing…but she was so beautiful, the mayor should have been first. What a waste (Murdoch, 2016)." After intense backlash from the global community, Duterte claimed he was only joking. Bad joke or not, such a suggestion functions to normalize rape culture and implies that such treatment of women is acceptable.

In 1998 Duterte's wife, Elizabeth Zimmerman, filed for divorce. A psychological report prepared for the court proceedings by Dr. Natividad Dayan concluded that Duterte suffered from "Antisocial Narcissistic Personality Disorder," and exhibited "gross indifference, insensitivity and self-centeredness, a grandiose sense of self-entitlement and manipulative behaviors, and pervasive tendency to demean, humiliate others and violate their rights and feelings" (2016). The documents reveal a deeply unsatisfying marriage for Zimmerman, marked by Duterte's flagrant infidelity and violent behavior. The report continues to assess Duterte's personality, punctuated by destructive behaviors and a near-total inability to accept responsibility for his actions. "As it is, he has poor capacity for objective judgment. He fails to see things in the light of facts, or at least from the point of view of most people. He interprets his actions solely from his own viewpoint, which is blemished by his personal needs, biases, and prejudices" (Lozada, 2016).

As a hypothesis, it is possible that Duterte's apparent ambivalent feelings towards women stem from his relationship with his mother, who is reported to have been very strict with him. She also could be considered to have put him in harm's way by sending him to a school where he was reported to have been sexually violated. Perhaps it is difficult for Duterte to deal with the conflicting feelings he has towards women. While he appears to regard them as a group with respect by instituting several programs for women in his country and government, he might also have difficulty tolerating the seemingly contradictory feelings, such as dislike or hatred, that he has about women. This internal struggle could cause him to project the tough, crusty, "rough guy" part of himself onto certain women, particularly in the form of misogynistic language—consider when he responded to a reporter's question about his health with, "How's your wife's vagina? Is it smelly? Or not smelly? Give me a report" (Chen, 2016).

Other Reasons for Duterte's Popularity

Duterte remains popular thanks to his independent leadership goals, which stand apart from his particular party affiliation. His current political aims are underpinned by the same philosophical approach he took early in his career as mayor of Davao City, which was by all accounts admired.

Duterte's goals included helping 6.1 million Filipinos out of absolute poverty, enacting the Philippines' Universal Health Care Act, and offering disadvantaged Filipinos the opportunity to earn a college degree for free, all of which he achieved in his first term. Polls find citizens report feeling more secure because of his hardline stance on drugs, and in 2020 the Duterte government enjoyed an approval rating of over 70 percent.

Duterte is also free to lead without heeding the dictates of a political party. This is in stark contrast to leaders like Trump, who needed (and had) the support of the U.S. Senate at every turn of his presidential term but lost his official power when his bid for a second term ended. Now, Trump must work behind the scenes with members of the House and the Senate if he wants to remain the head of the Republican Party. But Duterte's path also strays significantly from the political routes previously taken by other populist leaders, largely because of the Philippines' position as a nation living in the legacy of colonialism and "often brings up abuses from the colonial era in his anti-American rants" (Chen, 2016). He also lays blame for much of his country's problems on the current U.S.-Philippines relationship.

How Donald Trump is Like Rodrigo Duterte

In many ways Donald Trump is like Rodrigo Duterte. Both men can be rude, brash, and offensive, and they each demand unmitigated praise while pontificating to their followers. Donald Trump seems to become energized by "preaching to the choir" at the rallies he holds for his base; Duterte, like Chávez, another domineering leader who came from leftist political beginnings, "…can deliver a televised address for hours, his speech peppered with cuss words and confrontational language" (Webb and Curato, 2018, p. 49). They both are misogynistic as well: Trump has spoken disparagingly to women in and out of professional settings while Duterte jokes about raping women.

Trump and Duterte also share an appetite for attention, especially when in a crowd, and seem to thrive on being melodramatic. Trump, for his part, used social media to stroke his ego, posting outrageous and provocative tweets for years. That is, prior to his being banned from Twitter because of his behavior on January 6, 2021, when he incited many of his followers to storm the Capitol of the United States, an attack on democracy which resulted in five deaths and over $2.5 million in damage. The independently run Trump Twitter Archive reports that the former president's account either tweeted or retweeted over 56,000 tweets before his account was permanently suspended on January 8, 2021 (Trump Archive).

A few of the most outrageous include:

> On gun control: "No matter what you do – guns, no guns – it doesn't matter. You have people that are mentally ill. And they're gonna come through the cracks. And they're going to do things that people will not even believe are possible."
>
> Meet the Press, April 10, 2015

> On global warming: "It's really cold outside, they are calling it a major freeze, weeks ahead of normal. Man, we could use a big fat dose of global warming!"
>
> Donald J. Trump (@realDonaldTrump) October 19, 2015

These statements are good examples of a one-body projective identification wherein Trump projected aspects of himself onto others. In this case, we do not know if the recipients "accepted" the projections or if they stood up to Trump somehow.

We also do not know the extent of the interaction on social media, but what matters is that Trump is constantly attempting to get rid of a part of himself that he can not tolerate. Furthermore, I suspect he believes that if he has an effect on the other person, it is due to his own omnipotence.

In addition to illustrating projective identification, these statements are untrue. Mentally ill individuals are not the only people who have used guns to kill others. People who own guns and kill people come from various backgrounds and are in various states of mental health. While some might have mental health issues, it is inaccurate to attribute all or even most gun violence in the United States to unaddressed mental health concerns. For example, police officers are among those who kill people, sometimes with little or no provocation, and with firearms that are acquired and owned legally.

Regarding the tweet about global warming, Trump is projecting his ignorance and lack of knowledge about the climate crisis onto his followers. It is absurd to say or imply that because it is cold outside, global warming should be encouraged or is not a problem. At the current rate, "the point of no return," when substantial portions of the earth are projected by many scientists to be uninhabitable, may be reached by 2035. Here, as was frequently the case during his presidency, Trump substituted knowledge he did not have with ludicrous statements that he thought were inspirational. They were often, as is the case in this instance, a projection of his lack of knowledge instead. When he does not know something, rather than admitting to it, he tends to say outrageous things with the hope of getting attention. Unfortunately, he is often successful.

After Trump's expulsion from Twitter, Facebook, and other social media platforms, directly resulting from his behavior prior to the insurrection, he briefly established a personal blog page, "From the Desk of Donald J. Trump," on which he could continue posting his thoughts (Breuninger, 2021). The webpage was scrubbed after only a month but included choice comments about Congressperson Liz Cheney (R-WY), a vocal critic of Trump:

> **Donald J. Trump** 9:36am May 12, 2021
> Liz Cheney is a bitter, horrible human being. I watched her yesterday and realized how bad she is for the Republican Party. She has no personality or anything good having to do with politics or our Country. She is a talking point for Democrats, whether that means the Border, the gas lines, inflation, or destroying our economy. She is a warmonger whose family stupidly pushed us into the never-ending Middle East Disaster, draining our wealth and depleting our Great Military, the worst decision in our Country's history. I look forward to soon watching her as a Paid Contributor on CNN or MSDNC!
> (Save America, 2021)

This attack is yet another illustration of Trump's thinking, rather than being about anything that Liz Cheney stands for or has stated publicly. Following the 2020 election, Cheney was stripped of her House Republican leadership post—but that closed-door voice vote by her colleagues was retaliation for her failing to go along with lies about the election's legitimacy, and her general criticism of Trump's past behavior, rather than anything to do with her personality or politics.

In contrast to the way Trump used social media to create drama, Duterte earns widespread positive attention—and even Hollywood-inspired nicknames like "The Punisher" and "Duterte Harry"—from his actions, particularly those that are related to drug wars and killing drug dealers. For many everyday Filipinos, the situation, with its overriding themes of revenge, betrayal, and dynastic family intrigue, can feel more like a soap opera than government affairs:

> Daily revelations and entanglements are discussed while people watch the live streams or television broadcasts in living rooms, malls or restaurants, or listen on the radio while travelling on public transport.

Such conversations mix with celebrity gossip and conversations about television as part of the fabric of daily life; people speculate about the twists and turns of each day's events and consider the personal enmities and family histories behind political disputes.

(Pertierra, 2017)

The Good, The Bad, and The Ugly: Duterte's Leadership

It can be hard for Westerners to imagine why Duterte is so popular given his outrageous behavior, which includes saying atrocious things to anyone who gets in his way, sanctioning an untold number of extrajudicial killings, being extremely misogynistic, as well as taking a myriad of other actions which would be intolerable to most people. Indeed, the International Criminal Court weighed whether to open a full investigation into Duterte's role in suspected, "crimes against humanity of murder, torture and the infliction of serious physical injury and mental harm," including over 8,000 people accused—not yet convicted—of involvement in the illegal drug trade (Gutierrez, 2020).

Duterte is a complex man. On one hand he can be violent, meting out corporal punishments to curb drug use in the Philippines, as well as in the language he uses to speak about anyone he deems morally questionable or compromised. As brutal as the actions that he endorses are (and some of his own, as well, particularly in his early career), the words he chooses have a huge impact on Filipino society.

Yet Duterte maintains a surprising level of popularity. This national response seems to be counterintuitive, but I believe there is an explanation to be found in the day-to-day mindset of an average Filipino, for whom physical safety is a top priority. Duterte won the presidential election on a campaign to stop the rising tide of deadly violence in the country. In the nine months following his election, more than 2,500 people were killed by the police, plus about another 3,600 by vigilante groups (Lamb, 2016). But many citizens claim they're fine with the bloodshed, an eye for an eye, so to speak.

References

Breuninger, K. (2021). Trump blog page shuts down for good. CBNC, June 2. www.cnbc.com/2021/06/02/trump-blog-page-shuts-down-for-good.html.

Buendia, R. (2021). Populism in the Philippines: Its roots, rise, results, limitations and perils. PinkerPolitik, March 1. wrn.pinterpolitik.com/region/populism-in-the-philippines-its-roots-rise- results-limitations-and-perils/#.

Bulent, K. (2020). Rodrigo Roa Duterte: Jingoist, misogynist, penal populist. European Center for Populism Studies, September 17. www.populismstudies.org/rodrigo-roa-duterte-a- jingoist-misogynist-penal-populist.

Chen, A. (2016). When a populist demagogue takes power. *The New Yorker*, November 13. www.newyorker.com/magazine/2016/11/21/when-a-populist-demagogue-takes-power.

Clara Ferreria, M. (2021). After Duterte, the Philippines may get more Duterte. Bloomberg Opinion, June 21. www.bloomberg.com/opinion/articles/2021-06-21/p hilippines-duterte-is- working-to-stay-close-to-power-when-presidency-ends.

Ellis-Petersen, H. (2019). Philippines: Rodrigo Duterte orders soldiers to shoot female rebels 'in the vagina.' *The Guardian*, February 12. www.theguardian.com/world/2018/ feb/13/philippines- rodrigo-duterte-orders-soldiers-to-shoot-female-rebels-in-the-vagina.

Goldman, R. (2016). 'I cannot lie,' Rodrigo Duterte says, confirming he did kill people as mayor. *The New York Times*, December 16. www.nytimes.com/2016/12/16/ world/asia/philippines- rodrigo-duterte-confirms-killings-davao.html.

Gutierrez, J. and Jett, J. (2019). Rodrigo Duterte says he 'cured' himself from being gay. *The New York Times*, June 3. www.nytimes.com/2019/06/03/world/asia/duterte-gay. html.

Gutierrez, J. (2020). *Court finds evidence of crimes against humanity in the Philippines. The New York Times*, December 15. www.nytimes.com/2020/12/15/world/asia/p hilippines-duterte- drugs-icc.html.

Lamb, K. (2016). Thousands dead: the Philippine president, the death squad allegations and a brutal drugs war. *The Guardian*, April 2. www.theguardian.com/world/ 2017/apr/02/philippines- president-duterte-drugs-war-death-squads.

Lozada, A. (2016). Understanding Duterte: What a psych report says. ABS-CBN News, April 20. https://news.abs-cbn.com/halalan2016/focus/04/19/16/understa nding-duterte-what-a-psych- report-says.

Murdoch, L. (2016). Rodrigo Duterte lashes out at Australia after missionary rape joke. *The Sydney Morning Herald*, April 20. www.smh.com.au/world/rodrigo-du terte-lashes-out-at-australia- after-missionary-rape-joke-20160419-go9pg5.html.

Paddock, R. (2017). Becoming Duterte: The making of a Philippine strongman. *The New York Times*, March 21. www.nytimes.com/2017/03/21/world/asia/rodrigo-du terte-philippines-president- strongman.html.

Pertierra, A. (2017). In the Philippines, celebrity, melodrama and national politics are deeply entangled. *The Conversation*, January 25. https://theconversation.com/in-the-p hilippines-celebrity-melodrama-and-national-politics-are-deeply-entangled-69656.

Ranada, P. (2017). Duterte, the benevolent sexist? *Rappeler*, March 11. www.rappler. com/newsbreak/in-depth/duterte-women-empowerment-sexist.

Reuters. (2020). Philippines' Duterte scores record high rating, despite virus crisis. October 5. www.reuters.com/article/us-philippines-duterte/philippines-duterte-scor es-record-high- rating-despite-virus-crisis-idUSKBN26Q0YK.

Santos, A. (2018). The price of 'machismo populism' in the Philippines. *The Atlantic*, June. www.theatlantic.com/international/archive/2018/06/duterte-kiss-philippines/562265.

Save America. The Website of Donald J. Trump. www.donaldjtrump.com/alerts.

The Trump Twitter Archive. www.thetrumparchive.com.

Webb, A. and Curato, N. (2018). Populism in the Philippines. *Populism around the world: A Comparative Perspective.* Cham: Springer, p. 49. https://doi.org/10.1007/ 978-3-319-96758-5_4.

Chapter 11

Pugnacious Populism in Erdoğan's Turkey

This chapter explores the democratization of modern Turkey and some of the ways recent reconsolidation of religion and religious institutions with state policies blocked its economic and social development. Turkey's Democratic Party won its first free election in 1950. Prior to that time, the Turkish government spent many years shifting from a religious focus to a more secular one. For example, after the final fall of the Ottoman Empire which occurred from 1918 to 1920, the Grand National Assembly declared Turkey to be a republic in 1923. Thereafter, a secular party gained control of the country, banning Islam from the constitution in 1928. However, the early 21st century's ascent to power of Recep Tayyip Erdoğan, a forceful leader, "who rose from the conservative, religious working class that most resented westernized secularism" (Carlotta, 2019) to become Prime Minister (2003–14) and later President (since 2014), strengthened Turkey's turn toward Islamic rule.

Prior to Erdoğan's victory, movement toward full democratic transition was on a solid trajectory throughout most of the late 20th century, and in 1987 Turkey applied to become a member of the EU. While the nation waited until 1999 to be recognized as a candidate, France and Germany eventually stalled the negotiation in 2007 because of Erdoğan's strongman actions, which included intensifying conflict with the government of the Kurdish ethnic minority, repressing democratic protests, and taking, "more and more authoritarian decisions in his country and making provocations towards the EU" (Lourenço, 2019).

Islam was another major issue that caused some EU-member countries to hesitate when considering Turkey's application. In other words, religion had a re-birth in Erdoğan's Turkey and is playing a more central role in everyday life. That seemed to rub some EU-member countries the wrong way.

When Erdoğan was campaigning to be Prime Minister, he ran as a reformer. He claimed to want to help the Kurds regain some of the rights that had been taken away from them by various leaders over time, both in Turkey as well as in Iraq.

DOI: 10.4324/9781003202387-12

He also needed the support of the Kurdish populace to win his initial bid for the presidency and would not have been successful without their support. Kadri Gürsel—a Turkish reporter who was arrested in 2016 for alleged ties to terrorist organizations and subsequently sentenced to eleven months in prison—reported the following in 2014:

> If Erdoğan wants to be elected in the first round, he needs Kurdish votes. Such votes, however, do not come for free. The kind of victory Erdoğan wants requires that he meet some of the Kurds' demands and provide convincing promises for others yet to come. This cannot be disputed. In the first round of balloting, Kurds hold the key for Erdoğan.
>
> (Gürsel, 2014)

Despite his promises to look out for the interests of the Kurds—the group which secured his victorious run for President of Turkey—he lost interest in the minority's plight and began to take a more authoritarian stance. As this shift was occurring, the political party founded by Erdoğan in 2001, the Justice and Development Party (AKP), gained more and more power. The AKP was initially conceived as a populist party representing a range of views, mainly those of conservatives but also those of some liberal groups. Many Turks felt let down by the formerly popular Kemalist politics that focused on a homogeneous country rooted in Turkish identity while disavowing the religious beliefs and principles of the fallen Ottoman Empire.[1]

As Erdoğan was making this shift from a reformer to a religious leader, he abandoned the Kurdish cause while beginning to curry favor with Turks who were part of the far-right Nationalist Movement Party (MHP), which adheres to Turkish ultranationalism and has strong skepticism towards its place in a united Europe and the West. They dislike the Kurds intensely, believe them to be inferior, and think MHP adherents are the only *true* Turks. They also espouse anti-Americanism and dislike Armenians.

Shifts in Modern Turkey's Leadership

As stated earlier, following the dissolution of the Ottoman Empire in the early 20th century, modern Turkey shifted from a secular-leaning leadership to being governed with more of an emphasis on religion and religious traditions. During periods when non-religious leaders have led the country, the concept of *laiklik* was an important idea that informed the way governments have been run. *Laiklik* is somewhat but not exactly like Western secularism. It is not, according to scholars, "a formal separation between religious and political authority and institutions, but rather it has been a positivist state ideology to engineer a new homogeneous and stratified society" (Yavuz and Öztürk, 2019).

While aspects of *laiklik* were informed by Jacobin *laïcism,* which was more radical in nature, the term is related to the modern French concept of *laïcité.* However, it differs from both in important ways. Kemalists used Turkish *laiklik* as the most important tenet of the Republic's philosophy, eager to have it draw "the boundaries of public reasoning and [function] as a new form of civic religion to provide moral norms and political principles" (Yavus and Ozturk, 2020, p. 4).

Although the concept of *laiklik* is neither mentioned in the Constitution nor an official policy of the Turkish government in 2021, it was integral to Turkey at one time when the country was thought to be a on the way to becoming a robust liberal democracy. However, after Erdoğan won his first presidential election, his Justice and Development shifted from a secular government to one that accepted, if not embraced and promoted, the incorporation of Islam in civic affairs. This move effectively supplanted Kemalist nationalism. In the process of moving from a populist movement that was purported to be in the name of the people, a more autocratic way of governing began to take shape which included a clamp-down on the media. In several ways, this shift appeared to be a move reminiscent of the practices of the Ottoman Empire.

Turkey morphed into a "U.S.-style executive presidency—minus the Supreme Court and Congress" (Aydintaşbaş, 2017) and "he biggest jailer of journalists in the world" (Amnesty International, 2017). Thus, Erdoğan's justification of policies with reference to an Islamic mandate all point to a conflation of religion with the national vision (Yavus and Ozturk, 2019).

Hence, it appeared that Erdoğan's use of religion to develop or alter governmental policies was one of the actions that caused the collapse of democracy in Turkey. Specific examples of this preference include changes in Turkey's welfare system, which provided more for people with conservative values than to those who attempted to hold onto democratic ideas or had beliefs that were not in line with the religious doctrine espoused by the government. This included the closing of secular public schools to promote religious Imam *Hatip* ("Cleric Teacher" in Turkish), schools that "teach the national curriculum, but roughly half their courses are religious and their core classes—those which a student must pass to matriculate—are the Quran and Arabic" (Carlotta, 2018). Another profound division in modern Turkey occurred when Erdoğan exacerbated a wedge between what Turkish media term White Turks—those urban elites who fill state bureaucratic posts, academia, and corporate office—versus the Black Turks, those uneducated, avowedly religious country inhabitants, who Erdoğan said were the disadvantaged people of his country and who were aligned with the AKP. Erdoğan, in a classic populist move, aligned himself with the Black Turks, and in a speech on June 11, 2013, branded the elites as out of touch with the needs of the people of the country:

According to them, we don't understand politics. According to them, we don't understand art, theater, cinema, poetry. According to them, we don't understand aesthetics, architecture. According to them, we are uneducated, ignorant, the lower class, who has to be content with what is being given, needy; meaning, we are a group of negroes."

(Ferguson, 2013)

This systemic use of splitting, blame shifting, and projective identification draws a clear line between the "authentic" (i.e., the uneducated "Black" Turks), versus the elites. Erdoğan pitted himself and the values held dear by him and members of his party against the fancy urbanities—it is a well-worn populist trope and, as we've seen elsewhere in this book, a hallmark of defenses employed by populist leaders onto groups. In other speeches, Erdoğan extols his outsider status and simple ways—a man whose sole interest is to remove corruption from Turkish politics and make things great again.

Erdogan's use of projective identification extends beyond Turkey's own population towards Armenians in his refusal to recognize the Armenian genocide, which is another major issue that remains problematic for Turkey's advancement on the world stage. The genocide in Armenia, beginning with events that occurred on April 24, 1915, is still officially denied by Turkey's government as well as by other countries that apparently do not want to publicly criticize the nation (President Biden was the first U.S. president to acknowledge the genocide). I have previously written on this topic about the effects of this obfuscation, in which repair and the possibility of healing have not been possible because of massive denial, so disparagement, hatred, and animosity prevail (Messina, 2019, p. 127).

After the Coup Attempt

When looking at the political atmosphere in Turkey today, it is important to consider the 2016 coup attempt which Erdoğan claimed was initiated and led by Fethullah Gülen, a former political associate-turned opposition leader who fled for Pennsylvania, where he now lives in self-imposed exile. The coup attempt was not solely a secular versus religious struggle; many Muslims who followed Gülen were involved in previous attempts to overthrow the Erdoğan government. Known as "Gülenists," the government labeled them as terrorists.

Gülen does not follow fundamentalist Islamic anti-Western and anti-capitalism points of view and instead is pro-business and believes in science. He does not appear in public but remains involved in helping people in Turkey by frequently sending audio and video clips sharing his views on contemporary Turkish politics back to people in his homeland from Pennsylvania. According to Gülen, "[Erdoğan] always had this vision of being the single most powerful person" (Filkins, 2016). It is important to note that Erdoğan and his party's thinking toward secularism and democracy had evolved significantly over the years:

"In the beginning of their political careers, they put up a façade of a more democratic party and leadership. And they appeared to be people of faith. And therefore we did not want to second-guess their motives. We believed their rhetoric."

(Filkins, 2016)

The Media

As in nearly all populist-led countries, the media in Erdoğan's Turkey has been—and remains—tightly controlled by the government. Mistreatment of reporters in the press has been so egregious that the situation led eleven countries to band together to make it clear that the targeting of journalists was unacceptable.

Over the last three years, two types of statements have been made by many people on a consistent basis. One is "freedom of the press in Turkey is often limited," and the other is "journalists in Turkey have been prevented from doing their jobs." Neither circumstance is new, however. After the 2016 coup attempt, many journalists left Turkey, and hundreds of others were jailed. Media groups were also taken over or had to close. Despite journalists having rights enshrined in the Turkish constitution, these rights have been disregarded in recent times.

Hallmarks of Erdoğan's Leadership

Splitting, blame shifting, and projective identification have become rampant in Turkey and are observable across several political settings. One of the obvious ways these mental manipulations have emerged seems to involve the relationship between Erdoğan and Gülen, two leaders who at one time were friends.

Reportedly, when speaking of Gülen's attempts to unseat him, Erdoğan talked about being betrayed by Gülen. In 2014, during a speech at "The Great Turkey Symposium," an event hosted by the Confederation of Public Servants' Trade Unions, Erdoğan invoked a story about a man, who, if given the choice of being stabbed in the back or stabbed through the stomach would prefer the latter. "You deem him a friend, but you may not know and notice that the person you deemed a friend has been marketing his will, comprehension, homeland, and nation to dark circles," Erdoğan said to the crowd (Hürriyet Daily News, 2014).

This treatment of Erdoğan's former ally exemplifies splitting, the defense mechanism that accompanies projective identification. In this case, Erdoğan began to see his former friend in a different light, perhaps at some point ten years ago when, Gülen became a definitive adversary: a wholly "bad" person who needed to be destroyed. Erdoğan became unable to see any positive qualities in the man who had previously been his supporter; nor was he able to integrate various good qualities that he had once recognized in the former Turkish cleric, but instead now saw him exclusively as a major enemy.

Erdoğan is known for doing whatever it takes to silence the opposition. In his eyes, anyone who does not entirely agree with him represents the opposition by default. He is known for suspending people's passports to force them back to Turkey for punishment. Often, this reaction occurs simply because someone said something critical of him. Anyone with a legitimate political following with the potential to democratically unseat Erdoğan is seen as a dangerous adversary. The threat posed by his enemies must be eliminated at all costs.

To that end, Erdoğan's worst nightmare is Gülen, even though he is in hiding from the budding dictator and mostly keeping to himself in his frail old age. Despite living in the United States, Gülen still enjoys significant influence in Turkey. As a result, Erdoğan has been trying to get Gülen extradited for years but has been unsuccessful because the United States will not extradite without a valid criminal reason, which the Turkish government has thus far been unable to provide. Erdoğan blamed Gülen in part for the attempted coup and used that rationale in his extradition appeal in 2016, but the US government refused his request (Chappel, 2017). In the interim, those suspected of supporting the Gülen movement have been arrested.

With regard to projective identification, Erdoğan seems to exhibit traits he has accused Gülen of possessing. For example, Erdoğan has made numerous attempts to silence his adversaries, yet he pronounces that people suspected of working against him were traitors and would-be assassins (Fanack, 2016). This belief on Erdogan's part applies to Gülen who does not agree with him and will not be silenced. Because of his convictions, Erdoğan has said that Gülen is a harmful person who should be stopped.

At first glance, one might wonder why Erdoğan has such a strong reaction to Gülen, who fled Turkey and has lived in the United States for over two decades. If one assumes that people who employ projective identification as a defense mechanism have narcissistic traits—which is usually so—it is also important to know that such people also need to be in control one hundred percent of the time. In Erdoğan's case, as long as Gülen causes him to suspect that he could lose his dominant position as the leader of Turkey, he will feel threatened. In an opinion piece for *The Washington Post*, Gülen expressed sadness that:

> "the Turkey [he] once knew as a hope-inspiring country [is] on its way to consolidating its democracy and a moderate form of secularism has become the dominion of a president who is doing everything he can to amass power and subjugate dissent."

> (Gülen, 2017)

This is the type of statement that more than likely leads Erdoğan to feel Gülen is still a dangerous opponent who could threaten his power in Turkey.

Furthermore, since underneath a thin veneer of self-confidence, narcissists have a profound fear of being seen as weak, imperfect, or as someone who "doesn't measure up," they often experience intense anxiety. That is, unless or until they are able to project these feelings onto another person, so they are is not experienced by the original projector. Hence, when Erdoğan projects his anxiety onto Gülen, he might well experience some relief when claiming the failed coup to be "a gift from God" (Taspinar, 2016).

Erdoğan also appears to have trouble accepting that Gülen still maintains a significant following in Turkey even from his home-in-exile in a small town in the Pocono Mountains in Pennsylvania. Having people in Turkey who adore Gülen is most likely unacceptable to Erdoğan since he demands total loyalty and cannot stand that people in his country like and admire Gülen. As a hypothesis, it seems as though since some countrymen obviously and proudly prefer Gülen to Erdoğan, Erdoğan cannot tolerate feeling that he is not the mighty leader admired by *all* people in Turkey. Given his demand for unwavering admiration, he could be projecting this demand for absolute control onto Gülen by claiming he deserves to be hunted down and destroyed. Accordingly, if Gülen absorbs the projection and has not "given it back to Erdoğan," it is conceivable (though not necessarily likely) that he indeed moved to the U.S. and continues to live there because he feels inferior or less than Erdoğan in terms of power—because he has identified with what the President of Turkey foisted onto him.

One can imagine that Erdoğan cannot stand the thought of being seen as someone who is weak or "less than." However, it seems likely that he is viewed as inferior by those who think Gülen is a strong leader. If that it is case, he could project feelings of inferiority onto Gülen.

Erdoğan's Continued Alliance with the Nationalist Party in 2021

President Erdoğan is working with his far-right Nationalist Movement Party (MPH) to draft a new constitution for the Turkish government that is supposed to be available for public debate in 2022. The new plan includes installing a new, pro-MPH judiciary following a years-long purge of judges and prosecutors under Erdoğan's watch (Reuters, 2020). The revised constitution is slated to become law in 2023 to commemorate the 100th anniversary of the end of the Ottoman Empire (Reuters, 2021).

According to Devlet Bahçeli, President of the MPH since 1997, "this constitutional proposal is the democratic torch of the 100 years that lies ahead, a move by our people to build and reclaim the future" (*Middle East Monitor*, 2021). The MHP also wants to ban the pro-Kurdish Peoples' Democratic Party because it claims the Kurds are a threat to the unity of Turkey. This will be a difficult feat though, as the MHP, even with its allies, does not have the numbers to call for a referendum despite constituting a parliamentary majority.

Rights groups and Turkey's Western allies have criticized what they see as increasing authoritarianism under Erdoğan, especially since the 2016 coup attempt that prompted sweeping crackdowns on his perceived opponents in the civil service, education, the military and elsewhere. Turkish authorities say the measures were necessary for national security. Further, the coup attempt served as an excuse to crack down on anyone and any institution expressing a dint of dissent: as of March 2019, Erdoğan has ordered 500,650 people investigated, nearly 100,000 arrested, 3,003 schools and universities closed, 319 journalists arrested, and nearly 200 media outlets closed (Turkey Purge, 2019).

Only time will tell if a new constitution becomes the law of the land in Turkey in 2023. While opposition to the proposed changes coming from various rights groups in Turkey and from the Kurds is currently strong, Erdoğan is a dedicated strongman who reportedly wants to rule Turkey for the rest of his life. Whether he will succeed is yet to be seen.

Note

1 The Kemalist reforms represented a political revolution away from the Ottoman Empire to the establishment of the nation of Turkey. Organizers believed only a republican regime could best represent the wishes of the people.

References

Amnesty International (2017). Turkey: Journalists around the world demand release of 120 +jailed colleagues.www.amnesty.org/en/latest/news/2017/04/turkey-journalists-around-the-world-demand-release-of-more-than-120-jailed-colleagues.

Aydintaşbaş, A. (2017). Turkey's constitutional referendum: What you need to know. European Council on Foreign Relations, April 7. https://ecfr.eu/article/commentary_turkeys_constitutional_referendum_what_you_need_to_know_7268.

Carlotta, G. (2019). Erdoğan's plan to raise a 'pious generation' divides parents in Turkey. The New York Times, June 18. www.nytimes.com/2018/06/18/world/europe/erdogan-turkey-election-religious-schools.html.

Chappel, B. (2017). Turkey's Erdoğan suggests swap: Jailed U.S. pastor for Turkish cleric. NPR, September 29. www.npr.org/sections/thetwoway/2017/09/29/554451339/turkeys-Erdoğan -suggests-swap-jailed-u-s-pastor-for-turkish-cleric.

Dressler, M. and Mandair, A. (2011). Secularism and Religion-Making. Oxford University Press.

Ferguson, M. (2013). White Turks, black Turks, and negroes: The politics of polarization. Jadaliyya, Arab Studies Institute. www.jadaliyya.com/Details/28868.

Filkins, D. (2016). Turkey's thirty-year coup. The New Yorker, October 10. www.newyorker.com/magazine/2016/10/17/turkeys-thirty-year-coup.

Gülen, F. (2017). The Turkey I no longer know. The Washington Post, May 15. www.washingtonpost.com/opinions/global-opinions/the-turkey-i-no-longer-know/2017/05/15/bda71c62-397c-11e7-8854-21f359183e8c_story.html.

Gürsel, K. (2014). Turkey's Kurds key to Erdogan's presidency bid. Al-Monitor, June 10. www.al-monitor.com/originals/2014/06/gursel-turkey-kurds-peace-pkk-ocalan-akp-diy arbakir.html.

Hürriyet Daily News (2014). Turkish president Erdoğan: I was fooled, betrayed by Gulen. December 26. www.hurriyetdailynews.com/turkish-president-erdogan-i-wa s-fooled-betrayed-by-gulen-76156.

Lourenço, C. (Trans. by Järviniemi, J.) (2019). Turkish EU accession: Where are we? The *New Federalist*, March 25. www.thenewfederalist.eu/turkish-eu-accession-where-are-we?lang=fr.

Messina, K. (2019). *Misogyny, Projective Identification*. Routledge, p. 127.

Middle East Monitor (2021). Turkey: Erdogan ally drafts new constitution for AK Party to consider. May 5. www.middleeastmonitor.com/20210505-turkey-erdogan-a lly-drafts-new-constitution-for-ak-party-to-consider.

Reuters (2020). How Turkey's courts turned on Erdogan's foes. May 4. www.reuters. com/investigates/special-report/turkey-judges.

Reuters (2021). Erdogan's nationalist ally prepares draft Turkish constitution. May 4. www.reuters.com/world/middle-east/erdogans-nationalist-ally-prepares-draft-turkish-constitution-2021-05-04.

Taspinar, O. (2016). The failed coup and Turkey's Gulenist predicament. Brookings Institution, August 9. www.brookings.edu/opinions/the-failed-coup-and-turkeys-gu lenist-predicament.

Turkey Purge. Monitoring Human Rights Abuses in Turkey. https://turkeypurge.com.

Yavuz, M. and Öztürk, A. (2019). Turkish secularism and Islam under the reign of Erdoğan. *Southeast European and Black Sea Studies*, 19:1, 1–9, doi:10.1080/ 14683857.2019.1580828.

Yavuz, M. and Öztürk, A. (2020). *Islam, Populism, and Regime Change in Turkey*. Routledge, p. 4.

Yilmaz, I. (2021). The AKP's Authoritarian, Islamist Populism: Carving out a new Turkey. European Center for Populism Studies. www.academia.edu/47762750/Yilma z_The_AKP_s_Authoritarian_Islamist_Populism.

Chapter 12

Common Traits Among Populist Leaders

There is much debate about the types of populism that exist in contemporary society, as well as the personalities of populist leaders. Most are charismatic, strongman types who recognize some facet of what the downtrodden people in their respective nations have lost. They repackage the loss or losses as something the country must have to thrive and perhaps even survive.

Populist leaders described in this book are cut from this type of cloth. They frequently proclaim they are for the "people" and rally against the "elite." They also often imply and sometimes even say they are like "saviors" who will right all wrongs and then give back to their followers what is truly theirs.

These ideas entice those people who feel left out of mainstream politics or believe they have been disenfranchised from the "in" group. Followers are attracted to this type of personality because these leaders often charm and mesmerize their followers. They also make promises that sound wonderful, but once in office, most of the promises are not kept. Trump, for example, delivered on about a quarter of his 102 campaign promises (Greenberg, 2021). Once in power, he moved on to his next plan which involved seeking and obtaining more control.

Power is another essential driving factor, even from an early age for most populists. For example, Hungary's prime minister, Viktor Orbán, has been described as insatiably power-hungry. Donald Trump, who lost the 2020 presidential election, maintains such a strong desire to remain president of the United States that he fabricated a story about the election by claiming it had been stolen from him. No credible evidence of fraud was ever found, and further, "officials in the Trump campaign were aware early on that many of the claims...were baseless" (Feuer, 2021). To make matters worse, even in the fall of 2021, he was still trying to prove he won the 2020 presidential election.

Then there is Turkey's president, Recep Tayyip Erdoğan, who wants to keep his position as president until he sees fit to leave. Even back in 2016, he was drafting referendums to change the constitution to provide the president with sweeping power and the potential to serve three terms (Makovsky, 2017).

DOI: 10.4324/9781003202387-13

Populist Leaders' Narcissistic Traits and Their Relationships With Others

Many populist leaders frequently possess common narcissistic personality traits. Owing to a deep-seated sense of insecurity that is defended against by bravado, showiness, and proclamations of their greatness, they have a strong need to be praised and admired which they feel entitled to receiving, owing to their innate sense of superiority and grandiosity. They also feel entitled to getting the acclaim they seek. This includes caring about themselves while having little or no capacity to be empathic towards others. They are also haughty and arrogant, filled with a sense of self-importance. Oftentimes, they are pros at exploiting others.

Because images these leaders project to others are different from what they believe to be true about themselves—if they can ever acknowledge what they really think—they are prone to experience criticism and defeat as a significant psychological injury. This state of mind can lead to feelings of emptiness and thoughts about being less-than others. However, since narcissists cannot easily tolerate these feelings or thoughts, they often get angry and attack those who have caused them to feel they have failed or are inferior.

Interpersonal relationships with narcissists are generally superficial, owing to the one-sided nature of connections with another person or other people. What matters to narcissists concerns what is best for them, not for others. The farce of caring is for show, to boast to admirers. Genuine concern for others is insincere. Demonstrations of caring about people are only emotional façades constructed to enhance the show. Trump, for example, loved rallies with large, cheering crowds of people who appeared to love him. When asked they often said it was because they could identify with his rhetoric. He made them feel special, as if they were part of something big and something important. He treated his base like they were members of his exclusive country club in Florida, for example. However, it was all a farce.

Narcissists always think they know the right answer as well. They must preserve the image of being all-knowing to keep their true sense of inferiority at bay. Challenging them is not a satisfying endeavor. Just as they cannot tolerate defeat, they also will not put up with being questioned. They must preserve their fragile egos to maintain their fantasies of being the best and the smartest person they know so they can nurture their illusions of grandeur. They also exaggerate and frequently tell lies which allows them to manipulate others. This behavior has increased, owing to the ability to reach millions of people through social media. Fake news and disinformation can now reach followers quickly. There is no limit to the amount of propaganda that can be sent to followers who await information from those who control their thinking. Although Trump has been temporarily banned from access to millions of his admirers by Facebook and permanently from Twitter, he and his team are planning a comeback. Trump campaign adviser Jason Miller told Fox News's

#MediaBuzz in March 2021 that Trump would be "returning to social media in probably about two to three months with, "his own platform" (Goodwin, 2021).

Populist leaders also frequently rewrite history when their message differs from what has been said or done by past leaders. This has included removing statues of famous leaders whose contributions are not valued by the current populist leader, reprinting history books so younger generations will not know about the true history of their country as well as other acts of reframing the past.

Much like magical stories children are told, populist leaders of countries must also be the best whether what they portray is accurate or not. It's also not hard for them to find people who believe them because many of their devoted fans have heard fantastical stories in the form of fairy tales from a very young age.

Many or most people hear fairy tales when they are young, but all are not likely to fall for the lies populists may tell. For other followers, there's something compelling about a populist's rags-to-riches story so many will fall for the populist rhetoric, but clearly, that's not the case for everyone. Dysfunctional personalities rule the day in a number of fairy tales, while the protagonists—overlooked for much of the story—are endowed with special gifts.

Early experiences formed by hearing childhood fairy tales about the specialness of superheroes and villains set the stage for believing in *special* leaders who proclaim their greatness on a regular basis. In some ways, populists are like these characters in fairy tales, they must be superior to others at all costs. Some followers are also equally primed to accept narcissistic leaders and their exhortations because of lingering fantasies from childhood about characters in fairy tales.

Whether narcissists are prime ministers or presidents, they thrive on the opportunity to be in the limelight and to be the "best" no matter what it takes to get that message across. They also often have a need to put others down and to be the *most* important, smartest, and very best person they know which often necessitates denigrating others.

The Complexities of Narcissism

While many populist leaders have narcissistic personality traits, it is important to keep in mind the fact that narcissism is a complicated condition. The range of this character trait goes from healthy narcissism on one end of the spectrum to a severe condition recognized by the psychiatric community as a personality disorder.

People with healthy narcissism take care of themselves. They set personal boundaries and do not allow others to take advantage of them. At the other end of the narcissism spectrum, people can cause a great deal of suffering for anyone in a relationship with them, whether it's professional or personal.

Other less known features and behaviors exhibited by people on the narcissism spectrum are not as obvious as the ones mentioned above or those associated with the well-known features of narcissists; the ones most people recognize such as boastfulness, self-aggrandizement, demanding to be the center of attention and other traits that over-state their sense of importance. Ava Green of Napier University and her colleagues interviewed domestic partners of narcissists and determined two types of people shared common traits that identified them as narcissists.

Narcissistic partners who displayed standard, grandiose features were likely to react with violence in response to threats to their self-esteem, typically when demands of entitlement, admiration and perceived authority were not met. These relationships were described by participants as swift and vicious – they charmed and disarmed, and subjected partners to abuse, often quite overtly, to defend themselves against the slightest injury or ego-threatening situations (Green, 2019).

Green and her team also found that other types of narcissists do not react in the same way. In the case of *vulnerable* narcissists, these researchers found that they had an intense fear of being abandoned. Rather than lashing out when emotionally injured, they tended to be clingy. This suggests that relationships with more vulnerable narcissists may be slower and more insidious, and potentially more harmful. In these cases, the manifestation of narcissistic characteristics was found to be more subtle, leading to sulky, passive aggressive abuse of partners in response to fears of being abandoned (Green, 2019).

Narcissists also most often do not accept responsibility for their actions. They place blame on others, frequently employing splitting, blame shifting, and projective identification as mechanisms of defense to divide people into good and bad groups while shifting blame for their actions to others because they do not want to or cannot tolerate taking responsibility for their own behavior.

The Use of Primitive Mechanisms of Defense

Examples of splitting can be seen in countries that have populist leaders who attempt to demonize immigrants or others who they dislike intensely. Prime Minister Viktor Orbán of Hungary has labeled Syrian immigration as an invasion "of poison." In India, Prime Minister Narendra Modi has allowed violence against the country's Muslim population to soar. Philippines President Rodrigo Duterte has called on citizens to kill criminals and drug users. And in Brazil, President Jair Bolsonaro has promised to rip away all land and protections from the country's "smelly" Indigenous communities.

These heads of state use psychological tools to address the economic distress and other concerns of a population affected by globalization. For several idiosyncratic reasons, they manage to justify putting more power in their own hands. They also blame designated "others" such as immigrants who they have identified as being less-than the people they govern.

Splitting is First Step in Process

Splitting occurs when a person cannot accept that there are good qualities *and* bad qualities in the same person or group of people. This person must put people in a good category *or* a bad category. The same concept applies to groups of people. Splitting of this type is like living in a black or a white world without any gray.

Then, There is Projective Identification, and Often Blame Shifting

Splitting is most often followed by projective identification which is an unconscious process that allows a person to get rid of some aspect of his or herself that is intolerable by projecting it onto someone else. The result is that this person—I will call him or her—"A", feels like the unwanted quality is gone which often leads to temporary relief. The receiver of the projection, say this person is "B", often feels stunned initially and does not know what happened. Eventually, however, this person may start to believe the negative characteristic actually belongs to him or her (This process also applies to projections that are foisted upon groups of people).

This type of behavior is what populist leaders engage in. They point fingers at those people who oppose them and blame them for their actions. The shifting of blame is closely relate to projective identification with one major difference. While it is a mental maneuver that is often used by people who control and manipulate, as mentioned throughout this book, it is a more conscious process.

Populism and Xenophobia

Splitting, blame shifting, and projective identification are among the mechanisms involved in the hatred, many populists feel towards immigrants in their countries. Reasons vary, as do the groups that are hated, but it is usually the case that people from one culture begin to discriminate against others from another culture, a movement often initiated by a leader who is on the rise in terms of popularity.

In many democratic countries, populists in power or vying for it intensely dislike or hate Muslims. Others in places like Hungary still discriminate against people of Jewish decent as well. While each situation is different, common narratives connect people across countries and their negativity towards Islam and its followers. Much of the hatred is thousands of years old and goes back to the differences among Muslims, Jews, and Christians.

Many American hate Muslims because of the terrorist attacks on September 11, 2001. They seem to believe jihadist radicals are representative of the Muslim world at large. But reasonable people know that one fanatical group in any culture does not characterize all members of the group. Why hate innocent men, women and children who were also appalled and saddened by the devastation that resulted from the attack that destroyed the World Trade Center?

I suspect most Americans would be appalled if they thought the KKK was considered to represent mainstream beliefs.

Populist Leaders and Cults

It is often useful to learn about various movements within any given society from former participants who were part of the group. Reading Steven Hassan's insights about cults yields valuable insights. Now a mental health professional, Hassan was recruited by members of Sun Myung Moon's Unification Church when he was a college student in the 1970s. He says it was only through luck and the help of his family that he was able to regain freedom from the cult he was tricked into joining. He wrote in *The Cult of Trump,* after studying mind control for many years, that Trump's strategies mirrored Moon's techniques:

> Like Moon, Trump commands, and even demands, devotion and adoration from his audiences, but I also saw telling differences. Trump's over 500 rallies are far more choreographed and staged-managed than Moon's mass assembles ever were. Rousing patriotic music heralds his appearance onstage, while enthusiastic supporters stand by him cheering. Trump's rallies are strangely more intimate. Part of Trump's effectiveness is the way he talks to the audience, taking them into his confidence with personal asides, talking about how misunderstood and maligned he is by the media.
>
> (Hassan, 2020, p. xiii)

After a quiet reception, Hassan's book gained fresh interest after the January 6 insurrection. His message sounded the alarm about Trump's cult-like leadership. Hassan's prescription for extricating loved ones from a cult-like mindset is to maintain relationships and express support—easier said than done for most of us.

Poverty and Early Aggression Can Contribute to Development of Narcissism

Many factors contribute to the development of narcissism in populist leaders. Whether one can attribute being poor or having a poor parent to narcissism that develops later in life is variable, sometimes poverty sets the stage for this disorder to emerge later in life, but this is not always the case. However, many populist leaders mentioned in this book experienced some level of poverty when they were young. They almost always exhibited early aggressive tendencies as well.

In Trump's case, poverty is not obvious. It was his mother who was extremely poor, not Trump. He keeps the fact that she came from an extremely impoverished background in Scotland a secret. More than likely, this is because he has trouble tolerating the fact that his mother was a poor immigrant and worked in a menial job when she came to America as a domestic worker in the home of a New York millionaire. Instead of being proud of his mother's good fortune, Trump must be ashamed of her background because it sullies his heritage.

Volumes can and have been written about Trump's other narcissistic characteristics. One of the most blatant is his lack of empathy for others. He also has a constant need for approval and affection from members of his base but does not care about their well-being. This was evident when he insisted on having indoor rallies during the pandemic. Some Trump supporters—notably former Republican presidential candidate turned Trump supporter, Herman Cain, died from COVID-19 after attending a Trump rally unmasked.

Viktor Orbán

Viktor Orbán's family was very poor when he was a young boy. He and his siblings all endured a particularly harsh childhood. They worked in the field feeding animals and gathering vegetables to help their family. At times they had no access to running water. Whether or not this object poverty contributed to his aggression is unknown. But, by his own admission, he was a problematic young boy.

Daniel Ortega

Many of Ortega's family members, including his mother, were imprisoned, so he learned about aggression at a very early age. Ortega was also sent to prison when he was 15 years old. He was tortured then released which was followed by a period of exile in Cuba. There he received guerrilla training before secretly returning to Nicaragua in 1979.

Jair Bolsonaro

The town where Bolsonaro grew up was rough, where problems were routinely settled with gunfights. For this reason, the children often took cover under their parents' bed. Eventually, he went to a military-affiliated preparatory school. After he was discharged from military service as an adult, he entered politics where he developed a reputation for being extremely aggressive and demanding.

Rodrigo Duterte

As a child, Rodrigo Duterte was emotionally neglected. This would explain why he was thought to be a tough guy at an early ago who was involved in street fights and other disruptive ways of acting which led to his expulsion from two schools. Because of this behavior he was severely beaten by his parents though it was mainly his mother who disciplined him because his father was absent a fair amount of the time. It also has been reported that he was molested by a priest when he attended a Catholic school. This event could have caused him to be traumatized; an experience that he may not have psychologically worked through.

Narendra Modi

For much of his early life, Narendra Modi was poor. It is likely that he was exposed to situations that made him feel inferior to others because he was part of a low caste. Because his mother washed dishes to make money and his father sold tea on a cart at a train station, it seems quite likely that he encountered people who talked down to him or caused him to feel inferior. Assuming he had difficulty tolerating these feelings, he might have projected them onto Muslims, making them feel their status in India was inferior to Hindus. This mechanism could also have lessened Modi's feeling of being inferior to others that he most likely experienced at various times in his life. By casting off this sense of himself as marginal, while attributing it to Muslims, he might have relieved himself, at least temporarily, of feeling like a second-class person.

Recep Tayyip Erdoğan

Erdoğan came from a humble background. He was born in a poor Istanbul neighborhood. As a boy, in order to make money he sold watermelon, lemonade and sesame buns in a rough area of the city. At this time in his life he attended an Islamic religious school. When he was in high school, he gave passionate speeches about Islam which may have laid the foundation for his penchant to turn Turkey into a more religious country than it was prior to his ascent to power.

What Populist Leaders Had in Common as Children and Adolescents

By no means are narcissists always from poor, abusive families, but poverty and abuse can lead to feelings of shame and humiliation. When this is the case, narcissistic tendencies or a narcissistic personality disorder can develop later in life. This can set the tone for a less-than-optimal way of operating when it comes to taking responsibility for one's behavior in life.

In terms of shame, no one generally likes the feelings that are associated with it. They also tend to conceal the events that were originally connected to it. At times, they become filled with rage. Projecting these negative feelings onto someone else or others is an unconscious defense mechanism that can occur when these individuals cannot tolerate their own feelings or thoughts, including shame. They may become bullies, for example, who tease and scapegoat others to escape bad feelings.

Studying bullies reveals that they have frequently been taunted and teased by others at some time in their lives. Rather that dealing with this negative affect in a more direct way by seeking help from others, they most often project their bad feelings onto those who are vulnerable. In that way, they bully versus being bullied which, at least temporarily, alleviates the pain or negative feelings they initially experienced. As long as this type of person is perceived by others as being the best at everything, the status quo remains intact. If, however, this inwardly fragile person is narcissistically injured, the situation can rapidly change since the individual being described can quickly become filled with rage (as described above) that is directed toward the person who caused the psychological injury. The reaction can be quite aggressive since being wrong, less-than or losing is intolerable to narcissists, especially those with a full-blown narcissistic personality disorder.

Narcissists also have a need to win because losing can evoke feelings that were experienced in childhood or adolescence. This occurs since being seen as perfect is essential if one is to maintain a façade of perfection. This same idea applies to lying. Always being right is imperative to narcissists no matter how it is achieved because it keeps the fake persona they exhibit in place which covers up their actual weaknesses or truth deficit.

This type of self-focus does not allow for empathy to develop since getting one's own needs met is what matters. This mindset goes hand-in-hand with feelings of entitlement since the budding narcissist believes he or she is special. This, of course, is a defense against feeling inferior which is something that cannot be tolerated. Being special, the smartest and the best at everything they attempt to do is what holds narcissists with these characteristics together and keeps their pseudo self-worth intact, at least until they experience the next narcissistic injury. They also have a need to scapegoat others instead of accepting responsibility for their actions.

An Example of Early Aggression in a Narcissistic Populist Leader

Trump is a good example of how early aggressive behavior can lead to narcissistic character traits in adulthood. In the second grade, he hit a teacher, giving him a black eye. Why would he do that? Although no one will ever know with certainty because Trump does not tell the truth, it is nearly impossible to know his precise motivation. However, one can speculate that his early relationships as a toddler with a harsh father and unavailable mother contributed to his narcissistic personality disorder. Since he was bullied and ridiculed when he was a boy, Trump eventually embodied these attributes. He also followed in his father's footsteps and became much like the other leaders profiled in this book; an aggrieved aggressor-in-chief.

References

Feuer, A (2021). Trump campaign knew lawyers' voting machine claims were baseless, memo shows. *The New York Times*, September 21. www.nytimes.com/2021/09/21/us/politics/trump-dominion-voting.html.

Fitzpatrick, D. (2016). *The dark history behind Donald Trump's hair.* National Memo, June 12. www.nationalmemo.com/dark-history-behind-donald-trumps-hair.

Freud, S. (1922). *Group Psychology and the Analysis of the Ego.* Vienna: International Psychoanalytic Publishing House.

Goodwin, J. (2021). Trump is returning to social media in a few months with his own platform, spokesman says. CNN, March 22. www.cnn.com/2021/03/21/media/donald-trump- social-media-network/index.html.

Green, A. (2019). *Narcissism—and the various ways it can lead to domestically abusive relationships. The Conversation*, June 5. theconversation.com/narcissism-and-the-various- ways-it-can-lead-to-domestically-abusive-relationships-116909.

Greenberg, J. (2021). Trump ends his term as president with half of his campaign promises unachieved. Poynter, January 20. www.poynter.org/fact-checking/2021/trump-ends- his-term-as-president-with-half-of-his-campaign-promises-unachieved.

Hunt, H. (2016). *The Last Tycoon: The Many Lives of Donald J Trump*: Brattleboro, VT: Echo Point Books and Media.

Kluger, J. (2014). *The Narcissist Next Door:*New York, NY: Riverhead Books.

Lendvai, P. (2017). *Orban: Hungary's Strongman.* Oxford University Press.

Makovsky, A. (2017). Erdoğan's Proposal for an Empowered Presidency. Center for American Progress, March 22. www.americanprogress.org/article/erdogans-proposal-empowered-presidency.

Mudde, C. and Kaltwasser, R. (2017). *Populism: A Very Short Introduction.* Oxford: Oxford University Press.

Salmi, N. (2020). How populist leaders around the world rule by division. Matador Network, June 20. https://matadornetwork.com/read/populist-leaders-around-world-rule-division.

Chapter 13

Social Media's Stronghold on People Globally

It's Time to Hold Big Tech Accountable

The idea that our social interactions online are independent and unencumbered by the psychological maneuverings of anonymous engineers is false. Further, the very design of social media platforms provides unfettered opportunities for users to project their hateful feelings onto anyone they choose. This allows users to continuously spew vile material of all types without repercussions. Real change can only happen if social media companies are forced to change.

As I hope I have demonstrated throughout this book, populist leaders exert and maintain control when they dominate the microphone, which can include silencing dissidents and creating "news" outlets that are little more than propaganda vehicles. With social media, populists control the narrative in its entirety. Given how users psychologically respond to various types of virtual stimuli, social media is a particularly effective medium for those who employ splitting and projective identification to maintain control of their victims.

Regular consumers of social media are inundated with harmful messaging that reinforce whatever the person doing the projecting is trying to convey. To make matters worse, social media consumers already have a hard time extricating themselves from their devices, giving populist leaders an ideal platform to feed stories and ideas on an endless loop, almost like a virtual intravenous drip.

People might be hearing more about the deleterious effects of social media, but I wonder if some users are simply too far gone to notice. Still, the riot that took place on January 6, 2021, shocked even the most conservative and right-wing citizens in our country: Pew Research surveyed 5,360 U.S. adults asking respondents to share their reaction to the rioting on the U.S. Capitol. Thirty-seven percent reacted with anguish, horror, and shock, while 14 percent "expressed surprise, incredulity, or embarrassment that such an event could happen in the United States" (Hartig, 2020[1]). It feels as though there is a desire for change but putting action behind intent is so much harder when people are regularly bombarded with lies, false information, and fake news. We Americans have been involved in an unhealthy relationship (namely, with Donald Trump) which has damaged our mental health, and the psychological manipulation wrought via social media only compounds the issue.

DOI: 10.4324/9781003202387-14

Trump is no longer in office but still lurks in the swamplands in America, operating with the sole intent, it seems, to oppose and undermine the Biden administration and perhaps even run for office in 2024. Twitter might have stripped him of his account, but he remains the de facto Republican king-maker. Trump did not create the algorithms that are creating so many problems associated with fake news, but he and many of the other populists featured in this book are pros at manipulating social media.

In America, Trump normalized propaganda, disinformation, and fake news. These new ways of getting information are now embedded in our culture. Many media consumers are desensitized to much of it. The algorithms that lead people down dark paths of sensationalized information are controlling the minds of many Americans and as well as others around the globe. This way of getting information must be reassessed.

While no one, especially freedom-loving Americans, wants to believe they have lost free will, most of us do not control our social media and the kinds of news and information we consume. Social media engineers employ pervasive psychological techniques to whet people's appetite to stay on their platforms, and it is not because they care about user experience; they care about increasing ad revenue.

Social media barons want to make money. They do not care whether you've reunited with your long-lost high school sweetheart, but they will do everything they can to keep you hooked on staying in touch with each other online. They do this by controlling what users see in their feeds, and how often. Early Facebook investor Roger McNamee, said in his book, *Zucked: Waking Up to the Facebook Catastrophe*:

> Facebook has used surveillance to build giant profiles on every user and provides each user with a customized Truman Show, similar to the Jim Carry film about a person who lives his entire life as the star of his own television show. It starts with "what they want," but the algorithms are trained to nudge user attention in the direction that Facebook wants. The algorithms choose posts calculated to press emotional buttons because scaring users or pissing them off increases time on site.
>
> (McNamee, 2019, p. 9)

This type of mental manipulation causes users to want more and more of what they are "fed" by social media engineers who are hired by owners and top managerial personnel to entice Facebook followers to stay on the site as long as possible (the same system is used on other platforms as well). The longer they stay, the more likely they are to buy what sponsors are selling, which makes billions of dollars for the top brass who run social media companies and for the companies that sell them ads. In an interview on PBS, McNamee said recognized just how bad our predicament is:

What never occurred to me, and which I really struggle with every single day, is that conscious choices and priorities of the company put in motion forces that have undermined democracy, have undermined our economy, have undermined the public health of our citizens, and have actually done the same in countries around the world. It never occurred to me that anything I was involved in would ever—I've been really careful about my choices. I've consciously turned down companies that I knew would be financially successful because I struggled with their value system. I did that with Uber; I did that with Spotify; I did that with Zynga, knowing they were going to be successful but feeling like the value systems of those companies, they might be fine for a lot of people, but they weren't fine for me.

And I never had that sense about Facebook. I was never worried that they were going to go across the line, and I punish myself every day over that issue now, because obviously, if the harm is great enough, it doesn't matter that you didn't intend it.

(Jacoby, 2018)

Based on what McNamee has said about the motivation of those in charge of Facebook, it is understandable why social media is so irresistible; people naturally crave acceptance. Online, people transform into whomever they choose via avatars and Photoshop, all in the name of securing "likes" and "friends."

In addition to McNamee, former Facebook, Apple, and Google employees—among them "Social Dilemma" documentarian Tristan Harris and creator of the Facebook "Like" button Justin Rosenstein—have been sounding the alarm for years on the deliberately addictive mechanisms meant to hook users, especially children. At a TED conference in 2017, Harris laid out several examples of how tech engineers make their products as irresistible as possible:

A simple example is YouTube. YouTube wants to maximize how much time you spend. And so what do they do? They auto play the next video. And let's say that works really well. They're getting a little bit more of people's time. Well, if you're Netflix, you look at that and say, well, that's shrinking my market share, so I'm going to auto play the next episode. But then if you're Facebook, you say, that's shrinking all of my market share, so now I have to auto play all the videos in the newsfeed before waiting for you to click play. So, the internet is not evolving at random. The reason it feels like it is sucking us in the way it is, is because of this race for attention. We know where this is going. Technology is not neutral, and it becomes this race to the bottom of the brain stem of who can go lower to get it.

(Harris, 2017)

We now know social media engineers have learned a great deal about how our brains can be trained and shaped by our environment. Persuasive technology and behavioral modification shape attitudes and behaviors, and, as the partners at the Center for Humane Technology point out, "when we engage in persuasive technology repeatedly, it begins to train us: our thoughts, feelings, motivations, and attention start to replicate what the technology is designed to produce" (Center for Humane Technology, 2017). We might know that scrolling endlessly through our social media feeds is bad for our mental health, but we do it anyway—it has become too hard to turn away.

The techniques designed by social media experts that cause people to crave what their advertisers are selling are particularly effective because humans hate feeling left out to the point that we will go to extreme lengths to conform. A study in *Nature* revealed that, "...high confidence leads to post-decision accumulation becoming "blind" to disconfirmatory evidence (Rollwage et al, 2020)." Further, these scientists observed that "the strongest confirmation bias [occurred] when people were already confident in their decisions" (2020). In plain English: people will believe what they want to believe and will go to tremendous lengths to confirm those beliefs. We saw this happen after the 2020 US presidential election, when people who believed Trump won wanted to confirm their beliefs that the election was stolen. The more they learned, the more they wanted to know, and they gathered social media friends in the process. The same phenomenon can be said for people who mistrust the COVID-19 vaccine, claiming the want to engage in their own research to confirm whatever it is that they believe is so injurious about the vaccine.

Darrell West, a senior fellow at the Center for Technology Innovation and author of *Divided Politics, Divided Nation: Hyperconflict in the Trump Era* (Brookings Institution Press, 2020) explored the role of misinformation on social media in the lead-up to the January 6 insurrection, where he found that:

> "Trump supporters continue to spread outright lies. People I know argue that the violence was committed by ultra-liberal antifa supporters who infiltrated what they claimed was a peaceful Trump protest. Others are telling their friends to shut off the automatic update feature of their phones because the operators are going to remove Trump's access to the emergency broadcasting system."
>
> (West, 2021)

These were not mere falsehoods popping up at random: these lies turned into a justification of violence in the name of Trump, a man who, from their standpoint, was being framed by fake news. Further, knowing what we know about the addictive power of social media, telling people that what they believe is false does nothing—people can self-select their own facts and friends that will confirm everything they already think they know to be true.

Though Americans cast an historic number of ballots in the 2020 presidential election—Joe Biden won 81.2 million, and Trump won 74.2 million by a difference of seven million votes, Trump insisted that he won. He also created a false scenario that claimed the election was stolen from him—and he did not start sharing this theft theory the night of the elections; Trump had been saying since 2016 that his loss would be due only to fraud. Here's a quick recap of some of his highlights:

2016 primary and general election:

> "Ted Cruz didn't win Iowa, he stole it. That's why all of the polls were so wrong and why he got far more than anticipated. Bad!" (Twitter)

In the general election, even after Trump won the Electoral College, he claimed he also won the popular vote, which he did not, but cried fraud anyway:

> "In addition to winning the Electoral College in a landslide, I won the popular vote if you deduct the millions of people who voted illegally."

In 2020, via Twitter:

> "I WON THIS ELECTION, BY A LOT!"

> "They are finding Biden votes all over the place—in Pennsylvania, Wisconsin, and Michigan. So bad for our country!"

On the corrupt practice of mail-in voting two days after Election Day:

> "I've been talking about mail-in voting for a long time. It's—it's really destroyed our system. It's a corrupt system...."

Social media has a very dark side. According to McNamee (others have said this as well), "I had spent a career trying to draw smart conclusions from incomplete information, and one day in 2016 I started to see things happening on Facebook that did not look right. I started pulling on that thread and uncovered a catastrophe" (McNamee, 2019). Mark Zuckerberg *might* have started out wanting to connect college students to each other (his motives actually might not have been so innocent) but now unfortunately the big guys like Zuckerberg are making millions on retaining the attention of viewers, which turns into lucrative advertising revenue.

This mechanism promotes conspiracy theories as well, with some alterations. While Proud Boys might not buy anything, they push their ideas and get followers to believe outlandish and dangerous scenarios.

We cannot condemn social media completely—it *could* be a vehicle for positive change. This is complicated, and I am not suggesting it could be done overnight. But, if the powers that be were not so greedy and cared more about our planet, for example, positive change could happen. In the meantime, until governments decide to regulate social media, there are ways to take control of what we consume online. Here are a few:

Turn off notifications (Go to *Settings* > *Notifications* or swipe left on any incoming notifications and select *Manage* > *Turn Off*. Have you ever thought about why notifications are red? It's not by chance: red is powerful and can sway behavior. (Martinez-Conde and Macknik, 2014)

Even if the content isn't important, a red notification symbol suggests users should check it out ASAP. This simple switch will help reclaim focus.

Delete "Toxic" apps. If you want to log into Facebook, do it the old-fashioned way—take the time to type in the URL. Better yet, delete your profiles entirely—these programs profit off your distraction.

If you stay social, choose to reduce distracting information—avoid clickbait by unfollowing outrage-driven groups and delete polarizing media outlets from your newsfeed. Programs like Facebook Newsfeed Eradicator and uBlock Origin help reduce online distractions so that you can get the best out of these social sites without getting drawn into rabbit holes of nonsense.

How Projective Identification and Blame Shifting Fit into the Picture

A scant number of people run social media companies. They hire engineers to create algorithms that drive people to become addicted to social media. These top-level owners, managers and their teams of highly trained experts are the masterminds behind the manipulation of millions of people (McNamee, 2019). They are the ones who are projecting aspects of themselves—their need for power—onto groups of their users. The recipients are the group who believes they are the powerful people who need to save the country (the Insurrectionists, for example,) This same idea applies to any group of followers who believe the disinformation and conspiracy theories that are fed to them by social media engineers who create easily digestible and algorithms. As a result of this process, users come to believe erroneous information they have been led to believe is the truth. Instead, the actual truth is out of their reach if they only use social media as a source of news. This means that social media users are manipulated and are recipients of the projected parts of people who are running the show at Facebook, Twitter, Google, etc. (I should clarify that I think the masterminds are the people who profit and project greed, not the actual engineers employed by these firms—they are just doing their jobs.)

So, the avaricious, greedy, power-seeking gurus get rid of these characteristics by projecting them onto the Proud Boys, Incels, Truth Seekers, etc., who
then act to "save the day" and our country. The algorithm creators and
backers wash their hands of the negative traits. In the case of the Insurrection,
those who were duped to riot now face prison sentences.

Let's look at a one-on-one example of projective identification as it applies
to individuals and populist leaders to further illustrate the mental maneuvers
associated with projective identification: If a dishonest husband went home
and suggested to his wife that she take some type of illegal action to hustle
someone for money, she might be startled at first. However, if he continued to
press her, eventually she might steal to feel closer to her husband and more
loved by him. However, if she goes too far and gets caught, she is likely to go
to jail, while her husband remains innocent and unaffected—he might even
go so far as to suggest that she's always been a thief. Populists on social
media engage in similar behaviors: first, splitting occurs—assigning people to
good or bad groups—then, projective identification can occur. Blame-shifting
can also be part of the mix if the the projector and/or the recipient are consciously aware of what they are doing. Populists can suggest that they are
being swindled or cheated by another group, and wouldn't it be nice if something were done about it—what patriots those people who stand up and act
would be! (This is also an example of stochastic terrorism, which I have
explored in this book as well.) Some users who hear that kind of rhetoric
repeatedly might eventually act on those words.

Below are some of the reasons people become radicalized and how we can
bring our friends and family members back to their communities.

The Need to Find Meaning and Affiliation

After meeting basic needs, most humans want to do things that make them
feel good, whether that's helping others, creating art, or anything that affords
people the opportunity to enjoy a sense of accomplishment and satisfaction;
living a life of meaning is important to mental health. When these needs are
not met through socially acceptable avenues, some people will turn to cults or
radical extremist groups. Purposeless people find meaning by taking on the
causes of charismatic leaders, and that can have positive and negative results.

People want to belong—it is human nature. When they are a part of a
group, they feel more connected. This affiliation can come from church
groups, clubs, school, work, or other organizations that emphasize common
goals.

When people feel left out, disrespected, or rejected, they might join groups
that espouse less respectable intentions. People also join groups that support
causes that are intended to harm those who have rejected them.

While the need to find a purpose in life and belong to a group are ancient
human needs, much of the meaning and human connections in the past were

found on a local or regional level. If this was not possible, those who could move did so in hopes of finding what was unavailable in their hometowns. Today, with the proliferation of social media, nearly everyone can become part of any number of disparate groups in a matter of minutes. While there is tremendous positive potential in this technology, much of this interaction can turn negative quickly, especially with nefarious group leaders who capitalize on the opportunity to recruit new members from around the world.

Consider QAnon, the once fringy disproven far-right conspiracy theory that turned into a global movement. Since Trump's defeat, QAnon continues promoting baseless allegations that Democratic politicians (led by Hillary Clinton) and Hollywood celebrities are Satan-worshipping pedophiles who traffic in children for deviant purposes. Trump, according to lore, was elected to stop these sex-crazed deviants. QAnon believers waited for the "Great Awakening" when evildoers would be brought to justice. Even when the prophecies do not come to pass, Q followers find some kernel of an idea or concept upon which to hang their beliefs. Perhaps most disturbing is the reach of QAnon theories; according to a poll conducted by the Public Religion Institute and the Interfaith Youth Core, 15 percent of Americans agreed with a QAnon tenet that "the government, media and financial worlds in the U.S. are controlled by a group of Satan-worshipping pedophiles who run a global child sex trafficking operation" (Public Religion Research Institute, 2021). Taken too far, our natural desire to belong can be exploited with surprising ease.

Social Media Gone Awry

One reason why Zuckerberg created a social media platform was to bring people together so they could have meaningful connections with others. Contemporaries claim that Zuckerberg never imagined what Facebook would become (McNamee, 2019). The early rules governing the new platform were straightforward: "…listen to your users, stay simple, be reliable." He apparently never thought it would become a weapon of exploitation.

Much has changed since the early days of Facebook and other social media platforms. Today, algorithms limit what users see because their Facebook feeds are based on what users "like" while excluding what "is." A user must make a deliberate decision to find people shunted by the algorithm. If you have Facebook, consider your own experience: Who among your friends shows up at the top of your news feed? Most likely, you see profiles of people who come from the same background as you, share the same views as you, and enjoy the same activities. You have got to work to find people who differ—and that is by design.

Social media platforms use persuasive psychology to influence their users. One major psychological maneuver used in this process includes behavioral modification. In some cases, this mechanism can lead to radicalization. The

British- based Office for National Statistics found that young people aged 16–24 are the second-heaviest users of computers, making them prime targets for radicalization and recruitment (Prescott, 2015). A 2013 paper published by the nonprofit policy research organization RAND Europe examined the role of the internet in the radicalization of 15 British-based terrorists and extremists. "Evidence from the primary research conducted confirmed that the internet played a role in the radicalization process of the violent extremists and terrorists whose cases we studied" (von Behr, Reding, Edwards, and Gribbon, 2013). Key elements of the internet's ability to radicalize people include its 24/7 availability and the ease with which it facilitates like-minded behavior. Exploiting a shared grievance, whether real or imagined, has also been found to be a major factor in what qualities pull people towards extremism (Scrivens, 2020). In sum, radicalization on the internet is a massive problem with no easy solution.

What Can be Done to Bring Radicalized People Back to Their Former Lives?

There are no simple answers to this question and experts often disagree on the best approach. One thing is clear, more research is needed to solve this problem. Despite the overwhelming odds, some people who have followed the dark road to radicalization have come back. This deradicalization is most likely to occur, according to some experts, with the assistance of people who have had similar experiences—those who have been radicalized themselves but returned to their former lives (Scrivens, 2020).

It is also possible that social media companies that started out with good intentions could change the way they operate. Instead of enticing users to soak in one conspiracy theory after the other, they could encourage people to post higher-quality content. Current algorithms could be monitored by experts to find and discard harmful content.

No matter how we proceed, it is clear that changes need to be made if our democracy is going to survive since like it or not, it is a privilege and not a right.

Given the power of social media platforms, what can be done to stop the momentum of this phenomenon or if it can be stopped is of serious concern. An assessment published by the MIT Technology Review is not so optimistic: in "It's too late to stop QAnon with fact checks and account bans," journalist Abby Olheiser affirmed what many of us feel to be true: That Twitter is "perfect as a megaphone for the far right: its trending topics are easy to game, journalists spend way too much time on the site, and—if you're lucky—the president of the United States might retweet you." QAnoners are "proficient" at playing the Twitter game and based on the way the platform's algorithm works, Twitter functions more like a marketing campaign for QAnon: Content is created to be seen and interacted with by outsiders." (Ohlheiser, 2020). Even when sites like 8chan and Reddit tried to shut down QAnon activity, the group simply moved to other social media platforms. To limit the influence of extreme groups will require a joint effort by all social media platforms, and it does not seem like that is going to happen any time soon (2020).

How Intermittent Reinforcement Hooks People

Intermittent reinforcement is a conditioning and manipulation method that rewards people at unexpected intervals. The 20th-century psychologist B.F. Skinner studied the behavior and concluded that people will learn a new behavior (positive or negative) faster when every correct response is reinforced through continuous reinforcement. Mastering that behavior is achieved and maintained through reinforcement that is delivered intermittently. This means that we work less hard when we can predict that a reward is forthcoming. When the timing of the reward is unpredictable, humans repeat the behavior that led to the reward with greater interest and derive greater pleasure in the prize once it is bestowed (Skinner, 1938).

Intermittent reinforcement is often employed by malignant narcissists who manipulate their victims—sporadic moments of tender affection "rewards" the victim while creating a false sense of normalcy, thereby manipulating the victim into sticking around in the hopes that these intermittent rewards will become more predictable. We see a similar relationship with social media consumers. Someone who clicks on an image or page that has been suggested by a social media platform will either pique a user's interest or not, but the flow of information will be relentless. This process modifies user behavior. Operant conditioning—a learning methodology that employs rewards and punishments for various behaviors—is at the root of our collective obsession with technology and is why we compulsively check our phones and hit "refresh" to see if we will be rewarded with a new text message or social media update. The cycle can be broken, but just like gambling or drinking, this is a tough habit to break.

"The analogy between the gambler and the social-media junkie is hard to avoid," said Tristan Harris in 2016. "When we get sucked into our smartphones or are distracted, we think it's just an accident and our responsibility. But it is not. It is also because smartphones and apps hijack our innate psychological biases and vulnerabilities" (Harris, 2016). We might be checking our smartphones 150 times a day on average, but Harris claims there is no way we are doing that with intention; rather, we have been conditioned into an abusive relationship that we cannot pull ourselves away from, even when we know better.

The Addictive Need to Be Liked

People want to be accepted and at times crave attention. The more others "like" us, the better we feel. Since you can be whatever you wish to be on social media by projecting an image of your choice, it is highly likely that those who ordinarily would not be accepted by their peers can have hundreds if not thousands of "friends."

By suggesting what social media users' accounts might like, platform engineers manipulate what pops up to entice users to stay online for as long as possible. After endlessly participating in this process, people start to crave the constant stimulus they get from following social media. They also now belong to groups with other like-minded people. Some of these people might be legitimate friends, but most will not.

Manipulation and Dark Psychology

Dark psychology was coined in 2006 by Michael Nuccitelli, Psy.D. to describe people who prey on others. It is a form of psychological manipulation, and people who engage in this behavior are categorized by psychiatrists, psychologists and other mental health professionals as having Cluster-B personality disorders. People in this category include those with Antisocial, Borderline, Histrionic and Narcissistic Personality Disorders and exhibit one or more of these disorders. Such people are often deceitful, impulsive, have little or no capacity for empathy, and have a strong need for attention and maintain an outsized sense of self-importance. Narcissists often embody these traits.

Abusers who prey on disenfranchised people are often themselves the victims of abuse or rejection. Troubled as they might be, they read people well. Abusers choose people who they know are vulnerable and use strategies that have been proven to suck others into their world. Dark psychology has found its natural habitat online, where people suffering from personality disorders can mine the well of manipulation with impunity.

Can Social Media Platforms Change?

Back to the big question: Can social media become a positive force versus primarily a negative, destructive one that manufactures and perpetuates the dissemination of disinformation? Change is possible, but it will not be easy. Social media could be designed in society's best interest, but currently its major purpose is purely commercial, designed for profit. Since it is the case that social media platforms have been the sole news source for millions of people around the world, perhaps it is important for the companies that develop and maintain these platforms to be held to standards similar to those applied to newspapers and other traditional news outlets. But can this be done? Have social media companies grown so much that it would be impossible to reign them in? According to an article published by the Brookings Institute in 2019, the process would be difficult:

The sheer volume of content shared on social media makes it impossible to establish an editorial system. Consider Twitter: it is estimated that 500 million tweets are sent per day. Assuming each tweet contains an average of twenty words, the volume of content published on Twitter in one single day will be equivalent to that of *The New York Times* in 182 years.

(Yaraghi, 2019)

While changing the way social platforms operate might be hard, launching Mars rovers and sending people to space are also challenging endeavors, yet we are undeterred in those efforts. Why is social media so much more challenging? Perhaps it is important to think about and develop ways to curtail a phenomenon that could destroy our democracy as well as our planet. Harris suspects that our social media problem is:

"the problem *beneath* so many other problems in our society. If you care about inequality, racial justice, climate change... if you care about most of the issues we face, you will see that they depend on what people *think* about those issues and that's where social media is causing so many problems. If we can get the world to realize that we can all come together because no one wants a world where it's impossible to agree and democracies just fall apart and collapse into themselves."

(Mbe, 2020)

In addition, what Twitter provides users is different from TikTok's offerings, so one platform agreeing to one set of standards does nothing for the rest of the digital universe.

Disinformation and propaganda are bad for our mental health and equally bad for our democracies. According to Chris Fox of BBC.com, many world leaders are thinking about how to regulate social media because of the threats of disinformation on the fragile concept of democracy (Fox, 2020). The Forum for the Information and Democracy published a report that outlined non-binding recommendations to 38 countries that are interested in working together to stop what it called "informational chaos that poses a vital threat to democracies" (2020). Fighting global information chaos would make it necessary for social media platforms to create a *statuary build code* that would require participants to submit their plans for review by trusted scientists in much the same way that a company would submit a new kitchen appliance for the purpose of having its safety reviewed before it was mass produced. Algorithmic functioning would also be evaluated. The report suggests that social networks should display corrections to every person exposed to misinformation or lies.

This chapter offers an actionable guide that could be helpful if people in charge of social media platforms implemented some of these ideas as well as those that have been suggested by people like Triston Harris and Roger

McNamee, among others (Working Group on Infodemics, 2020). In a general sense, it includes transparency, accountability, quality, and safety standards. These standards are followed by nearly every other industry on the planet, which suggests they could be created and enforced in our digital world.

A significant problem with social media is that *relative* truth is valued over universal truths. This issue is causing a divide that could lead to a split from which we might not be able to recover. Tim Kendall, former president of Pinterest, has indicated that the situation is so bad it could lead to a civil war, saying that:

> "our democratic institutions and public discourse are underpinned by an assumption that we can at least agree on things that are true. Our debates may be about how we respond or what values we apply to a particular problem, but we at least have a common understanding that there are certain things that are manifestly true."
>
> (Fox, 2020)

What about Freedom of Speech?

The meaning of free speech has become muddled over time. Western democracies enjoy the freedom of speech, but that is not the same as enjoying unfettered access to anyone, anywhere, offering up unending hate and vitriol—that is abuse.

Despite how destructive social media is today, the good news is that there are few people who run the show. If we could encourage these leaders to become more conscientious about what they are doing, which includes the possibility of destroying our democracy, there might be hope in spite of the obvious catastrophic conditions they are creating and perpetuating. Tristan Harris says "the current technology we have doesn't give us a choice. We are forced to use inhumane technology. That said, we often say this problem is like climate change" (Harris, 2020). Yet, according to Harris, only 100 people are at the top of the most consequential tech companies—these are the people who need to be convinced to change what they are doing.

What Else Could Turn Around the Spread of Disinformation Perpetuated by Social Media?

The simple answer is to reveal and change the way algorithms work; to share the formula with a standard-setting board of trusted scientists, mathematicians and social ethicists who can determine the best use of these technologies. Verifying posts for accuracy via human and artificial intelligence could also be helpful. Making social media companies responsible for what users post could help curtail sensationalized and fake news. Blocking users who violate company guidelines is another strategy that could help make people who post on social media more responsible. Finding a way to accurately determine what is true—objective reality—and promote what we "know" about our world versus conspiracy theories is one of the most essential changes that needs to be made. Social media companies should be fined for breaking rules, once they are established. By create a cabinet-level position to have oversight of the internet including social media platforms to stop the destruction of our democracy would also be a new approach that could help remedy many of the problems that currently exist.

A Challenge to Mark Zuckerberg

While watching news clips how the rich and famous celebrated the 4th of July in 2021, I saw a short piece about Mark Zuckerberg. He was on an electric surfboard holding up an American flag. I thought to myself, this guy could change the world. He did something that started an information revolution that became a global destructive force, and he made billions of dollars in the process. Now, with his expertise and years of experience in technology, he could certainly find a way to make social media a force for good and not evil. He has got the funding and knowledge, why not do something meaningful for mankind? I believe what matters is what one contributes to the world, little things and big ones. Zuckerberg could be remembered as one of the great contributors of the 21st century instead of a self-centered, isolationist who only cares about himself. What do you think, Mark? The first option sounds awesome. People will never forget what you did that went awry. But, you would be a much more significant contributor to this world if you ameliorated one of the worst threats to our planet that has ever existed.

To date, history reveals a man consumed with his creation with little regard for consequences. According to *The Crimson*, Harvard's newspaper in 2003, then-undergraduate Zuckerberg was accused of "breaching security, violating copyrights, and violating individual privacy by creating the website, www.fa cemash.com. When notified by administrators that he was in hot water, Zuckerberg wrote an email to the Crimson saying that:

> "I understood that some parts were still a little sketchy and I wanted some more time to think about whether or not this was really appropriate to release to the Harvard community."
> "Issues about violating people's privacy don't seem to be surmountable."
> (Kaplan, 2003)

Hopefully, Zuckerberg will figure out how to protect people's privacy and develop ways to shield Facebook's users from lies, disinformation and conspiracy theories that threaten our democracy. Consistently enforcing of deplatforming—expelling and banning of a person, group, or business from a platform—for violations would be a great start.

References

Center for Humane Technology (2017). How social media hacks our brains. www.humanetech.com/brain-science.

Fox, C. (2020). Social media: How might it be regulated? BBC News, November 12. www.bbc.com/news/technology-54901083.

Harris, T. (2016The slot machine in your pocket. Der Spiegel International, July 27). www.spiegel.de/international/zeitgeist/smartphone-addiction-is-part-of-the-design-a-1104237.html.

Harris, T. (2017). How a handful of tech companies control billions of minds every day. TED Talk transcript. www.ted.com/talks/tristan_harris_how_a_handful_of_tech_companies_control_bil lions_of_minds_every_day/transcript.

Harris, T. (2020). We're 10 years into this mass hypnosis. *52 Insights*, September 6. www.52-insights.com/interview-social-media-tristan-harris-were-10-years-into-this-mass-hypnosis.

Hartig, H. (2021). In their own words: How Americans reacted to the rioting at the U.S. Capitol. Pew Research Center, January 15. www.pewresearch.org/fact-tank/2021/01/15/in-their-own-words-how-americans-reacted-to-the-rioting-at-the-u-s-capitol.

Jacoby, J. (2018). Transcript of interview with Roger McNamee. PBS, February 26. www.pbs.org/wgbh/frontline/interview/roger-mcnamee.

Kaplan, K. (2003). Facemash creator survives ad board. *The Harvard Crimson*, November 19. www.thecrimson.com/article/2003/11/19/facemash-creator-survives-ad-board-the.

Martinez-Conde, S. and Macknick, S. (2014). How the color red influences our behavior. *Scientific American*, November 1. www.scientificamerican.com/article/how-the-color-red-influences-our-behavior.

Mbe, V. (2020). A conversation with Tristan Harris, co-founder and president of the center for humane technology. *Thought Economics*, October 29. https://thought economics.com/tristan-harris.

McNamee, R. (2019). *Zucked: Waking Up to the Facebook Catastrophe*. Penguin Press.

Ohlheiser, A. (2020). It's too late to stop Qanon with fact checks and account bans. *MIT Technology Review*, July 26. www.technologyreview.com/2020/07/26/1005609/qanon-facebook-twitter-youtuube.

Prescott, C. (2015). Internet access – households and individuals. Office for National Statistics, UK. www.ons.gov.uk/peoplepopulationandcommunity/householdcharacter istics/homei nternetandsocialmediausage/bulletins/internetaccesshouseholdsandindivi duals/2015-08- 06.

Public Religion Research Institute (2021). Understanding Qanon's connection to American politics, religion, and media consumption. May 27. www.prri.org/resea rch/qanon-conspiracy-american-politics-report.

Rollwage, M., Loosen, A., Hauser, T.U., Moran, R., Dolan, R.J., and Fleming, S.M. (2020). Confidence drives a neural confirmation bias. *Nature Communications*, 11(1), 1–11.

Scrivens, R. (2020). Former extremists play a key role in combatting extremism. Rantt Media, November 16. https://rantt.com/how-to-deradicalize-extremists.

Skinner, B. (1938). *The Behavior of Organisms*. New York: Appleton-Century-Crofts.

von Behr, I., Reding, A., Edwards, C., and Gribbon, L. (2013). Radicalization in the digital era: The use of the internet in 15 cases of terrorism and extremism. RAND Europe, p. xii. www.rand.org/content/dam/rand/pubs/research_reports/RR400/RR453/RAND_RR453.pdf.

West, D. (2021). The role of misinformation in Trump's Insurrection. Brookings Institution. www.brookings.edu/blog/techtank/2021/01/11/the-role-of-misinformation-in-trumps-insurrection.

Working Group on Infodemics (2020). Forum on Information & Democracy. https://informationdemocracy.org/wp-content/uploads/2020/11/ForumID_Report-on-infodemics_101120.pdf.

Yaraghi, N. (2019). How should social media platforms combat misinformation and hate speech? Brookings Institution. www.brookings.edu/blog/techtank/2019/04/09/how-should- social-media-platforms-combat-misinformation-and-hate-speech.

Chapter 14

Pandemic Blame Game, Or Politicians Behaving Badly

As of May 2022, some 515 million cases of COVID-19 had been confirmed, including 6.24 million deaths since the pandemic began in early 2020. When this volume arrives on bookstore shelves, I know that these numbers will be, sadly, already out-of-date. This is despite the fact the former President Trump said on numerous occasions that it was totally under control and added insult to injury by claiming there were very few cases in the United States. While cases were rising and people were dying he also said it was going away.

The facts are quite different. The Delta variant was dubbed one of the most contagious respiratory viruses in humans and was the primary driver behind the fourth wave of infections that swept through the world. Then the Omicron variant came along and was even more contagious. All of these findings lead to a natural question: how did we get here? Some of it is obvious: Areas with low vaccination rates experienced the highest case spikes and deaths, and early vaccine export bans kept resources in wealthy countries. Even after the World Health Organization launched COVAX, an endeavor aiming to provide global equitable access to vaccines, some countries still do not have enough vaccines, and still others, many in Africa, have none at all (Larson, 2021).

As discussed in other chapters, projective identification and blame shifting has plenty to do with how leaders managed the coronavirus pandemic. One of the most far-reaching examples of projective identification occurred when President Trump first addressed the impending consequences posed by COVID-19, but he was not the only global leader who badly mishandled the pandemic. This chapter will examine how he and other leaders, whose mismanagement was rooted in unconscious projective identification, caused many people to die who could have survived with more conscientious leadership. Shifting the blame to other people also played a major role in how the pandemic was mismanaged.

Some of the worst transgressions can be credited to Donald Trump, Narendra Modi, and Recep Tayyip Erdoğan, leaders who already use divisive rhetoric to confront and tear down those around them, and that talent helped them successfully shift blame for the pandemic onto targets within the country as well as in other countries. They shirked responsibility, while, shockingly,

DOI: 10.4324/9781003202387-15

retaining a sizeable portion of the electorate on their sides. These leaders style themselves as "wartime presidents" who are "fighting an invisible enemy" (Trump at daily coronavirus pandemic briefing, 2020), but when it came right down to it, none of these men (and they are all men; female leaders like New Zealand's Jacinda Ardern, Taiwan's Tsai-Ing-wen, and Germany's Angela Merkel led their countries through the crisis with greater empathy and compassion than their male populist counterparts), actually took up the proverbial charge and led the way through this crisis.

How Trump viewed and handled the COVID-19 pandemic in the U.S. is, unfortunately, the perfect case study for how he looks at the world around him and his role within it, and is why this chapter devotes a significant amount of space to him—much of this chapter hails from my book on the Trump presidency where I discuss, among other topics, his role in mishandling the pandemic. That material has been updated here, and it is worth including in this book because I believe Trump laid the groundwork for how other populist leaders addressed the pandemic in their countries by legitimizing quack cure-alls, deflecting blame, and engaging in psychological warfare.

Projective identification can emerge in a number of ways when a person in authority deals with a complex, alarming, or unpredictable situation. This often includes blame-shifting, gaslighting and minimizing as well as when one engages in a type of magical thinking wherein a person "decides" that something is true and then navigates in the world acting as if the 'fantasy' they created is a fact. Trump and key members of his administration engaged in these thought processes starting in February 2020, when it first became apparent that a novel coronavirus could wreak havoc on America's citizens and economy, not to mention their global standing.

The results were devastating and led to confusion, frustration, and loss of trust so extensive in the midst of a pandemic that the effects caused millions to be sick and thousands to die needlessly because of Trump's fantasy that COVID-19 was very well contained in the United States. He "decided" what was happening and thereafter believed it, despite it being false. He then projected that dangerous falsehood onto the American people.

COVID-19 is the disease caused by the SARS-CoV-2 novel coronavirus that was first identified in Wuhan Province, China, and Trump's insistence on calling it things like the "Chinese virus," "Wu Flu," or "Kung Flu," revealed his penchant for name-calling and bullying. While it might be true that the COVID-19 pandemic did not originate on U.S. soil, once community spread in the U.S. was identified, the responsibility for how the virus was handled lay squarely on the shoulders of American leadership. Alarmingly, the Trump administration's continuous broadcasting of denigrating statements and accusations about Asians led to a stark increase in anti-Asian harassment and assault (Anti-Defamation League, 2020).

Once it became clear that the COVID-19 epidemics in China and Italy made inroads in the U.S., Trump began shifting blame for any negative outcomes away from himself—a tactic he never relinquished, even as a private citizen. As it became clear that death and mortality from COVID-19 in the U.S. was caused by a knotty combination of failures in public health policy and lapses in personal judgment—some of it undeniably preventable—Trump vehemently denied any of it was his fault.

In contrast, some leaders around the world, faced with the possibility of severe outbreaks, did not mince words when speaking of the seriousness of their situations. South Korean President Moon Jae-in warned of "a grave turning point" in the virus' spread (BBC News, 2020). China's President Xi Jinping acknowledged "shortcomings" in China's response and said lessons must be learned from the country's "largest public health emergency."

While this next claim might appear to be an objective statement of fact, it is actually a laser-like refocusing of blame onto a single individual. Trump has no shortage of white whales, including TikTok and the U.S. Postal Service, but none so bedevilling as his presidential predecessor, Barack Obama, whom he repeatedly accused of having left him "nothing" with which to fight the coronavirus pandemic. A quick fact-check shows that the Obama Administration left office with intact pandemic response plans and relatively robustly staffed and funded public health agencies (Timm, 2020).

Unsurprisingly, these claims came to include Joe Biden as the two faced off in the run-up to the 2020 presidential election.

A tweet from September 3, 2020, shows Trump's target-creep:

> Sleepy Joe Hiden' was acknowledged by his own people to have done a terrible job on a much easier situation, H1N1 Swine Flu. The OBiden Administration failed badly on this, & now he sits back in his basement and criticizes every move we make on the China Virus. DOING GREAT JOB!
>
> (Trump archive, 2020)

But bullies will be bullies. Not having the ability or opportunity to directly affront the 44th President of the United States, Trump so profoundly resented Obama that he is alleged to have hired an actor resembling him to participate in a video in which Trump "ritualistically belittled the first black president and then fired him" (Orden, 2020).

"It's going to disappear. One day it's like a miracle—it will disappear." Trump's February 27, 2020, declaration at the White House was nothing more than gaslighting. In June 2020, as cases were surging in new hotspots daily, Trump was still saying this. But rather than "fade away," cases rose (Halon, 2020). Were people seeing things that were not there? Was the news coverage of medical personnel and patients not real? Were we starting to think, like the female protagonist who is abused by her husband in the 1920 film *Gaslight,* we were going crazy? In this particular case, it is likely Trump was trying to reassure supporters who might have been on the fence about whether it would be safe to attend a large rally in Tulsa, Oklahoma, where neither social distancing nor face coverings would be required.

When a person in a leadership position expresses a conviction or a mood, their appointees often blindly parrot and even amplify their sentiments. Echoing Trump's claims of the low level of threat the virus posed were people in his cabinet, including Vice-President Mike Pence, who in June falsely stated, "We are flattening the curve" (Qiu, 2020). In April 2020 Trump's son-in-law, Jared Kushner, was enthused about the country beating COVID-19 and the economy and life in general coming "roaring back again" by summer (Lahut, 2020). By July, however, the U.S. was clearly still overwhelmed by the virus as people continued to deal with an extended series of outbreaks. Some public health officials called this phase "a second wave," with death tolls setting daily records.

Additionally, the virus has disproportionately attacked people of color across all age groups, even in younger cohorts where age is usually a positive factor in avoiding death. For example, based on data received on June 6, 2020, among those aged 45–54, Black and Latino death rates were, according to the CDC, at least six times higher than for whites (Ford, 2020). Some political observers have posited that Black lives were put on the line to ensure the economic engine of the U.S. does not falter (Server, 2020). Ultra-conservative pundits even argued that the death tolls were not so bad when it became clear that more nonwhites were dying than whites.

When Mike Pence was put in charge of the U.S. Coronavirus Task Force in February 2020, many observers noted the irony in the appointment: Few politicians have as poor a record on public health as he did at the time. Aside from being a lifelong advocate of policies denying women reproductive health services, early on in his career he was a vocal apologist for Big Tobacco, downplaying the link between smoking and lung cancer, and as governor of Indiana he enabled the worst outbreak of HIV the state had ever seen by severely cutting public health funding and delaying the establishment of needle exchange programs (Westman, 2020). "We've tested more than any other country combined," declared Trump erroneously in May 2020 (Luthra, 2020).

Once it was out in the open that the U.S. was facing a major public health emergency, and Trump had changed his tune to openly acknowledge as much, then the more familiar braggadocio Trump has come to be associated with came raining down, fast and furious. In early March 2020, amidst a widespread testing shortage, Trump claimed, "Anybody that needs a test, gets a test. We—they're there. They have the tests. And the tests are beautiful" (Trump, March 2020). By May he enthusiastically lobbed inflated numbers about U.S. testing:

"This week, the United States will pass 10 million tests conducted—nearly double the number of any other country. We're testing more people per capita than South Korea, the United Kingdom, France, Japan, Sweden, Finland, and many other countries—and, in some cases, combined."

(Trump, May 11, 2020)

These responses were examples of blatant exaggeration which is a polite way of saying that Trump was lying, or, if we want to be more generous, knowingly stretching the truth about what level of testing the U.S. had both the capacity for, and the political will to carry out. This is the same person who, during his 2016 campaign, said, "We will honor the American people with the truth, and nothing else" (Trump, 2016).

In reality, the countries that had early success beating back the virus did so through robust testing campaigns the likes of which we did not see in the U.S. for months. While abundant testing—in both symptomatic and asymptomatic people—works to control the virus if it is followed by contact tracing and other public health measures, it can also be very alarming, or very sobering, depending on how one looks at it.

More Testing Equals More Cases

On several occasions, Trump said that he did not want to bolster testing capabilities in the U.S.—because he did not want to see more cases recorded (McDonald, 2020). Not only is this a superbly misguided way to approach an infectious disease, but were he a doctor, he might be facing malpractice suits for negligence. His approach since the early days of the pandemic has included measures to cloud transparency and with it, the appearance that he is not to blame, as when he insisted that travelers on a cruise ship—many of them elderly and sick with COVID-19—that had docked in California be kept on the ship, saying, "I like the numbers being where they are. I don't need to have the numbers double because of one ship that wasn't our fault" (McFall-Johnson, 2020).

Take Hydroxychloroquine

The bottom line is that, like anyone who is fundamentally insecure, Trump was and probably still is on a constant hunt for anything—positive or negative—to be remembered by. Accordingly, he periodically pushed various treatments, however unsubstantiated, dubious, or downright dangerous, in the hope one of them would be his legacy. While medical experts were sounding alarms about the potential risks for some individuals who were taking or thinking about using hydroxychloroquine to either treat or prevent COVID-19, Trump reported his experience as an early adopter of the untested drug: "I get a lot of tremendously positive news on the hydroxy," he said, adding, "What do you have to lose?" (Karni and Thomas, 2020).

An April White House fact sheet noted that 28 million tablets of Hydroxychloroquine had been shipped across the country from the Strategic National Stockpile (Trump, April 2020).

There are worse examples of Trump and various people—for one, the MyPillow CEO Mike Lindell, who Anderson Cooper called a "snake oil salesman"—in his circle who promoted dangerous prophylaxes and treatments for COVID-19, including, injecting bleach, (Rogers and Hauser, 2020) and taking oleandrin (Swann, 2020). They would be laughable if not for the ease with which they seemed to result in the Food and Drug Administration weakening their own regulatory standards to push some of them through, their relationship to various financial stakeholders, and most tragically, the people who hurt themselves by following bad advice.

At Warp Speed: With the Vaccine Came Hesitancy

The Trump administration enthusiastically claimed victory for the vaccine. The idea that one would be ready before the November election, even giving orders for personnel and health care facilities to be mobilized, the "October Surprise" was never likely to materialize. For a leader to fast-track public health interventions that have life-saving potential is not necessarily a bad thing, but in this case, the results could have proven deadly. Authorizing the speeding up of trials could have led to skipping safeguards and regular safety protocols. And forcing state health authorities to put in place large scale immunization capabilities before there is an actual vaccine to distribute is arguably a diversion of resources that would be better aimed at known virus mitigation efforts like enhanced testing.

Scared that a rush to approval would jeopardize the public's already wavering confidence in a new vaccine's safety, for the first time in U.S. history, a group of drug companies vowed not to release any vaccine that did not meet the usual rigorous safety and efficacy standards required for new drugs (Thomas, 2020). The damage was already done, however, as studies showed that fewer than half of Americans said they would get a vaccine if it was available—and that held true, despite the superb efficacy of the drugs. During the summertime surge of the fourth COVID-19 wave in the United States, fully 99.2% of people who were hospitalized or who died from the virus were unvaccinated—a stunning testament to the efficacy of the vaccinations (Johnson and Stubbe, 2021).

Operation Warp Speed provided $18 billion in funding for the development of vaccines and encouraged the public-private partnership of the development of vaccines at an unprecedented pace. The Pfizer vaccine, which was 95% effective against the early strains of the virus, did not receive government funding, but did secure a $2 billion dollar contract to produce 100 million doses. Moderna was allocated up to $955 million from the federal government for the development of its vaccine which ultimately showed a 94.5% efficacy against the early strains. Of course, it is a tribute to human ingenuity that these vaccines were developed so quickly and with such efficacy, and Trump should be proud of such an achievement, however, he could not help himself from claiming near-total credit.

Trump's polarizing message brought the anti-vaxxer movement to the forefront of the presidential election and remains a significant roadblock to stopping further spread and mutation of the virus—we are now at a point where the lambda variant might be immune to those vaccines developed at lightning speed.

Trump undermined public confidence in vaccines, and Americans remain skeptical at their peril. Is it fair to say that the Biden administration has also facilitated this divide by politicizing vaccination and flip-flopping on the rationale behind mask mandates? Of course, but Joe Biden is not a populist and certainly does not promote dangerous elixirs like bleach to cure COVID-19. The anti-vaxxer movement has grown in the United States in various forms since at least the end of the 19th century with the creation of the Anti-Vaccination Society of America in 1879 (Novak, 2018), but Trump made it political. Recall that Trump was absent when Mike Pence rolled up his sleeve for his televised jab, that was not a mistake; his presence would have legitimized the vaccine for millions of Americans. "Trump helped re-energize the anti-vaccine movement," said vaccine expert Dr. Peter Hotez. "And now he wants to pivot and make this his greatest accomplishment" (Stolberg, 2021). Trump's ability to sway perception is unquestioned; just imagine the shift in vaccination rates if he came out and wholeheartedly supported vaccinations.

Trump was not the only world leader to bungle the coronavirus response. On Modi's watch, India became the epicenter of the global pandemic in May 2021, when 400,000 new cases were being reported per day, with 3,500 daily reported deaths—numbers, by most accounts, that underestimate the true toll (Slater, 2021). The Center for Global Development estimates that the real death count from COVID-19 as of July 2021 ranged from 3.4 million to 4.9 million (Anand, Sandefur, and Subramanian, 2021).

Modi ordered a complete, 21-day lockdown in March 2020, just months after it seemed the virus was on the wane. In a country of 1.3 billion people, this sudden order caught many Indians off-guard, jobless, and hungry. Hospitals were overwhelmed with patients and ran out of oxygen. People died outside hospitals (NDTV, 2021). Makeshift funeral pyres burned throughout cities and the countryside, while millions of newly unemployed migrants returned to their villages where they hoped to find food and water. Some died en route (Pathi, Salliq, and Nessman, 2021).

In February 2021 Modi declared victory over the virus: "It can be said with pride that India not only defeated COVID-19 under the able, sensitive, committed and visionary leadership of Prime Minister Narendra Modi, but also infused in all its citizens the confidence to build an "Atmanirbhar Bharat,'[Self-Reliant India]" a press release declared prematurely for Modi's Bharatiya Janata Party (Bharatiya Janata Party Press Release, 2021). Unfortunately, that celebration came too early. India began reopening in June 2020. As emergency hospitals were being dismantled, Modi announced plans to upgrade permanent healthcare infrastructure: building more oxygen plants and getting more people vaccinated. But many of those planned updates did not happen, most of the population remained unvaccinated, and the country faced another surge without the necessary upgrades or tools to do battle with the virus.

In March 2021 Modi dedicated most of his monthly radio address to apologizing to the citizens of India "for tough decisions" as he called them, acknowledging that the lockdown was acutely felt by:

"my poor brothers and sisters...They [the poor] must be thinking what kind of Prime Minister is this who has locked up all of us. I specifically ask forgiveness from them. But looking at the world, this looks like the only option."

(Phukan, 2020)

It appears that Modi and his officials did not advise state ministers of their decision to enact a countrywide lockdown, according to a BBC investigation that found "no evidence of key experts or government departments being consulted prior to the lockdown being implemented" (BBC, 2021).

In April 2021 Modi addressed a crowd of supporters at a campaign rally in West Bengal: "I have never seen such a huge crowd before! Wherever I can see, I can only see people. I can see nothing else" (Pathi, Salliq, and Nessman, 2021). Though spring 2021 brought another surge in cases, a climbing death toll combined with a botched vaccine rollout, Modi did not call for another lockdown, nor did he cancel the aforementioned rally, cricket matches, or a massive Hindu festival. The situation became so dire that the vice-president of the Indian Medical Association, Dr. Navjot Dahiya called Modi a "super spreader" for allowing such large gatherings to happen. In a classic move of projective identification, Modi shifted responsibility for the pandemic response by laying the burden on local and state governments—states like Uttar Pradesh—that were ill-equipped to handle the pandemic on their own.

As the death toll and case numbers rose, Modi and his cabinet downplayed the severity of the problem. When vaccines became available, only 9 percent of Indians were at least partly vaccinated—and this in a country whose citizens trust vaccinations. "The problem is not that we can't trust these vaccines," explained Caravan magazine reporter Chaht Rana, "the problem is that we did not communicate in a way that instills faith in these vaccines" (Harris, 2021).

For a while, government officials attempted to keep stories about hospitals at capacity and lack of oxygen out of the news. For example, two starkly different narratives about the pandemic have emerged from the state of Uttar Pradesh, which shares a border with Nepal. Reports coming out of the region suggested that there were oxygen shortages at regional hospitals (Dahiya and Goel, 2021). Government representatives, meanwhile, claimed that there was "no shortage of oxygen" but rather that "black-marketeering and hoarding" was to blame. In truth, a black market popped up for oxygen, but volunteers eventually stepped in to distribute free oxygen cylinders to those in need. "It's very clear that both the central and state governments have failed, and so it's up to small NGOs and civilians to try and step in and do what we can. But it's not enough, it's not even nearly enough to fill the gap," said Mohit Arora of Sewa Satkar Trust, an organization providing as many oxygen cylinders as it can to meet some of the overwhelming demand (Ellis-Petersen, 2021).

To tamp down criticism, Modi's government successfully petitioned Twitter to block posts critical of his response to the pandemic, citing the country's Information Technology Act of 2000. Though the posts remain visible outside of India, the Ministry of Electronics and Information Technology told CNN that these posts were fomenting panic by "using unrelated, old and out of context images or visuals, communally sensitive posts and misinformation about Covid-19 protocols" (Madhok and Suri, 2021). One of the blocked posts, written by opposition leader Moloy Ghatak, said:

"India will never forgive PM @narendramodi for underplaying the corona situation in the country and letting so many people die due to mismanagement. At a time when India is going through a health crisis, PM chose to export millions of vaccine to other nations."

(Ghatak, 2020)

Dissent might have been quieted, but Modi's mishandling of the pandemic created an unnecessary economic and social disaster on top of what the virus wrought. India's post-pandemic economic recovery was stifled due in large part to the real death toll numbering in the millions rather than the official hundreds of thousands, as well as a devastating second wave of the virus.

Erdoğan's Handling of Pandemic Costs Lives, Consolidates Power

For some populist leaders, there's nothing like an old-fashioned crisis to consolidate power, and Turkey's Recep Tayyip Erdoğan is no exception. After a failed coup attempt in 2016, Erdoğan's primary objective became focused on rooting out dissent wherever it appeared. During the pandemic, Erdoğan authorized the government to enforce Article 217 in the Turkish Penal Code to investigate:

"any person who publicly provokes the public to disobey the law and such provision is capable of disturbing public peace, shall be sentenced to a penalty of imprisonment for a term of six months to two years or a judicial fine."

(Turkey Penal Code, Part 5, Article 217 (1))

A 2005 provision to that article increases the penalty by "one half" if the offences "are committed through the press or broadcasting." Social media and traditional news outlets were natural targets, and Amnesty International found that the government has targeted journalists, doctors, and other critics under the auspices of this law:

"Between 11 March [2020], when the first positive cases of the infection was declared, and 21 May, the Cyber Crimes Unit of the Interior Ministry alleged that 1,105 social media users had made propaganda for a terrorist organization, including by 'sharing provocative Corona virus posts.'"

(Amnesty International, 2020)

Amnesty spoke to detainees—journalists and doctors, mostly—who reported that they increasingly felt pressure to self-censor and to downplay the severity of the situation. It is also much easier to blame citizens for the pandemic than to take constructive criticism or actually put effective policy measures in place.

Throughout 2020, Erdoğan blamed international anti-Turkish conspiracies for the downfall of the Turkish economy and for his mishandling of the pandemic. "We see ourselves as an inseparable part of Europe. However, this does not mean that we will bow down to overt attacks to our country and nation, veiled injustices, and double standards," he said in a speech to his Justice and Development Party (Dettmer, 2020).

It appears that Erdoğan threw caution to the wind in March 2021, when thousands of ruling party supporters joined him in an Ankara stadium. Erdoğan spoke for nearly two hours, but said he cut his speech short to prevent unnecessary exposure to the coronavirus (AP News, 2021). In the same month Turkey tallied over 15,000 new coronavirus cases in a single day, which did not prompt Erdoğan to impose any new restrictions to stem the surge. "We decided to continue the current practice in our cities in today's meeting and to closely follow the developments," he said to reporters (Reuters, 2021). A year later, the country would report 59,000 new cases in a single day, showing that any mitigation strategies had not worked.

The full extent of the pandemic on Turkey remains unclear; outsiders asserted that Erdoğan's government did not do enough to discourage congregate gatherings and mask-wearing (Cookman, 2021). The government inflated how many people were vaccinated as well; in April 2021, Turkey's health minister claimed that the country "has administered the most [vaccinations] in the world," which is not supported by any global data (Cookman,

2021). In contrast, the country was ranked the second-worst in the world for its response to the pandemic (Bekdil, 2021). Consider, for example, the inexplicable restrictions imposed on the 82 million Turks:

> The government launched a "stay at home" campaign but kept workplaces open. The 65+ age group was banned from public travel but not from flying. They were not allowed to go out for groceries but were free to go to the mosque .... Shopping malls were allowed to open...while joggers were fined.... Eateries could remain open but were not allowed to play music.
>
> (Bekdil, 2021)

While Erdoğan crowed that his political rallies attracted thousands of people, he banned the Health Ministry from releasing the number of coronavirus cases. Such information would confirm what many already suspected: that the actual number of cases and deaths was much higher than reported, and that the economy would be stymied as a result. And yet, Erdoğan blamed the rest of the world for its failure to get a grip on the pandemic.

Caring, Compassion, and Mentalization: Empathy Can Save Lives

Though most of this book has focused on projective identification as employed by populist leaders, I believe it is important to provide a counterbalance to those narratives to demonstrate that hope does exist. Mentalization—the ability to listen to various viewpoints and understand the mental state of others—is a powerful tool in helping people out of crisis, as demonstrated by Anthony Fauci, former director of the Centers for Disease Control, and Ardern, the Prime Minister of New Zealand.

Early in the pandemic, Anthony Fauci frequently shared information that was at odds with what Trump said, but he did not attempt to personally attack the president: For example, Fauci said it was "absolutely wrong and inappropriate" to call COVID-19 the "Chinese coronavirus" (Haltwanger, 2020). As a lead member of the White House Coronavirus Task Force, Fauci is not only a widely respected physician and scientist, but he is a deeply empathetic person. "I don't want to embarrass him," he said about Trump.

> "I don't want to act like a tough guy, like I stood up to the president. I just want to get the facts out. And instead of saying, 'You're wrong,' all you need to do is continually talk about what the data are and what the evidence is."
>
> (Haltiwanger, 2020)

Fauci is the consummate practitioner of mentalization, taking profound care to listen before he speaks and to make room for expression of opinion contrary to his own. But in this situation, he also maintained his integrity by avoiding exaggeration, euphemisms and, of course, outright untruths.

While giving a commencement address in May 2020, Fauci illustrated flawlessly how important mentalization is to growth and healing, when he told the graduating seniors:

> "I am profoundly aware that graduating during this time and in this virtual way — unable to celebrate in person this important milestone in your lives with your friends, classmates and teachers — is extremely difficult. I deeply empathize with the situation in which you find yourselves."
>
> (Dwyer, 2020)

New Zealand Prime Minister Ardern's leadership during the pandemic has been particularly lauded. Researchers point to her style of communication, which she uses to motivate and unify, and "where a delicate blend of language use and intonation conveys *direction, meaning and empathy* (while still pulling no punches)" (Wilson, 2020). Ardern has explained the role of compassion in her leadership style:

> "It takes courage and strength to be empathetic, and I'm very proudly an empathetic and compassionate leader. I am trying to chart a different path, and that will attract criticism, but I can only be true to myself and the form of leadership I believe in."
>
> (Ardern, 2020)

Her country kept its borders closed to the rest of the world and, as of publication, will only begin to welcome vaccinated visitors from low-risk countries in 2022. Speaking about her role during the pandemic, Ardern did not shirk an ounce of responsibility to, or solidarity with, the people of New Zealand, saying:

> "The worst-case scenario is simply intolerable. It would represent the greatest loss of New Zealanders' lives in our country's history. I will not take that chance. The government will do all it can to protect you. None of us can do this alone."
>
> (Ardern, 2020)

References

Amnesty International (2020). Turkey: Stifling free expression during the COVID-19 pandemic. June 16. www.amnesty.org/en/latest/campaigns/2020/06/turkey-stifling-free-expression- during-the-covid19-pandemic.

Anand, A., Sandefur, J., and Subramanian, A. (2021). Three new estimates of India's all- cause excess mortality during the COVID-19 pandemic. The Center for Global Development, July 20. https://cgdev.org/publication/three-new-estimates-indias-all-cause-excess- mortality-during-covid-19-pandemic.

Anti-Defamation League (2020). Reports of anti-Asian assaults, harassment and hate crimes rise as coronavirus Spreads. www.adl.org/blog/reports-of-anti-asian-assaults-harassment-and-hate-crimes-rise- as-coronavirus-spreads.

AP News (2021). *Erdogan under fire for packed congress despite virus surge.* March 21. https://apnews.com/article/turkey-recep-tayyip-erdogan-coronavirus-pandemic-ankara- elections-a63b2af6c03c96d316df4e0a9518058d.

Ardern, J. (2020, March 21). *"COVID-19 Alert Level Increased,"* Speech to the people of New Zealand. www.beehive.govt.nz/speech/prime-minister-covid-19-alert-level-increased.

BBC News (2020). *Coronavirus: South Korea declares highest alert as infections surge.* February 23. www.bbc.com/news/world-asia-51603251.

BBC News (2021). *India COVID-19: PM Modi 'did not consult' before lockdown.* March 29. www.bbc.com/news/world-asia-india-56561095.

Bekdil, B. (2021). Turkey: How not to handle a pandemic. The Begin-Sadat Center for Strategic Studies. Bar-Ilan University. https://besacenter.org/turkey-how-not-to- handle-a-pandemic/.

Bharatiya Janata Party Press Release (2021). Resolution passed in BJP national office bearers meeting at NDMC convention centre, New Delhi. February 21. www.bjp.org/en/pressreleasesdetail/4491198/Resolution-passed-in-BJP-National- Office-Bearers-meeting-at-NDMC-Convention-Centre-New-Delhi- ?__cf_chl_jschl_tk__=pmd_mLtkXGvl3Lfvllxj1dhe9evQ9eSE4dGsHILJkkj8S.U-1632499827-0-gqNtZGzNArujcnBszQk9.

Cookman, L. (2021). What is the real extent of Turkey's COVID-19 crisis? Al Jazeera, April 14. www.aljazeera.com/news/2021/4/14/what-is-the-real-extent-of-turkeys-covid-crisis.

Dahiya, H. and Goel, K. (2021). Yoga says, 'no oxygen shortage in UP,' but here's a reality check. *The Quint*, April 29. www.thequint.com/coronavirus/yogi-adityanath-says-no- oxygen-shortage-in-uttar-pradesh-ground-reports-differ.

Dettmer, J. (2020). Will Erdogan complain about anti-Turkish conspiracy become self-fulfilling prophecy? Voice of America, December 3. www.voanews.com/europe/will-erdogan-complaint-about-anti-turkish-conspiracy-become-self-fulfilling-prophecy.

Dwyer, C. (2020). Anthony Fauci: 'Now is the time…to care selflessly about one another. NPR, May 23. www.npr.org/sections/coronavirus-live- updates/2020/05/23/861500804/anthony-fauci-now-is-the-time-to-care-selflessly-about- one-another.

Ellis-Petersen, H. (2021). 'People phone up pleading,'" the volunteers battling India's oxygen crisis. *The Guardian*, April 28. www.theguardian.com/world/2021/apr/28/people- phone-up-pleading-the-volunteers-battling-indias-oxygen-crisis.

Ford, T., et al. (2020). Race gaps in COVID-19 deaths are even bigger than they appear. Brookings Institution. www.brookings.edu/blog/up-front/2020/06/16/race-gaps-in-covid-19-deaths-are-even-bigger-than-they-appear.

Ghatak, M. (2021). Twitter. https://twitter.com/GhatakMoloy/status/1384385821956923393?ref_src=twsrc%5Etfw%7Ctwcamp%5Etweetembed%7Ctwterm%5E1384385821956923393%7Ctwgr%5E%7Ctwcon%5Es1_&ref_url=https%3A%2F%2Fwww.theverge.co

m%2F2021%2F4%2F24%2F22400976%2Ftwitter-removed-tweets-critical-india-censor -coronavirus.

Haltiwanger, J. (2020). Dr. Fauci said he would never call coronavirus the 'Chinese virus,' which Trump insists on doing. *Business Insider*, March 23. www.businessinsider.com/fa uci-said-he-would-never-call-coronavirus-the- chinese-virus-2020-3.

Halon, Y. (2020). Trump tells 'Hannity' Coronavirus is 'fading away' ahead of controversial Tulsa rally. Fox News Flash, June 17. www.foxnews.com/media/trump- ha nnity-coronavirus-fading-away-tulsa-rally.

Harris, M. (2021). The Trumpiness of India's COVID surge. Slate, April 29. https://sla te.com/news-and-politics/2021/04/india-covid-surge-modi-government- trump.html.

Johnson, C. and Stubbe, M. (2021). Nearly all COVID deaths in the US are now among unvaccinated. AP News, June 29. https://apnews.com/article/coronavirus-pa ndemic-health- 941fcf43d9731c76c16e7354f5d5e187.

Karni, A. and Thomas, K. (2020). Trump says he's taking hydroxychloroquine, prompting warning from health experts. *The New York Times*, May 18. www.nytim es.com/2020/05/18/us/politics/trump-hydroxychloroquine-covid- coronavirus.html.

Lahut, J. (2020). Jared Kushner said the US would be 'really rocking again' by July 7. *Business Insider*, July 10. www.businessinsider.com/kusher-rocking-again-by-july- quote- coronavirus-states-reopening-2020-7.

Larson, K. (2021). Vaccine deserts: Some countries have no COVID-19 jabs at all. AP News, May 9. https://apnews.com/article/africa-coronavirus-vaccine-coronavirus-pa ndemic- business-government-and-politics-2d5eab50c1ef8bd63b1a48331f4c3025.

Luthra, S. (2020). Trump's claim the US tested more than all countries combined is 'pants on fire' wrong. KHN, May 1. https://khn.org/news/trumps-claim-that-u-s-tes ted-more- than-all-countries-combined-is-pants-on-fire-wrong.

Madhok, D. and Suri, M. (2021). Twitter blocks posts in India critical of Narendra Modi's COVID-19 response. CNN Business, April 26. www.cnn.com/2021/04/26/ tech/twitter- covid-india-modi-facebook/index.html.

McDonald, J. (2020). Trump falsely says COVID-19 surge 'only' due to testing, misleads on deaths. FactCheck.org, June 25. www.factcheck.org/2020/06/trump-falsely-sa ys-covid-19-surge-only-due-to-testing-misleads-on-deaths.

McFall-Johnson, M. (2020). Trump said he wants to keep grand princess cruise passengers on the ship so that US coronavirus numbers don't 'double.' That strategy failed in Japan. *Business Insider*, March 6. www.businessinsider.com/trump-keep-pa ssengers-on-grand-princess-cruise-ship-coronavirus-2020-3.

NDTV (2021). Former diplomat died of COVID after long wait outside hospital, his wife says. April 29. www.ndtv.com/video/news/left-right-centre/former-diplomat- die d-of-covid-after-long-wait-outside-hospital-his-wife-says-584482?rdr=1.

Novak, S. (2018). The long history of America's anti-vaccination movement. *Discover*, November 26. www.discovermagazine.com/health/the-long-history-of-americas-anti- vaccination-movement.

Orden, E. (2020). In tell-all book, Michael Cohen says Trump hired a 'faux-Bama' before White House run. CNN, September 6. www.cnn.com/2020/09/05/politics/m ichael-cohen- book-trump-white-house/index.html.

Pathi, K., Salliq, S. and Nessman, R. (2021). India's virus surge damages Modi's image of competence. AP News, May 5. https://apnews.com/article/india-sports-cor onavirus-pandemic- health-d38a9060e8a115a5389f816b857cd481.

Penal code of Turkey. Part 5. Offenses against public peace. Article 217 (1). www.
venice.coe.int/webforms/documents/default.aspx?pdffile=CDL-REF(2016)011-e#:%
7E:text=(1)%20Turkish%20law%20shall%20apply,have%20been%20committed%2
0in%20Turkey.&text=then%20this%20offence%20is%20presumed%20to%20have%
20b een%20committed%20in%20Turkey.
Phukan, S. (2020). Coronavirus: I apologise for tough steps, says Narendra Modi in
Mann ki Baat. *The Hindu*, March 29. www.thehindu.com/news/national/pm-addres
ses-first- mann-ki-baat-amid-covid-19-lockdown/article31197188.ece.
Qui, L. (2020). As cases surge, Pence misleads on Coronavirus pandemic, Pence misleads on Coronavirus pandemic. *The New York Times*, June 26. www.nytimes.com/
2020/06/26/us/politics/coronavirus-pence-fact-check.html.
Reuters (2021). Turkey's Erdogan says new pandemic measures not being considered as
cases rise. March 15. www.reuters.com/article/us-health-coronavirus-turkey/turkey
s-erdogan-says-new-pandemic-measures-not-being-considered-as-cases- rise-idUSKBN
2B72DT.
Rogers, K. and Hauser, C. (2020). Trump's suggestion that disinfectants could be used to
treat coronavirus prompts aggressive pushback. *The New York Times*, April 24. www.
ny times.com/2020/04/24/us/politics/trump-inject-disinfectant-bleach-coronavirus.html.
Server, A. (2020). The coronavirus was an emergency until Trump found out who was
dying. *The Atlantic*, May 8. www.theatlantic.com/ideas/archive/2020/05/americas-ra
cial- contract-showing/611389.
Slater, J. (2021). India sets pandemic record with more than 400,000 new cases; Fauci
says crisis is 'like a war.' *The Washington Post*, May 1. www.washingtonpost.com/
world/2021/05/01/india-coronavirus.
Stolberg, S. (2021). Trump claims credit for vaccines. Some of his backers don't want
to take them. *The New York Times*, April 4. www.nytimes.com/2020/12/18/us/poli
tics/trump- vaccine-skeptics.html.
Swann, J. (2020). Trump eyes new unproven coronavirus cure. Axios, August 16. www.
axios.com/trump-covid-oleandrin-9896f570-6cd8-4919-af3a- 65ebad113d41.html.
Thomas, K. et al. (2020). Pharma companies plan joint pledge on vaccine safety. *The
New York Times*, September 4. www.nytimes.com/2020/09/04/science/covid-vaccine-
pharma-pledge.html?referringSource=articleShare.
Timm, J. (2020). Fact check: Trump falsely claims Obama left him 'nothing' in the
national stockpile. NBC News, May 6. www.nbcnews.com/politics/donald-trump/fa
ct-check-trump-falsely-claims-obama-left-him-nothing-national-n1201406.
Trump, D. (2016). Transcript of Donald Trump at the G.O.P. Convention. *The New
York Times*, July 22. www.nytimes.com/2016/07/22/us/politics/trump-transcript-rnc-
address.html.
Trump, D. (2020). Press conference: Donald Trump joins the daily coronavirus pandemic briefing. March 6. www.youtube.com/watch?v=KSWcH_n8Bm8&t=1137s.
Trump, D. (2020). Remarks by President Trump after tour of the Centers for Disease
Control and Prevention. March 6. https://trumpwhitehouse.archives.gov/briefings- sta
tements/remarks-president-trump-tour-centers-disease-control-prevention-atlanta-ga.
Trump, D. (2020). Transcript: President Donald J. Trump has led a historic mobiliza-
tion to combat the coronavirus. White House Archives, April 14. https://trump
whitehouse.archives.gov/briefings-statements/president-donald-j-trump-led-   histor
ic-mobilization-combat-coronavirus.

Trump, D. (2020). Remarks by President Trump in a Press Briefing on COVID-19
Testing. White House Archives. May 11. https://trumpwhitehouse.archives.gov/
briefings-statements/remarks-president-trump-press-briefing-covid-19-testing/

Trump, D. (2020). Sleepy Joe Hiden' was acknowledge by his own people....Twitter.
The Trump Twitter Archive, September 3. www.thetrumparchive.com/?searchbox=
%22sleepy+joe+hiden%22.

Westman, N. (2020). Mike Pence, who enabled an HIV outbreak in Indiana, will lead
US Coronavirus response. *The Verge*, February 26. www.theverge.com/2020/2/26/
21155286/mike-pence-coronavirus-response-hiv.

Wilson, S. (2020). Pandemic Leadership: Lessons from New Zealand's Approach to
COVID-19. Leadership Special Issue, Volume 16, issue 3. https://journals.sagepub.
com/doi/full/10.1177/1742715020929151.

Chapter 15

Ecological Grief
Mourning a Changing Planet and Fighting Populist Denialism

Conservationist and author Aldo Leopold was one of the earliest observers to codify the phenomenon of grief associated with the disappearance of plants, animals, and ecosystems. In 1949 he said, "One of the penalties of an ecological education is to live alone in a world of wounds" (Global Citizen).

Today, humans across the globe confront losses in the natural world that have significantly altered their way of life, and these changes have mental health consequences as well. It is time to recognize, if not embrace, our collective grief for our imperiled planet, and mobilize our efforts to mitigate the damages before it is too late. Many populists feel otherwise. Some believe the idea of global warming is a clever hoax devised by elitist international cabals seeking to impose restrictive regulations and impinge on the sovereignty of nations. Other populists, sensing change among the voting electorate, have crafted "green policies" that argue for national unity rather than global cooperation in the fight against climate change.

But let's dispense with the falsehoods before examining ecological grief and how populist leaders are actively battling the very notion of climate change. Climate change is real. It is here, and it is killing us and our planet. It is hard to pick one event or part of the globe that reflects the rapid pace of environmental distress—there are so many proverbial and literal fires burning across the globe, it is hard to keep track of all of them. Ocean levels rise, once-in-every-200-year storms cripple major metropolitan areas, apocalyptic fires burn in places better known for their snow—the climate has altered and nearly all of it was predicted. In 1965 President Lyndon B. Johnson received a startling report written by some of America's top scientists. The topic of *Restoring the Quality of Our Environment* was not weapons, the Vietnam War, or chemical warfare, but rather how humans were rapidly baking planet Earth. Climate scientists Roger Revelle, Wallace Broecker, and others did not mince their words:

> The present rate of production of carbon dioxide from fossil fuel combustion is about a hundred times the average rate of release of calcium and magnesium from the weathering of silicate rocks. As long as this

DOI: 10.4324/9781003202387-16

ratio holds, precipitation of metallic carbonates will be unable to maintain an unchanging content of carbon dioxide in the atmosphere. Within a few short centuries, we are returning to the air a significant part of the carbon that was slowly extracted by plants and buried in the sediments during half a billion years.

(Revelle and Broecker, 1965)

How about this, also from the same paper:

Man is unwittingly conducting a vast geophysical experiment. Within a few generations he is burning the fossil fuels that slowly accumulated in the earth over the past 500 million years … The climatic changes that may be produced by the increased CO_2 content could be deleterious from the point of view of human beings. The possibilities of deliberately bringing about countervailing climatic changes therefore need to be thoroughly explored.

(Revelle, 1965, pp. 126–7)

The team predicted the melting of the Antarctic ice caps, rising sea levels, warming of the oceans, increased acidity of water, and other catastrophic events. In short, humans are responsible for the destabilizing and dramatic changes we are experiencing across the globe, and we have been aware of it for years.

Just this past year, according to the National Oceanic and Atmospheric Administration (NOAA), January 2021 in the United States was the seventh warmest in the 127 years since recording began. North America had its second-warmest January on record. Arctic sea ice was 6.5% below the 1981–2010 average and the ninth consecutive January with temperatures above the twentieth century average (National Oceanic and Atmospheric Administration, 2021). Great Lakes ice coverage was the smallest in decades. On January 25, an EF-3 tornado ravaged a Birmingham, Alabama suburb, leaving nearly ten miles of devastation. Tornadoes are usually atypical that time of year. Smoke from California wildfires reached the East Coast of the United States. North of the border, millions of shellfish boiled in their shells off the coast of Vancouver, British Columbia, during a July heatwave that also left dozens of humans dead (Yurk, 2021). In August 2021 Hurricane Ida leveled parts of Louisiana and killed people in New York and New Jersey, where flooding reached catastrophic levels. This is merely a sampling from one year in one part of the world. The climate crisis is not thirty years away, it is here, happening in real time.

In August 2021 the International Panel on Climate Change, an organ of the United Nations tasked with assessing climate change science, released a blistering report about the current state of the climate, confirming what many of us know in our bones: "Human-induced climate change is already affecting many weather and climate extremes in every region across the globe" (Intergovernmental Panel on Climate Change, 2021).

As climate change has increased the temperature of our oceans, hurricanes and tropical storms are more intense. The effects of tropical cyclones are numerous and well known. Stronger winds and heavier rains can cause severe flooding and destruction, which are predicted to occur with greater regularity through the twenty-first century. More powerful storms will also require more remediation efforts, which will be costly: according to the Center for Climate and Energy Solutions, eight of the ten costliest hurricanes on record in the United States have occurred since 2004, each resulting in billions of dollars in damage (Center for Climate and Energy Solutions, 2020).

In 2016 the Environmental Protection Agency released a paper entitled "Climate Change Indicators" and opened with searing lines echoing those written by President Johnson's climate scientists in 1965:

> The Earth's climate is changing. Temperatures are rising, snow and rainfall patterns are shifting, and more extreme climate events—like heavy rainstorms and record high temperatures—are already taking place. Scientists are highly confident that many of these observed changes can be linked to the levels of carbon dioxide and other greenhouse gases in our atmosphere, which have increased because of human activities.
>
> (Environmental Protection Agency, 2020)

Humans have been adding greenhouse gasses into the atmosphere at an increasing rate since the Industrial Revolution. NOAA's weather station on Mauna Loa in Hawaii recorded carbon dioxide at 419 parts per million in May 2021. That's the highest level in modern recorded history (National Oceanic and Atmospheric Administration, 2021). For comparison, the last time this much CO_2 was in our atmosphere was approximately 4 million years ago.

Though some world leaders might protest otherwise, none of this is the result of conspiracies carried out by a "Deep State;" in fact, French mathematician Jean-Baptiste Joseph Fourier (1768–1830) discovered the greenhouse effect in the 1820s. In *Théorie Analytique de la Chaleur* (1822) Fourier offers this introduction to the properties of heat conduction:

> Heat, like gravity, penetrates every substance of the universe, its rays occupy all parts of space. The object of our work is to set forth the mathematical laws which this element obeys. The theory of heat will hereafter form one of the most important branches of general physics...
>
> (Fourier, 1878)

Then, in mathematical pirouettes based on Newton's law of cooling, Fourier provides a fundamental equation for heat conduction and deduces that Earth's atmosphere acts like an insulator and that what gets trapped inside it heats the planet as well. The term "greenhouse effect" is not his, however; thank Swedish meteorologist Nils Gustaf Ekholm for conjuring that in 1901 (Ekholm, 1901).

As many of us bear witness to the death of our planet, we mourn. But how? Humans do not have processes in place to deal with the grief and anxiety that many of us feel. In *How We Grieve*, author and philosopher Thomas Attig explains that coping with loss is not passive, though we might feel helpless while in the moment. Loss of a loved one, he argues, requires relearning how survivors fit into the world. In the chapter entitled "Relearning the World," Attig offers an example where a couple's young son dies unexpectedly. After the funeral, the couple must relearn how to go through their days without their child.

> "It is difficult for Ed [the father] to find refuge from the pain. He is reminded of [son] Bobby wherever he turns...He sees Bobby's presence everywhere he goes....Ed cannot grasp just why or where he fits in...It is a struggle to discover, and make their own, ways of going on without him in that world. So much of what they had taken for granted in their lives is no longer sustainable, at least not in the way it was prior to Bobby's death."
>
> (Attig, 2010, pp. 103–106)

The death of a loved one, whether sudden or the result of years of illness, is difficult to accept, but can happen. As such, societies have mechanisms in place to deal with those losses. Death and mourning of loved ones are part of our culture—we are not immortal and expect that one day, we will all meet the same fate.

Losing people we love, Attig argues, means the world we once took for granted is no longer as it was. Those of us left behind must relearn our physical world, reexamine the places we took for granted and how they have changed. Although he does not examine the grief felt when natural disasters happen, I believe the process of environmental grief is similar. Let's consider the disappearance of the Amazon rainforest: somber images of clear-cut old-growth jungle replaced by palm oil trees can elicit feelings of great sadness and grief. Those sections of the Amazon will never, not even with the most aggressive feats of geoengineering, be restored to what they once were. Places that we once took for granted disappear, and there's no codified procedure for processing those feelings. Those feelings of anxiety and anger mingled with anticipation for the devastation to come are jumbled together and there is seemingly little any one human can do to change things. Without mourning rituals, these feelings of sadness, hopelessness, and anger seem out-of-place, misunderstood, or inappropriate, resulting in a kind of mental stasis where acceptance and closure never happen. Nor, then, is there healing or the cultivation of resilience.

In Attig's example, Bobby's parents find solace in the early days following their son's death by visiting his grave. "Different objects and places challenge each of us differently when we grieve," Attig writes. "The range of objects and places that challenge us is perhaps most affected by the nature of our relationship to the deceased." (Attig, 2010, p. 112) Keeping that premise in mind, how can a community effectively mourn the disappearance of a natural phenomenon? It turns out that relearning a relationship with a physical space is possible when reconciling eco grief: in 2019, two funerals were held—the first in Iceland, the other in the Swiss Alps—to mourn the loss of glaciers to climate change. The Okjokull glacier was the first of its kind in Iceland to be declared dead in 2014. The glacier once measured over 6.2 square miles, but by 2012 had dwindled to less than a quarter square mile. Researchers from Iceland and professors at Rice University organized the event, which involved trekking up a volcano near the site of the former glacier and memorializing the loss. Unlike an increase in carbon dioxide in the atmosphere, the disappearance of a glacier is tangible—satellite images from space confirm it— not to mention that barren rock covers land once frozen by ice is a physical manifestation that is impossible to ignore. "You don't feel climate change daily, it's something that happens slowly on a human scale, but very quickly on a geological scale," said a funeral attendee in a report published by *The Guardian*. "Seeing a glacier disappear is something you can feel, you can understand it and it's pretty visual," he said (Agence France-Presse, 2019).

Hardly a month later, hundreds of people dressed in black gathered in the Swiss Alps for another memorial, this time for the Pizol glacier, where a priest officiated, and mourners paid their respects by leaving bouquets of flowers where Pizol once loomed. Since 2006 the Pizol glacier lost nearly 90% of its volume and is the first glacier to be removed from the Swiss glacier surveillance network (Siad and Woodyatt, 2019). Had the pandemic not shut down in-person activities, would we have seen further such demonstrations through 2020 and 2021? Will there be more glacier funerals in the future?

Until recently, climate change was slow and abstract: it has been awfully hard to encourage people and governments to enact policies meant to prevent climate disasters when the pace of change seemed incremental or invisible (Cunsolo and Ellis, 2018). Winters with slightly less snow? No big deal, until thirty years goes by and residents of traditionally-snow-covered terrain find themselves with mud instead. This kind of slow or invisible change is hard to mourn in real time and also makes it challenging to mobilize efforts to combat it. If you cannot see it, it is hard to get upset about it.

Until you do. Until the day a farmer wakes up to fields inundated with river water. When fires burn so hot that they spawn their own weather systems. When a spring morning is eerily bereft of birdsong. When there's more plastic in the ocean than fish.

Researchers have coined new terms and phrases to identify these disorienting feelings of loss: eco-anxiety, environmental grief, ecoguilt. In a 2018 article that appeared in the journal *Nature*, scientists Ashlee Cunsolo and Neville Ellis agree that ecological grief is "an underdeveloped area of study" even though this kind of grief is an understandable and natural response to the ravages of climate change. Their paper posits that ecological grief is a type of mourning that deserves a more widespread recognition in part to help mourners process their grief and to find constructive outlets for their pain:

> [W]e anticipate, along with a small but growing number of scholars, that ecological grief will become an increasingly common human response to the losses encountered in the Anthropocene. To bear witness to ecological losses personally, or to the suffering encountered by others as they bear their own losses, is to be reminded that climate change is not just an abstract scientific concept. Rather, it is the source of much hitherto unacknowledged emotional and psychological pain, particularly for people who remain deeply connected to, and observant of, the natural world.
>
> (Cunsolo and Ellis, 2018)

The pandemic did not help matters: Mental health professionals reported a dramatic increase in negative mental health symptoms like depression, anxiety, and PTSD during the height of the pandemic (Panchal, Kamal, and Garfield, 2021). People's nerves are frayed. The climate crisis is testing all of us–including those whose job it is to listen and help others heal.

Some professionals say they are unequipped to help patients with this new kind of anxiety, finding themselves unable to find the right combination of words that could provide comfort (Whitcomb, 2021). A 2016 study conducted by researchers at Smith College found that over half of responding therapists felt ill-equipped to deal with patients in mental distress, owing to the climate crisis:

> The findings suggest that the internal reactions that therapists have to the topic of climate change may impact how they receive and respond to clients who talk about it in therapy, and also indicate that although the majority of therapists believe climate change is relevant to their field, many do not feel that that their training has equipped them to deal with the subject.
>
> (Whitcomb, 2021)

Moreover, the American Psychiatric Association anticipates that more people will be seeking mental health counseling as the crisis worsens. Therapists specializing in subspecialties, such as eco-therapy, are few and far-between.

It is easy to see why so many people feel hopeless and why funerals for glaciers feel appropriate. Extreme despair can impair our ability to make any changes, even small ones, so we as mental health professionals must find ways to encourage our patients to look beyond the horrible headlines and, if not overcome feelings of existential dread, then learn to channel those feelings into constructive action.

Processing Environmental Grief

Though in its infancy as a field, environmental mourning is growing. The nonprofit Good Grief Network, "…brings people together to metabolize collective grief, eco-anxiety, and other heavy emotions that arise in response to daunting planetary crises. Using a 10-Step approach…we run peer-to-peer support groups that help folks recognize, feel, and process their heavy emotions, so that these feelings may be transformed into meaningful actions."

Mourning our collective losses helps cultivate resilience while empowers participants to feel like they can enact meaningful solutions to the overwhelming number of environmental problems we face in our world today.

That being said, our world family as well as our children will all suffer untenable consequences if we do not change how we interact with the environment. "The danger is that unless we break with Exceptionalism and mourn our exaggerated sense of narcissistic entitlement, we may pay them lip service with kind words but throw them overboard as our zone of sacrifice while we carry on with carbon-intensive life as usual" (Weintraub, 2021, p. 299).

We need leaders willing to face this crisis with clarity, to acknowledge the grief many in the global community are experiencing. President Johnson signed the Clean Air Act into law in 1963, and two years later he shared the disturbing findings of the Revelle report with the public. Further, the various conservation measures he enacted did improve air and water quality—we can thank him for reducing air pollution by 50 million tons since 1970—but he did not have the solutions (or the greater political will) necessary to tackle the daunting task of reducing carbon emissions (National Parks Service, 2020). Subsequent presidents addressed visible signs of pollution while the larger invisible threat grew unchecked. Our leaders do not have the luxury of tackling low-hanging fruit and hoping a future leader will get the job done. It is up to us.

Populists See Climate Change as Existential Threat to Their Power

To say that it is infuriating to see the can kicked down the road is an understatement—those fifty-year-old predictions that stunned Johnson are now coming to pass—and it is clear that previous administrations chose to defer action on this issue rather than address it. Former President Donald Trump

happened to be at the helm when these disasters began manifesting themselves in significant ways. He proved himself neither willing nor prepared to
address this issue, or at the very least acknowledge its existence. His dismissal
of existing scientific data was dangerous for Americans for whom the effects
of climate change are already at hand.

Trump and his advisors politicized climate change, while Trump's expert
ability of shifting blame altered how we communicate with each other. These
behaviors made it nearly impossible to have an open and honest dialogue
about present and future environmental issues since even basic facts were
called into question under Trump's presidency, such as whether climate
change even exists (Trump dismantled 112 environmental rules during his
presidency). When facts are less important than ideology, there's little room
left for finding middle ground and even less hope of finding solutions that we
all need, no matter where we fall in our political beliefs—we are all breathing
the same air, after all.

The warning signs of the Trump administration's departure from the goals
set forth by the environmentally sensitive Obama administration began on
Trump's first day in office, when all references to climate change on the White
House website were removed and replaced with calls for "energy independence (Chreighton, 2017). Abrupt slashes to the Environmental Protection
Agency's budget for domestic programs were also a portent of what was to
come. Whether or not Trump believes the climate is changing in negative
ways is unclear. What is obvious is that he states his beliefs—both as president and as a private citizen—without adequate knowledge about the subject. Though hundreds, if not thousands, of scientists by now have shown
there are clear connections between human activity and global warming,
Trump decided not to heed their warnings.

If Trump were merely a passive climate change denier, then perhaps his
inaction would not be any worse for our country than the various panaceas
applied by previous presidents. Rather, he actively pressed the notion that
climate change is a fallacy. In a tweet from March 12, 2019, Trump quoted a
climate sceptic who misrepresented himself as a co-founder of Greenpeace:
"Patrick Moore, co-founder of Greenpeace: "The whole climate crisis is not
only Fake News, it's Fake Science. There is no climate crisis, there's weather
and climate all around the world, and in fact carbon dioxide is the main
building block of all life." @foxandfriends. Wow!" (Trump, 2019) Greenpeace
quickly issued a counter tweet saying that, "Patrick Moore was not a co-
founder of Greenpeace. He does not represent Greenpeace. He is a paid lob-
byist, not an independent source." (Moore's relationship with Greenpeace is
itself long and murky, but Moore remains very much persona non grata with
the organization.) But the damage was done: Trump's initial tweet was
retweeted some 32,000 times and liked by about 100,000 followers. Greenpeace's response was retweeted over 10,000 times. Actively denying climate
change is irrational and done at the expense of our existence as we know it.

Former President Trump also waffled on climate change, a behavior that confused his base as well as people around the world who followed him on social media platforms. At times he said that climate change did not really exist and was a costly hoax. Yet at other times he claimed to believe that it was an important issue that he cared about very much. With that type of leadership, how could a country make a positive contribution to cleaning up our environment?

Like all successful populists, Trump is charismatic—he understands how to talk to people and assure them that he is listening to them. And he speaks to more than the stereotypical base of white, poor, uneducated American men. Throughout his campaign, during his presidency, and now as a private citizen, Trump casts himself as an outsider, leading the people against a vast, frightening government conspiracy trying to force Americans to comply with burdensome programs. As such, his claims and his lies become irrelevant when wrapped up in theories of hijacked freedom and the American way. Data becomes meaningless and his stories about how cold the weather is or that climate change is a Chinese hoax are far more reassuring and relatable than the ominous threats of a warming planet. A lack of facts allowed Trump to weaponize misinformation and hurl it at those who would question him or debunk him with data.

It also helped Trump's political ambition that we are in the midst of an era when Americans are more inclined to doubt science—consider, for example, parents who refuse to vaccinate their children for fear of catching autism, even though there is no link between the two (Centers for Disease Control and Prevention, 2021). A recent Gallup poll found that the number of Americans who believe vaccines are important fell from 94 percent in 2001 to 84 percent in 2019. And though the majority of respondents said that vaccines are less dangerous than the diseases they prevent, 46 percent said they were unsure whether vaccines caused autism—down from 52 percent from Gallup's last poll in 2015, but still high enough to suggest that misinformation continues to influence the decision-making process.

Though hundreds of scientists agreed in the UN's report that climate change is a crisis of today, the grim assessment did not quite galvanize populist politicians as many global citizens might have hoped. Estimates issued by the World Resources Institute found that thirty percent of global greenhouse gas emissions emanate from countries with populist leaders: Brazil, India, and the Philippines among them (Dilbey, 2019). Internationally organized efforts to reduce carbon emissions are viewed by populists as direct attacks on their sovereignty.

In the recent past, right-leaning populists—Trump and Jair Bolsonaro among them—outright denied the existence of climate change. In 2019 members of Germany's Alternative für Deutschland (AfD) launched a campaign of climate change denialism, targeting sixteen-year-old Swedish environmental activist Greta Thunberg as a "climate protection hussy," and that international climate policy is "a 'pretense' for leaders to 'burden people with taxes'" (Deleja-Hotko, Müller, Traufetter, 2019). Climate change is a major topic in Germany, and AfD leadership cannot ignore it. But rather than acknowledge the facts about climate change, they are shifting the conversation by suggesting that human-induced climate change is a hoax and that any efforts to address the problem will bring economic disaster—a far greater and more immediate issue than fighting change we cannot always see.

But, as torrential rains and hellish fires become more commonplace, those once-invisible threats are now unavoidable. Sensing the shift among voter sentiment, populists have embraced a shift in tone and approach to the issue. Now, rather than saying that climate change does not exist, populist leaders argue that climate policies are internationally led threats against national sovereignty. Marine Le Pen's proposal to address climate change embraces a nationalist approach to tackling climate change that would not include international cooperation. According to a 2019 *The New York Times* assessment, Le Pen's environmental policy promotes [French only concerns versus global issues]

> the right's traditional idealization of the land and French national identity, [while] the National Rally's environmentalism focuses on the local—people living and working as much as possible in their own local communities. It encourages reigning in everything from material consumption and population growth as a way to conserve limited resources.
>
> (Onishi, 2019)

These policies fit perfectly into Le Pen's France-first objectives, such as limiting trade and immigration.

Hungary's Viktor Orbán has never been particularly known for his stance on climate change, largely because it has not been a significant political issue among Hungarians. But in 2019 he voted to veto the EU's carbon neutral by 2050 pledge (Harper, 2019). This about-face came just four days after Orbán's Minister of Innovation said at a ribbon-cutting ceremony for a solar energy plant that he supports Hungary going carbon-neutral (Tramas, 2019). Orbán's cabinet released a statement after his veto vote saying that the Hungarian government could not "responsibly support said proposal as long as we do not know what funds the European Union can make available for modernizing industry." This sounds more in line with Orbán's train of thought.

As with other populist leaders sensitive to the fears that climate change is real, Orbán's anti-climate change stance has evolved. Rather than lash out against immigrants as the root of all that ails the Hungarian people, climate policy is the international left-leaning scourge to keep Hungary from making economic progress.

Populist jockeying for power and blame shifting does not change the fact that the planet is warming and that we need to work together to fix it. Such disorder does not solve the grief and anxiety many people still feel. If my fellow mental health practitioners can help patients address and channel their grief into productive outlets, perhaps that larger, louder groundswell will be the necessary push to get all hands on deck.

References

Agence France-Presse (2019). Iceland holds funeral for first glacier lost to climate change. *The Guardian*, August 18. www.theguardian.com/world/2019/aug/19/icela nd-holds- funeral-for-first-glacier-lost-to-climate-change.

Attig, T. (2010). *Why We Grieve*. Oxford: Oxford University Press, 2nd ed.

Center for Climate and Energy Solutions (2020). Hurricanes and climate change. www.c2es.org/content/hurricanes-and-climate-change.

Centers for Disease Control and Prevention (2021). The National Center for Emerging and Zoonotic Infectious Diseases. www.cdc.gov/ncezid/index.html?CDC_AA_refVa l=https%3A%2F%2Fwww.cdc. gov%2Fncezid%2Fdw-index.html.

Creighton, J. (2017). All mentions of climate change were just deleted from the White House website. *Futurism*, January 20. https://futurism.com/all-mentions-of-clima te-change- were-just-deleted-from-the-white-house-website.

Cunsolo, A. and Ellis, N. (2018). Ecological grief as a mental health response to climate-change related loss. *Nature*, vol. 8. pp. 275–281. www.nature.com/articles/s41558-018-0092-2.epdf?author_access_token=UJYCnlw0zZieuYACw3AJQtRgN0jAj Wel9jnR3ZoTv0M Z8cLxe72VDW0esMFb0zEFM26k9KCrjCPa-wqxJcwmMgcIei5y7 ci3SN_gtpLunMy- I9r_Qst3A5V3rz96ScHSGy2dP3IB1DKK9qNem8yIrw%3D%3D.

Dejeja-Hotko, V., Müller, A., and Traufetter, G. (2019). AfD seeks votes by opposing climate protection. *Der Spiegel*, May 6. www.spiegel.de/international/germany/a fd-seeks-votes- by-opposing-climate-protection-a-1265494.html.

Dilbey, A. (2019). How to talk to a populist about climate change. *Foreign Policy*, March 29. https://foreignpolicy.com/2019/03/29/how-to-talk-to-a-populist-about-climate-change.

Ekholm, N. (1901). On the variations of the climate of the geological and historical past and their causes. *Quarterly Journal of the Royal Meteorological Society*, vol. 27, 1–61. http://nsdl.library.cornell.edu/websites/wiki/index.php/PALE_ClassicArti cles/archives/cl assic_articles/issue1_global_warming/n5._Ekholm__1901.pdf.

Environmental Protection Agency (2016). *Climate indicators in the United States*, 4th ed. www.epa.gov/sites/production/files/2016-11/documents/climate-indicators-2016-fact-sheet.pdf.

Fourier, J.B. (1822). *Théorie Analytique de la Chaleur*. Translated by Freeman, A. (1878). The Analytical Theory of Heat. Cambridge. https://books.google.com/books?id= No8IAAAAMAAJ&printsec=frontcover&dq=theorie+analytique+de+la+chaleur&hl =en&newbks=1&newbks_redir=0&sa=X&ved=2ahUKEwi9oPW5rsznAhXsRt8KHX aiAoIQ6AEwAnoECAYQAg#v=twopage&q=heat%2C%20 like%20gravity&f=false.

Global Citizen. (2021). www.globalcitizen.org/es/content/climate-anxiety-what-to-do/#!. February 9.

Good Grief Network. www.goodgriefnetwork.org/about.

Harper, J. (2019). *EU climate goals ditched as Warsaw and Budapest dig in.* DW, June 26. www.dw.com/en/eu-climate-goals-ditched-as-warsaw-and-budapest-dig-in/a- 49357554.

Intergovernmental Panel on Climate Change (2021). Climate Change 2021: The physical science basics summary for policymakers. Headline statements. A.3, p. 11. www.ipcc.ch/report/ar6/wg1/downloads/report/IPCC_AR6_WGI_SPM.pdf.

National Centers for Environmental Information (2021). State of the climate: Global climate report for January 2021. www.ncdc.noaa.gov/sotc/global/202101.

National Oceanographic and Atmospheric Research (2021). Carbon dioxide peaks near 420 parts per million at Mauna Loa observatory. www.epa.gov/sites/produc tion/files/2016-11/documents/climate-indicators- 2016-fact-sheet.pdf.

National Parks Service (1966) Lyndon B. Johnson and the environment. U.S. Department of the Interior. www.nps.gov/lyjo/planyourvisit/upload/EnvironmentCS2.pdf.

Onishi, N. (2019). France's far right wants to be an environmental party, too. *The New York Times,* October 17. www.nytimes.com/2019/10/17/world/europe/france-fa r-right- environment.html?searchResultPosition=9.

Panchal, N., Kamal, R., Cox, C., and Garfield, R. (2021). The implications of COVID- 19 for mental health and substance abuse. KFF, February 10. www.kff.org/coronavirus-covid-19/issue-brief/the-implications-of-covid-19-for-mental-health-and-substance-use.

Revelle, R., Broecker, W., et al. (1965). Restoring the Quality of Our Environment: Report of the Environmental Pollution Panel, November.

Siad, A. and Woodyatt, A. (2019). Hundreds mourn 'dead' glacier at funeral in Switzerland. CNN World, September 22. www.cnn.com/2019/09/22/europe/swiss-glacier- funeral-intl-scli/index.html.

Tramas, F., trans. by Kovacs, Z. (2019). What is behind Viktor Orban's climate change doublethink? Hu.com, August 28. https://index.hu/english/2019/08/28/hungary_climate_change_viktor_orban_fidesz_europ ean_union.

Trump, D. (2019). Patrick Moore, co-founder of Greenpeace:...Twitter, March 12. www.thetrumparchive.com/?searchbox=%22patrick+moore%22.

Weintraub, S. (2021). *Psychological Roots of the Climate Crisis: Neoliberal Exceptionalism and the Culture of Uncare.* New York: Bloomsbury Academic.

Whitcomb, I. (2021). Therapists are reckoning with eco-anxiety. *Scientific American,* April 19. www.scientificamerican.com/article/therapists-are-reckoning-with-eco-anxiety.

Yurk, V. (2021). Pacific Northwest Heat Wave Killed More Than One Billion Sea Creatures. *Scientific American,* July 15. www.scientificamerican.com/article/pacific-northwest-heat-wave-killed-more-than-1-billion-sea-creatures.

Conclusion

I started writing this book around the same time that Joe Biden won the 2020 presidential election. Donald Trump could not handle the truth and he continued to try to have the results changed with appeals to state legislators, attorneys general, and the Supreme Court. He also appealed to his base, which obliged his followers to storm the capitol building in what will be forever known as the Insurrection of 2021.

Despite such attacks, some Americans, including me, felt relief by spring 2021, that we might be able to heal the divide and move forward as a united country. I thought America came perilously close to becoming a populist country but was saved by Biden. Now, some months later, Trump is still in the picture—still contesting the results. Recently unearthed documents reveal that members of his reelection campaign knew in November 2020 that his claims of fraud were false. The Republican Party has not regained any credibility. Being a fair-minded party member seems to be a thing of the past. Some representatives continue to act as though Trump is at the helm. Are Republicans afraid of him, or is their deep desire for power driving their kowtowing? If nothing else, Trump remains the undisputed leader of the GOP, which brings him great power. Is he a cult leader in the true sense of the word? How much of this is polarization due to our decadelong addiction to consuming "news" on social media, whose algorithms are designed to point us to what many Americans seek which appears to be controversial and vitriolic posts?

According to Triston Harris, co-founder of the Center for Humane Technology, arguments get users going in online discussions and keep them engaged, which is exactly what the people who run social media platforms want. The longer a person stays on Facebook, for example, the more likely it is that he or she will buy something one of the sponsors is selling. He also said something must be done about this process before it is too late. I now believe American democracy is in trouble and our collective mental health is nearing a breakdown.

Not even a decade ago, many of us believed we could live together in a country where exchanging ideas was a civilized and crucial component to the

DOI: 10.4324/9781003202387-17

success of self-governance. This is no longer the case. It is as if we are teetering on the edge of cliff. If Trump or one of his protégées wins the election in 2024, our democracy will be lost. We will have fallen into a pit of populism where lies, deceit and conspiracy theories are common currency. If this happens, we will have a leader who cares about him self (a populist can be a woman but it is unlikely to be the case in 2024 in America). Believes he she is entitled to rule based on capricious whims versus law and order and cares little about the American people. Our democracy will have been broken beyond repair. If this happens, projective identification will have overtaken reason, trust, and truthfulness.[1]

To stave off this malignant form of government we must do whatever is possible to preserve our democracy. If there is any hope for America, we the people must fix this country as the preamble of the Constitution directs us to do: to, "promote the general Welfare and secure the Blessings of Liberty to ourselves and our Posterity, do ordain and establish this Constitution for the United States of America." How we go about that is not so clear, but I believe mentalization, which I will review shortly, can help.

In the United States, several additional factors led to the deepening political divide in America that started several decades ago: notably, with the advent of neoliberalism, a type of deregulated capitalism that transfers power from government-regulated entities to private industry. Where this mindset exists, the well-being of the people is shunted in favor of prosperity for a few.[2]

Neoliberalism worsened the inequality between the super-rich and everyone else. Powerful people who only cared for themselves made decisions that lined their pockets by fleecing those of working Americans. This also led to a type of radical individualism which effected the collective negative sense of community. People began to feel more isolated and lonelier which encouraged a retrenchment into tribal identities where splitting and projective identification flourish in the form of scapegoating and blame-shifting.

Another result of neoliberalism is trickle-down economics, a system that provides many opportunities for the wealthy to prosper. Members of this group secure very high salaries and receive substantial tax cuts for businesses as well as breaks when it comes to paying capital gains tax. There are also significant dividends for the wealthy. What is left trickles down to everyone else.

This financial concept considers the processes inherent in projection and projective identification wherein a person or group of people project undesirable characteristic they possess onto others who "buy" what they are told by the experts who run major financial operations worldwide. These officials sound as though what they are doing is for the sake of the masses but instead they are doing it for themselves as well as for others who share their level of wealth.

Since it is a conscious process, blame-shifting is also part of an intentional maneuver employed by Exceptions (Weintrobe, 2021) or super-charged narcissists who believe they are entitled to the riches of our planet. In the case of neoliberalism, projection of greed is often at play in conjunction with a sense of omnipotence that bolsters the defenses of those involved in the accumulation of inordinate amounts of wealth. They believe they are part of a privileged class who deserve the fortunes they have amassed. Some members of this group who have projected negative aspects of themselves onto those who are less fortunate thereafter accuse them of being greedy, begging for money, accepting handouts and/or living on public assistance. To the projectors of greed, the poor are thought to be money grubbing members of society who do not want to work for a living.

Psychoanalyst Sally Weintrobe sees it like this:

> Another reason why Exceptions [those people who benefit from neoliberalism] may be prone to paranoia is they may omnipotently 'deal with' any guilt at taking more than their fair share by mentally constructing a category of denigrated 'leechers and moochers'. Their own bad behavior can now be projected onto 'leechers and moochers'. This may stir further paranoid anxieties that the demonized 'other' will eventually retaliate. Exceptions may then redouble their efforts to self-idealize and demonize to shore up their defenses, increasing their dissociation from reality and from empathy towards the other.
>
> (Weintrobe, 2021, pp. 54–55)

So, what does all of this say about democracy in America in 2022?

Fareed Zakaria articulated this well on his news show Global Public Square (GPS), on August 1, 2021: "If political order is rare, liberal political order is rarer still." He also stated that "...liberal democracy is the Goldilocks form of government. It needs a state that is strong enough to govern effectively but not so strong that it crushes the liberties and rights of its people." We have the power to maintain this government if we can work together to keep it. Can we keep it? Can other countries hold on to theirs? Polarization will be a tough nut to crack.

Democracy at Risk in Tunisia: Projective Identification in Action Once Again

American democracy is not the only one on the ropes. The authors of the *Democracy Index 2020: In sickness and in health?* determined that, "in 2020 a large majority of countries, 116 out of a total of 167 (almost 70%) recorded a decline...compared with 2019" (Economist Intelligence Unit, 2021, p. 5). The analysis also revealed that the US "retained its 'flawed democracy status,'" owing in large part to the politicization of the pandemic, police violence, and the contentious presidential election (2021, pp. 6–7). The situation worsened during the pandemic when millions of people around the world were forced to shelter in place, creating anxiety and exacerbating existing tensions.

Tunisia is one such country where democracy is under attack. On August 1, 2021 Zakaria and Tarek Masoud, a member of Harvard University's Middle East Initiative, discussed the tenuous situation taking place in the only democracy in the Arab world: Tunisia's president, Kaïs Saïed, fired the Prime Minister along with other top officials and invoked a provision in the country's constitution that allows the president to take charge in certain dire circumstances. Such a move is only lawful if it is done in consultation with a special court that is supposed to settle problems among various branches of the government. As problematic as this move is, President Saïed seemed to be acting on Tunisian unrest and protests about the country's pandemic response.

Masoud, who has studied Tunisia's government, sounded alarmed but said it is too early to know if the only democracy in the Arab world has failed. Eric Goldstein of Human Rights Watch said that "it's ominous for human rights when a president claims constitutional backing for seizing enormous power and the next thing you know, police start going after journalists" (Yerkes, 2021).

Whether president Saïed used projective identification or blame shifting as a defense mechanism to justify his actions is not yet clear. Though like similar stories unfolding around the world, this one is far from over, and I suspect there will be ample information to examine in the future. But Saïed's actions contradict his earlier pledge to make changes while adhering to the constitution. Instead, he fired officials and consolidated power under the office of the President which is not consistent with democratic leadership. All eyes are on Saïed's next moves.

I also think there are important global implications for the populist movement in the US and in other parts of the world. It is a brand of thinking that has emerged throughout the world in the form of conservative-leaning populist nationalism: I believe understanding the psychological motivations behind these political decisions is important because it embodies the toxic elements of shifting blame.

This trend gained traction in America when Trump made his initial bid for the White House. From the beginning, his campaign was underscored by his lack of willingness to take responsibility for his behavior. Often, he shifted blame onto others. While he had positioned himself as being someone who was against the establishment, few people thought of him as a real contender for the presidency. Instead, many people thought Trump's his new zeal for politics was a publicity stunt.

Slowly, Trump began to gain favor with white supremacists, misogynists, racists, the alt-right and other people who felt disenfranchised from mainstream America. He and his growing cohort preferred to see those who attempted to uphold democratic ideas as "out to get" them.

Although he did many questionable things throughout his life, up until 2012 his behavior, though noxious, had limited impact on desperate groups of people. It mostly touched his immediate family, people who lost money owing to his failed businesses and those working for and with him. Then Trump was elected America's 45th President, and the world is quite possibly forever changed. Do the rest of us possess the psychological fortitude to combat his continued march forward? Can we give back these projections in the form of setting limits with Trump, trying him for the crimes he has committed and by saying "no" to any future attempt he might make to lead the country? The answer to these questions remains unclear.

Truth for Change: Real Fact Checking Could Make a Big Difference

Opinion has supplanted fact, thanks largely to social media and the massive amounts of information that can be sent and received in seconds. This is a global problem.

What people read on social media leads them to more and more information, much of which is of questionable origin. A good deal of it is fake. Facebook and other social sites buy the attention of its viewers to make money no matter what the consequences to the users might be.

The Wall Street Journal recently published a series of articles called "The Facebook Files" illustrating how far Facebook's leaders were willing to go to increase profits at the expense of users' mental health. The newspaper's investigation revealed how the social media Goliath ignored its own internal findings, including acknowledging that Instagram (a Facebook-owned entity) makes "body image issues worse for one in three teen girls," that they are "not actually doing what we say we do publicly," and that posts with the most reshares (and most eyeballs) are the most violent, misinformed, and toxic. Scheck, Purnell, and Horwitz, 2021). And, in a nasty little bit of elitism, Facebook shields millions of high-profile users from the company's rules. So, the louder one's megaphone, the more likely Facebook will look the other way. (Horwitz, 2021). Why? Eyeballs equal engagement which equals revenue.

Finding A New Path: Learning to Mentalize—A Way of Collaborating That Can Help Heal the Divide in America

Ready to unplug? Mentalization can help. When it occurs, people feel free to express themselves while allowing others to also do so. In this state, a person knows his or her view and *respects* others. When it is in play, all ideas are valued, and none are judged. Everyone has a voice and is free to express their beliefs. In an environment where people mentalize, personal, community, and corporate engagement become possible. This process is important whether people are in school, at work, on a playground, in a family setting, or part of a corporate environment.

Collaboration between and among people in different political parties is also possible when mentalizing is part of these exchanges. It involves a process where contributions from all participants are respected. This way of interacting facilitates optimal communication between and among people in most all settings. When all ideas are valued and respected, people feel engaged. It can also promote self-worth and can be observed in groups that collaborate effectively, in groups that participate in authentic engagement and with individuals. While projective identification lowers self-worth, mentalization helps people overcome its impact while learning how to respect the opinions of others.

Much like any other interpersonal conflict, moving on from longstanding political rivalries can be difficult, if not totally overwhelming. When insults are lobbed, aspersions cast, and characters are called into question—all age-old tactics in the world of campaigning—the effects can be disastrous. Lyndon Johnson left a sharp-tongued legacy which included calling Bobby Kennedy "snot-nosed," and "sonny boy." A century earlier, Aaron Burr and Alexander Hamilton's mutual enmity ended in a duel that proved fatal for Hamilton.

While arguments between friends or family members might blow over as easily as the air the words float on, for people duking it out in the 21st-century's political arena, any barbs leveled publicly are etched on the record in perpetuity, thanks to the internet.

When Biden chose Kamala Harris as his vice-presidential nominee and running mate earlier this year, a chorus of skeptical onlookers cried foul. *Didn't Harris call Biden a racist at the debate? Hadn't he called her a liar?* For the record: she did not, and he had not (Swenson, 2020). But the important thing is what they had been *perceived* as saying.

The mood has shifted between them, certainly. Biden now heaps praise on Harris, calling her "smart," "tough," and "experienced," while Harris responds in kind by applauding Biden's character. How did they manage this contretemps, and more importantly, how are they continuing to work together as a convincing team?

The simple answer is that Harris and Biden were doing what most people do who want to rise above previous conflicts or misunderstandings. They did what we all do when we want to move forward, undivided: they tried to understand what the other was thinking—where they were "coming from." We often speak about this kind of interaction as "seeing" each other. After a particularly meaningful or cathartic conversation, one might say "I felt seen or heard" by others while communicating. In these kinds of exchanges, each person puts their own doubts aside and takes the time to see—and accept—the other as the complex human being that they are.

The more technical answer is that they are practicing mentalization, defined by the American Psychological Association as "the ability to understand one's own and others' mental states, thereby comprehending one's own and others' intentions and affects."

Mentalization is easy and natural for many of us when the person we are dealing with holds the same opinions as us. But when there is discord in beliefs, mentalization becomes especially important because it allows us to hold two seemingly conflicting or incompatible ideas—our own and the other person's—in our minds simultaneously. This does not mean that we necessarily share a viewpoint—we can still disagree—but it does mean that we are each free to have and express our own opinions without judgment from the other. Both views are permitted. Being able to incorporate two perspectives or mindsets is the crux of mentalization.

When Biden chose Harris as his running mate, despite her earlier critiques of him, he was able to mentalize. When Harris responded to his request with "Absolutely, yes!" she was employing the same technique (Desjardins, 2020). They were *opening* the lines of communication, rather than shutting them down. Clearly, they will not always agree, but they developed a relationship wherein they can listen to each other in an atmosphere of respect without judging the other person as being inferior.

Though the concept of mentalization is centuries-old, the term came to prominence in psychological circles during the late 1960s in conjunction with discussions associated with attachment theory. Without healthy parent-child attachment, the ability to understand other people's emotions and mental states is difficult to achieve, and with it, the ultimate development of a healthy personality is still challenging but not impossible.

As a society, I think it is fair to say that many of us have forgotten how to talk to each other. Discussions now often quickly devolve into open rhetorical combat peppered with ad hominem attacks. We cannot go on like this, and we do not have to. But to achieve the repair and healing that is essential for progress, we need to actively dislodge the wedge that's been driven between groups that makes it incredibly difficult, if not impossible, to engage in meaningful dialogue and debate.

Being able to talk to those who maintain different viewpoints is important. Despite how difficult thoughtful debate can be, there are examples of growth and healing that mentalization enables, whether it is public figures like Nora Mulready accepting her nephew after admitting she had been wrong about gender transition in children (Mulready, 2020), or shifts in corporate mindsets as momentous as the owners of the Washington Redskins retiring its racist name in favor of the Washington Football Team.

We might not end up painting each other in the glowing terms Biden and Harris inevitably used as they worked to win the 2020 presidential election. However, we will end up in a better position to understand one another, and rather than thinking of ourselves as being on opposing teams, no matter what our political or personal affiliations are, we can start to envision ourselves as being on the same team. Our national survival depends on it.

While thinking about the concept of truth, I do think we need to be able to come together and agree on real facts; to find some way of identifying reality.

As Tristan Harris said in *The Social Dilemma*, if we cannot agree on what is *true…* "we are toast." Trump lost the election. To go along with his perception of winning in 2020, as many Republicans in Congress and Fox News reporters have done, is wrong. It is not true that Trump won his 2020 bid for re-election, it is false. While there is a place for perception and subjective reality, one's opinion or sense of something should not ever be mistaken for truth or reality.

Let's look at a simple example of observable truth versus factual data. Let's say, on a rainy day, someone in a green car hits a man with a blue suit. Four bystanders pulled the driver out of his car at a stop light and force him to sit on the curb until the police arrived. However you spin it, a drone filming from above would record what I outlined in the above sentence. There would be a green car on a rainy day whose driver hit a man with a blue suit. There would be images of four by-standers who forced the driver out of his car. There would also be footage of the driver sitting on a curb presumably waiting for the police to arrive.

When people attempt to recount stories of what they have witnessed, for several reasons the recall of events vary from person to person. This is the case because we all encode, store, and retrieve what we have witnessed differently. Contrary to what one might think, facts are less accurate when people share information before reporting it; a phenomenon known as *collaborative inhibition*. While this seems to be counterintuitive, it appears to occur because people are often afraid to report some parts of what they observed.

While the "truth" is hard enough to determine, owing to the complexities of human memory, conjuring up self-serving versions of it or producing fake news for personal or corporate gain for the purpose of manipulation is unconscionable.

Notes

1 As I have explained throughout the book, projective identification is an unconscious defense mechanism that causes people to project what they cannot tolerate about themselves onto others and thereafter act as if the quality, trait, or behavior resides within the other person or other people if a group is involved in this dynamic. In other words, they do not take responsibility for their own actions and instead shift blame to others.
2 Neoliberalism is a way of thinking and an economic system that gives power and control to a few people. It is also known as exceptionalism, which normalizes greed. It is exhibited by a small number of people.

References

Desjardins, L. (2020). Biden introduces Harris at a campaign event devoid of the standard pomp. PBS News, August 12. www.pbs.org/newshour/show/biden-introduces-harris-at-a-campaign-event-devoid-of-the-standard-pomp.

Economist Intelligence Unit (2021). Democracy Index 2020: In Sickness and in Health? The Economist Group. https://pages.eiu.com/rs/753-RIQ-438/images/democracy-in dex-2020.pdf?mkt_tok=NzUzLVJJUS00MzgAAAF_vPUJRGJqEff6tZdCW911wzD z7H_XFGzCSbtR_ZNnDKmUjHk8SAL4CwtHz8gonkxNyVPsqRFD-lGyRXEnZ joVzzBHQagRwI1vNTXzivgiJp-_Uw.

Mulready, N. (2020). I sympathized with gender-critical campaigners-until my nephew came out as trans. *The Independent*, August 27. www.independent.co.uk/voices/tra nsgender-gender-critical-recognition-act-jk- rowling-lgbt-a9687576.html.

Rocha, V., Merica, D., King, G. et al. (2019). The first Democratic debate, night 2. CNN Politics. www.cnn.com/politics/live-news/democratic-debate-june-27-2019/h_b381d219b3 3e3de6757b4feb63036316.

Scheck, J., Purnell, N., Horwitz, J. et al. (2021). The Facebook Files: A Wall Street Journal Investigation. *The Wall Street Journal*, October 1. www.wsj.com/articles/ the-facebook-files-11631713039.

Swenson, A. (2020). *Kamala Harris did not call Joe Biden a racist on the debate state.* AP News, August 11. https://apnews.com/article/fact-checking-9244041620.

Weintrobe, S. (2021). *Psychological Roots of the Climate Crisis: Neoliberal Exceptional- ism and the Culture of Uncare.* Bloomsbury Academic.

Yerkes, S. (2021). The Tunisia model in crisis: The president's power grab risks an authoritarian regression. *Foreign Affairs*, August 6. www.foreignaffairs.com/articles/ tunisia/2021-08-06/tunisia-model- crisis?utm_medium=promo_email&utm_source= lo_flows&utm_campaign=registered_us er_welcome&utm_term=email_1&utm_con tent=20210925.

Zakaria, F. (2021). How the delta variant might complicate the economic recovery convincing the unvaccinated to get their shots; teetering democracy in Tunisia; and, why one scholar wants a truth and reconciliation committee after the U.S. Capitol attack. Global Public Square, August 1. https://omny.fm/shows/fareed-zakaria-gps/a ugust-1-2021-on-gps-how-the-delta-variant- might-c#description.

Epilogue

As I am completing final edits of this book, Vladimir Putin is attacking Ukraine. He appears to have a need to shift blame for his attack filled with venomous rage onto courageous people who are willing to give up their lives to protect their country. Rather than owning his unbridled desire to covet and expand what he believes is his territory, Putin is projecting his aggression onto the West by claiming NATO is plotting to destroy Russia. To the contrary, Putin is the one who is literally pummeling Ukraine while millions of viewers from around the world watch; others are protesting. This is a classic example of projective identification that is being playedout in realtime in front of millions of people.

As we move through the next few years, it will be important to monitor populism and authoritarian rule as well as a few key factors that are likely to affect the remaining democracies in the world. The question on my mind is, will they continue, or will they falter? And, what can be done to ensure that democracy lives on?

Although many factors will determine whether self-government remains to be a part of life in America as well as in other parts of the world, one thing that is causing so many problems that must be ameliorated is the negative way in which internet platforms has altered how we communicate. Moving forward, it will be imperative for this way of sharing information to be regulated if democracies are to survive and flourish. Currently, misinformation and fake news have replaced truth, which is an essential part of living in a democratic society. Olivia So, a very bright 16-year-old whom I recently spoke with and who does not have accounts on Facebook, Instagram, Twitter, Snap Chat, or Tik-tok (but obviously understands it), put it thusly: "Social media creates relevance and relevance creates power." This power of which she speaks is one that incorporates control, dominance, force, and supremacy all of which are not part of a democratic way of life.

In the United States, the end of democracy was averted when Joe Biden won the presidential election in November of 2020. Although Donald Trump did not give up gracefully and incited the insurrection on January 6, 2021, the country dodged a populism bullet, this time.

DOI: 10.4324/9781003202387-18

Biden got off to a decent start. He saved countless lives by promoting COVID-19 vaccines. He started to narrow the gap between the salaries men and women receive for comparable work. He also signed a bill to help poor people gain access to legal representation and he signed The American Rescue Plan that will help millions of Americans make it through the pandemic. In addition, he revoked Trump's ban on Muslim immigration.

President Biden ended the war in Afghanistan, something most Americans thought was necessary. However, the way he did it—without an exit strategy—led many people to criticize him, including Trump and his followers. Polls taken in September 2021 found that most Americans disapproved of how he handled the withdrawal from Afghanistan.

As he continues his presidency, Biden appears to be doing things that even some Democrats do not support. One example of a surprising policy shift was a secret deal he made with the Australian government to sell them a nuclear submarine. This incensed the French government and President Macon because they had already struck a deal with the Australians for this same project. Biden's team muscled in and offered Australia a sweeter deal; a move on Biden's part that was viewed by the French in a very negative way causing them to recall their ambassador back from the United States.

On Global Public Square (GPS) on September 19, 2021, Fareed Zakaria said that Trump's selfishness as it related to international policy was thought to be an aberration. However, if Biden does not change his current way of operating and return to his former commitment to internationalism, according to Zakaria, he could essentially normalize Trump's foreign policy. This would be a disaster for the United States and would perpetuate Trump's mantra of "Make America Great Again." Zakaria believes that Biden's stance on this subject is close to the 45th President's mindset since he appears to be hanging onto the idea by talking about an "America First Policy" which is essentially the same. Why he is doing this is unclear, but we will need a course correction if our democracy is going to continue to thrive.

Could Redistricting Push Us Towards Populism? A Lot Depends on the 2020 Census

In order to ensure that our democracy remains intact, we must make sure all Americans are represented in Congress, not the old guard or white Americans but *all* Americans. This will include making sure the information gathered in the 2020 Census accurately represents our changing population.

At stake is how federal funds will be spent as well as how state and federal policies will be made. Most important of all is equal representation. If our citizens are represented fairly, our democracy has a chance of surviving. However, if redistricting occurs in an inequitable manner, the 2022 mid-term election could set the tone for an unfair presidential election in 2024. If this occurs, our democracy could be in jeopardy.

The possibility that the 2020 census data could be misused was recently published by the Union of Concerned Scientists. In this document, Coleman Harris, an expert on redistricting said the Census numbers are crucially important because they represent real people who live in real communities throughout America. They are not simply figures in rows and columns on a spreadsheet to be added and subtract for the sake of research. They represent people's lives.

Harris also said that misuse of the 2020 Census data would be most harmful to Black people, Latinos, and Indigenous groups, adding that such omissions could exclude these citizens from the political process in America.

This fear has led scientists to call for evidenced-based and fair redistricting; something all Americans have a responsibility to monitor so that our democracy can stay intact.

The 2021 Abortion Law in Texas: Is This Making Texas More Like a Populist Country?

Texas governor Greg Abbott introduced legislation to ban abortions in Texas after a fetal heartbeat is detected which usually occurs around six weeks after conception; a time when many women do not know they are pregnant.

This initiative was backed up by the Republican legislature and as of September 1, 2021, it became law. This occurred after the Supreme Court of the United States failed to stop this bill from going into effect.

What this means is that Abbott is running Texas much like a populist leader would run a country. He has taken the law into his own hands with the help of his supporters. This is despite the fact that in the United States women have a right to an abortion based on Roe vs. Wade. It is as if Texas no longer is part of the United States.

Abbott is not exactly a live free or die sort of governor. While he might appear to be on one hand, he reversed some of his own decisions when the heat was turned up. For example, he has enforced government mandates at times including an unpopular executive order in July 2020 requiring Texans to wear face masks in most public settings. However, this mandate was rescinded when Abbott was reprimanded by some of his fellow Republicans. He also required vaccinations for all school children for polio, measles, mumps, and rubella as well as for Hepatitis A, Hepatitis B, Varicella, and Meningococcal disease (MCV4) but announced plans recently that stated he intends to ban certain treatments such as hormone therapy and surgeries for transgender people.

Governor Abbott's penchant for cherry picking which Federal laws he wishes to follow while dismissing others that he does not like makes him seem like an authoritarian ruler versus a governor of a state. Texans are not his personal flock, but he treats them as such. Abbott once again provides an excellent example of this new and unfortunate trend in America. As a follower of Trump, he began to make proclamations about what people should and should not do that contradicted his earlier positions. As is the case with Trump, Abbott also began to disregard laws in America.

One example of his capricious behavior reared its ugly head when he prohibited government entities from mandating mask-wearing. He also tweeted on May 18, 2021, "Texans, not gov't, should decide their best health practices."

However, when it comes to a woman's right to choose what is best her body as well as for her family, Governor Abbott changed his tune by supporting the anti-abortion legislation in his state. This is extremely inconsistent as well as being unconstitutional. It is also the way populist leaders operate: Whatever suits their current needs is what occurs.

While the meaning of this behavior cannot be known with certainty, one hypothesis is that Governor Abbott is projecting feelings of disgust or distain towards women that he cannot tolerate onto pregnant women. Thereafter *they* are the anti-life people. This appears to be an excellent example of projective identification. Again, the *It's not me! It's you* theme emerges.

At the same time, Governor Abbott has not managed to contain COVID-19 deaths in his state, nor has he tried. Over 86,000 Texans have died from the pandemic, yet he wants to punish women who wish to make a personal decision to terminate a pregnancy, even in cases that involve rape or incest. This raises the question of who is doing something wrong. Shifting blame and refusing to take responsibility for his actions, which could cause a great deal of harm to other people, seems to be Abbott's *modus operandi*.

So, what is this inconsistency about? Why does Abbott pronounce that he believes in freedom of choice when it comes to decisions involving the health of Texans but not for the health of pregnant Texans?

Abbott's actions have cost the lives of thousands of people, owing not only to coronavirus deaths but also to the shortage of intensive care unit (ICU) beds. A U.S. Army Veteran who needed other medical services unrelated to COVID-19 was not able to find an ICU bed, owing to the large number of COVID-19 cases. Unfortunately, this man died.

On another note, Abbott is paralyzed and won $6 million dollars when he sued his homeowner's association because a tree fell on him when he was jogging. However, he has fought against the Americans with Disabilities Act numerous times. As Attorney General, he aggressively fought against efforts to force the state to comply with this Act. This is not a matter of opinion; it is a matter of fact.

Once again, the governor of Texas accuses people of taking advantage of the system, yet it appears that he is the one who shifted blame to other entities while refusing to take action or accept responsibility for his own behavior.

Critical Race Theory

If we are going to save our democracy, Americans need to take stock of what is occurring in the United States as it relates to the Critical Race Theory (CRT), a concept previously relegated to the ivy halls of academia that now is on the frontlines of culture wars.

Part of the reason for this misunderstanding is the complexity of the theory itself. To make matters even more confusing, since this theory was built on identity-based Marxism and historically had been studied in graduate school, it has become a lightning rod for many groups ranging from members of Congress to parents and educators who are focused on K-12 curricula.

People opposed to the CRT might have various reasons for their distrust or dislike of it. However, I believe it has become such a hot topic because it taps into personal feelings about race that are difficult to tolerate and discuss. When this dynamic exists, when a person cannot accept something about him or herself, whatever cannot be explored is often projected onto another person or other people. The mantra of *It's not me! It's you!* becomes the prevailing mindset. In this case, what is being projected are the facts about our shared history at a time when truth-telling is on the wane. People want to rewrite history; something that often occurs in populist-led countries.

It is a fact that white Americans stole land from Black Americans. White people have also refused to hire Black people. The latter group has been denied access to equal educational opportunities as well. While many White people have been able to realize the American dream, Black people for the most part have not been able to do so.

These are facts that recently have become the center of controversy in educational circles. To make matters worse, teachers who expose their students to this information are being criticized. Parents are also staging protests about the CRT. It is as if "the truth" about our shared history is no longer a topic that can be discussed.

The Environment: Serious Warnings and Ways Individuals Can Make a Difference

The Intergovernmental Panel on Climate Change (IPCC) recently released a study on climate change—the first in ten years—outlining the critical climate change problems facing humanity. According to the IPCC report, by 2040, the temperature will increase by 1.5 degrees Celsius (2.7 degrees Fahrenheit) and will continue to rise in the decades that follow at alarming rates unless concerted efforts are made to halt the current levels of carbon dioxide emissions. According to Professor Kim Cobb, "the changes we're seeing now are widespread. They're rapid. They're intensifying. They're unprecedented in thousands of years," says Cobb. "It's indisputable that these changes are linked to human activities" (Democracy Now, 2021).

Other problems we face include changes in the sea level that is predicted to rise by between 1 and 8 feet by 2100 because of melting ice and the expansion of seawater that is caused by the rise is temperature and the loss of ice in the Arctic ocean.

The IPCC also reported on droughts and heat waves and predicts that extreme heat waves that now occur once every twenty years will happen every two to three years by the end of this century. Hurricanes are also predicted to be worse in terms of their strength and intensity which will create more Category 4 and 5 storms.

While predictions are grim, the question of what individuals can do seems to be worth exploring, which some concerned environmental groups have done. Using a CO_2 calculator, the Brandenburg University of Technology in Germany found that turning the heat down by 1 degree Celsius saved 6 percent of the energy that it takes to heat buildings. Electricity consumption in private households also has great savings potential.

If small group effort makes a difference, what about individual contributions? Many people believe that a decrease in meat consumption and more bike riding, to use two examples, could help the dire situation we are facing today. If we all—friends and foes—did some things to preserve our planet some of the time, we might not need a savior on a white horse to gallop in and save us. Nor would we be reliant on some people doing the right thing all the time.

The Perpetual Need to be Vigilant: Keeping an Eye on Splitting, Blame Shifting, and Projective Identification if America is to Continue to be a Democracy

In nearly every country where populist leaders are in control, splitting, blame shifting, and projective identification are employed to divide and conquer the people they govern or rule. Now some Republican governors in the United States are following suit by creating their own rules that are not aligned with the U.S. Constitution. It is as if they are leading their own country versus being a governor of one of the 50 states in the United States.

Given that politicians in this country know what living in a democracy means, what happened to leaders who think they can do what they wish with the lives of other people without consulting them? Why is the Supreme Court not intervening when our Constitution is seriously challenged?

One answer is that Trump deeply polarized our country more than any other president in modern times. He did this by failing to take responsibility for his actions and instead blamed everyone else for his personal shortcomings. He also lied to the American public. According to the Washington Post Fact Checker he made false or misleading claims 30,573 times during the four years that he was President of the United States.

This behavior seemed to give some of his admirers in government positions a license to do the same things. They followed the cult of Trump and did what he did or what he told them to do. This process of blindly following the negative behavior of an unscrupulous president must be stopped. The cult must be disbanded and those who followed this leader must be brought back into the fold so that we all can be free to believe in our government once again as we reestablish faith in the words set out in the Preamble of our Constitution, which I offer here: "We the People of the United States, in Order to form a more perfect Union, establish Justice, ensure domestic Tranquility, provide for the common defense, promote the general Welfare, and secure the Blessings of Liberty to ourselves and our Posterity, do ordain and establish this Constitution for the United States of America."

To paraphrase Benjamin Franklin, we have a republic, if we can keep it. To do so will take all of us to be willing to see past our differences in the interest of creating something greater and better than any one of us could accomplish alone. I hope we are up to the task.

References

United States Constitution (1787) Preamble.
Washington Post Fact Checker. (2021). www.washingtonpost.com/politics/2021/01/24/ trumps-false-or-misleading-claims-total-30573-over-four-years.
Zakaria, F. (2021). Global Public Square (GPS), September 19.

Index

For Product Safety Concerns and Information please contact our EU
representative GPSR@taylorandfrancis.com
Taylor & Francis Verlag GmbH, Kaufingerstraße 24, 80331 München, Germany

www.ingramcontent.com/pod-product-compliance
Lightning Source LLC
Chambersburg PA
CBHW070323270326
41926CB00017B/3736